DIRTY LITTLE SECRETS AND REALLY BIG DEALS

DIRTY LITTLE SECRETS & REALLY BIG DEALS

Building Respect
One Hotel At A Time

THE BOB POMEROY STORY

by Madeline Hombert

Copyright © Pomeroy Enterprises 2010. All rights reserved.

No part of this book may reproduced, stored in a retrieval system, or, transmitted by any means without the written permission of the author.

Library and Archives Canada Cataloguing in Publication

Hombert, Madeline, 1944–

Dirty little secrets and really big deals : Building respect one hotel at a time : Bob Pomeroy's story / Madeline Hombert.

ISBN 978-0-9784995-0-1

1. Pomeroy, Bob. 2. Hospitality industry—Alberta, Northern—Biography. 3. Hospitality industry—British Columbia, Northern—Biography. 4. Hotelkeepers—Canada—Biography. I. Title. II. Title: Bob Pomeroy story.

TX910.5.P65H65 2008   647.94092   C2007-906563-5

Available through most Pomeroy Hotels, book distributors and stores or, by mail at:

Pomeroy Enterprises
Box 280, Grande Prairie, Alberta, T8V 3A4

$34.95 Cdn/US

If ordering by mail, please add $6.95 for shipping/handling to US or Canada. Be sure to quote the ISBN # 978-0-9784995-0-1 when ordering.

Printed in China.

Dedication

The book is dedicated to the children of Bob Pomeroy and especially to the memory of Tim Pomeroy—the son who never lived long enough to share in his father's ultimate success.

Foreword

When I was asked to write the foreword to this book about my father's life, I was reminded about some very valuable lessons he gave me over the years.

He told me that no one can create action like the leader; that at the end of the day, good or bad, right or wrong, a company is a personal reflection of an individual and that individual must always put his best foot forward. He taught me that a leader must get his team to believe, and, to do so, he has to believe more than all the team members combined. If a leader does these things on a regular basis, great things will follow. My father is that type of leader and, time and time again, great things follow him.

During the development and construction of my first "solo" project, the Pomeroy Hotel in Fort St.John, my father got me to focus; he motivated me; he showed me how to motivate my team. Then he gave me the help and support I needed to get the job done. At the Grand Opening dinner, he delivered a speech that would rival any speeches on leadership that I have ever heard. That speech, that particular instant, was the single most satisfying moment of my career. It was better than signing the deal, better than getting the financing completed, better than opening the Gaming Center, better than creating the new Pomeroy Hotel brand, better than any of it. It was that moment that made me believe in myself and in my family. My father's speech clearly defined him. It revealed not only everything he has accomplished but also the journey it took to arrive at his present status.

I am so proud to call this man my father; so proud and so fortunate to be at the helm of the company that carries our family name; so appreciative of all of the opportunity I have been given through his hard work.

I love him for all the things he has done for me, and I have long forgiven him for any of the things he missed doing. I love him for making me who I am; for giving me the legacy of a strong will and intelligent mind. I love him for the sacrifices he made for our family, and for the generosity he willingly shows to family and to everyone he meets. I love him for the unlimited energy and strong work ethic he taught us through his own example.

I hope this book helps people understand my father; helps them see how his strengths far overshadow his weaknesses; helps them recognize him for being an honest man, a great leader, and a sensitive human being with a great heart.

—Ryan Pomeroy

Introduction

This is the story of Bob Pomeroy and his success. It is a current story, a Canadian story, a real story. It is about the successful journey of a man who dreamt big—a man who still dreams big and who will not let those dreams die.

It is the account of a man who continues to prove that ambition, focus and an unrelenting drive to succeed can take an uneducated person from a background of abuse and uncertainty to a position of wealth and respect.

Money has come and money has gone. Deals have been made and deals have collapsed. The few times that Bob has hit rock bottom, he has pulled up his socks and bounced back higher than before. He's left behind the people who have done him wrong and he's generously shared his success with the ones who've stuck by him through good times and bad.

Like most success stories, this one includes some dark passages. Sixty-plus years of living and working in Canada's new northern frontier could not have been spent without incurring bruises and fortunes are rarely made without breaking a few rules. Although Bob has been able to charm his way out of most trouble, he has not led a charmed life.

This book has been written in two distinct parts; the first half being a candid, raw review of Bob's childhood and early life. There are troubling passages and there are funny passages—nothing has been sugar-coated. The honesty and the intimacy are obvious.

The second half is made much more powerful by the truths told in the first half of the book. It describes exactly how Bob turned ambition, intelligence, ingenuity and perseverance into a fortune.

This is not a "how-to" manual. More accurately, it is the telling of how one man turned opportunity into success. It is also an example of how fortunes may be built today in this country without the advantage of family money or an elite education.

—Madeline Hombert

First Half

"Dream lofty dreams and, as you dream, so shall you become"

—*JAMES ALLEN*, "AS A MAN THINKETH", COLLINS,1971

One

"Alone among all creatures, the species that styles itself wise, "Homo Sapiens", has an abiding interest in its distant origins, knows that its allotted time is short, worries about the future and wonders about the past."

—JOHN NOBLE WILFORD, NY TIMES 30 OCT 1984

A biography is never complete without including the genealogical roots of the family name. There are often disputes and inaccuracies because some births were not recorded and many records were made in good faith based on a person's statement at the time of immigration. Sometimes, errors were made in spelling of names due to a lack of education centuries ago. There are also instances where an illegitimate child registered the name of his father based on the mother's testimony.

Genealogy has become a passion with many people and thanks to DNA testing and international cooperation, family histories have become well validated. Much research was done about the Pomeroy history, both in England and in Canada.

The Pomeroy family began in Europe and the original family name was "de la Pomerai." Records begin with Radulphus de la Pomerai (1030 to 1102) in Normandy, France.

Radulphus de la Pomerai took an important part in the Norman Conquest of England and, for his allegiance and service to the King; he was awarded extensive lands and manors in the West Country. These lands included Berry Pomeroy in Devon. In fact, Radulphus was a Knight with William the Conqueror and his son, Henry De La Pomerai, married the natural daughter of Henry 1, King of England. The first Pomeroy spelling appears with Richard Pomeroy (1540–1612).

American roots show up with Eltweed Pomeroy (1585–1673) in Northampton, Massachusetts. A grandson of Eltweed, Joseph Pomeroy (1672–1712), moved on to Connecticut and then the family headed north to Camden East, Ontario where the 21st Great-Grandson, Daniel Pomeroy, was born and was registered in 1825. His son, Irwin Smith Pomeroy (1878–1946) moved to British Columbia and settled in the Fort St.John area.

There is no doubt that the Fort St. John Pomeroys are direct descendents of Eltweed Pomeroy but—and this is the big "but"—is Eltweed a direct descendent of the Devon Pomeroys or another branch of the family?

Richard Pomeroy of Devon was definitely tied to the royal family, as there are documents in England that record the full ancestral line. On his records, Eltweed's father is stated to be Richard Pomeroy. Record books in England state that Richard Pomeroy of Devon died childless so was Eltweed an illegitimate child of the Devon Richard Pomeroy or was there another Richard Pomeroy in England?

According to a researcher who has the most comprehensive facts and records, the DNA from Eltweed Pomeroy is ". . . different from a descendent from the current noble family." Further DNA evidence states that "Eltweed's DNA is the same as descendents from several old trees of the family that date back variously to around 1600–1700, and in parishes where there are records dating back to the 1550's, some of which are in the geographical vicinity of Berry Pomeroy Castle in Devon."

This evidence would allow the acceptance that Eltweed's family originated in England but there are gaps in the records that prevent any absolute and direct connections to the Devon-based Richard Pomeroy.

In a recent family compilation, for example, it shows a Henry Pomeroy as living from 1531–1559. In the very next point, it states that Henry's son Richard lived from 1560–1593. It also states that Richard was a minor child when his father died, leaving him as a ward of his uncle. It seems to be a contradiction to state that the son was a minor child BEFORE his father died and then in another statement claiming the birth and death dates of Richard to say that he was born AFTER his father died.

Records do show that Eltweed was the son of the Richard that lived from

1560–1593 but genealogists in England suspect that this was a different Richard altogether, not the Richard who was heir of Berry Pomeroy.

If Eltweed could eventually be established as a descendent of the original family tree that remained in Berry Pomeroy, then Bob Pomeroy could be listed among the direct descendents of King Henry I of England and a distant cousin of the late Princess Diana.

If, on the other hand, his ancestors are from another branch that migrated to Ireland, it might explain Bob's affection for Irish Pubs and the establishment of his Egan's Restaurants and Irish Pubs.

Whatever the current spelling may be and whichever branch of the family tree any Canadian Pomeroy descends from, the original de la Pomerai family came from the apple growing orchards of La Pommerai in the Calvados region of Normandy. The lands are in near proximity to Reims—the famed champagne producing region of France and there is still a Pommery family thriving there. ("Pommes de le roi" translates to "apples of the king" and the family's orchard was the supplier of apples to the King of France. In fact, the name of the specific species of apples was "Pomme-roi" or King of Apples in deference to their benefactor.)

In any case, it is just as interesting to realize that once upon a time, the De La Pomerai family began as orchard-keepers for the King of France. There is today a distant connection to Pommery Wineries in France. Although the current owner of the winery is not a direct Pomeroy descendant, she took the name in homage to the original orchards and family. The Pommery winery is arguably one of the finest champagne producers in Europe—a fitting connection for one of the finest hoteliers in Alberta!

MORE RECENT HISTORY

Irwin Smith Pomeroy, born in Maidstone, Ontario in 1878, moved west to Alberta and married his wife Minnie in 1902. After being a cook in Edmonton, then farming near Fort Saskatchewan, he finally relocated his family to Fort St. John, BC in 1928. Irwin and Minnie homesteaded on the land that eventually became the site of the Fort St. John airport. The couple had nine children—Helen, Ruth, Mary, Bill, Walter, Dan, Gordon, Ralph and Ross. After Minnie passed way in 1941, Irwin married Katharine Whitson. It was a brief marriage, however, as Irwin died in 1946.

Ross, born in 1921, was always known as "Scotty." He married Mandy

Millsap and their family included Marie (from an earlier relationship of Mandy's), Bob, Judy and Joan. Their only son, William Robert "Bob" Pomeroy, is the subject of this book.

Ross was also the name of Mandy's father. Although it was Grandpa Ross Millsap who became Bob's first larger-than-life hero, Uncle Ralph Pomeroy became Bob's mentor, teacher and friend. Grandpa Ross Millsap had a colorful past that captured the imagination of a young boy and helped him forget about his own unhappiness. Uncle Ralph Pomeroy had a stellar reputation that gave the young man stability and hope for his future. Both men taught him to dream big, follow his heart and never doubt his own ability.

Grandpa Ross Millsap came from Millsap County in Dallas, Texas. He admitted to being a horse thief and stories abound that validate his "wild man" reputation.

Before he left Texas—one step ahead of the law, as he would tell—he swept a ranchman's young daughter off her feet and convinced her to leave with him. Grandma Nelly was raised as a refined young woman and this streak of rebellion must have been the talk of the area for years.

After arriving in Canada, Ross sent letters to people in the US bragging about the huge land tracts he owned in northern Canada. He always told stories, embellished his adventures and his notoriety. In truth, he and Nelly homesteaded on a small tract outside of Fort St. John and raised 11 children.

Martha Olive ("Mandy") was the eldest daughter and she went to work as a domestic when she was barely nine years old. At 20, she was pregnant and unmarried. Showing amazing strength and will for the times, Mandy moved in with another family, gave birth to her daughter Marie and supported the child alone until she met and married the youngest Pomeroy son, Scotty.

The Pomeroy family had done well in the Fort St.John area. They had land, businesses, influence and, more than anything, respect. With a notorious father and her own stigma of being an unwed mother, being courted by one of the Pomeroy men would have finally brought social acceptance to Mandy Millsap's life. Circumstances aside, the marriage was based on love and family members still preserve romantic letters that Scotty wrote to Mandy during their courtship. Ross "Scotty" Pomeroy died in 1999.

Two

"Nothing is so soothing to our self esteem as to find our bad traits in our forebears. It seems to absolve us."
—*VAN WYCK BROOKS, A WRITERS NOTEBOOK, DUTTON* 1958

The Pomeroy family has always been an integral part of the Fort St.John community.

In 1928, Irwin Pomeroy, after living in Edmonton and then farming in Fort Saskatchewan, moved his family and homesteaded a large tract of land in the Fort St. John area. Irwin and his wife instilled in each of their nine children the firm belief that hard work is the only way to achieve success and community influence is a direct result of that success.

Even through the depression the family managed to keep the farm going and eventually Dan, Gordon and Walter each took a quarter-section as their own. (Bill suffered a paralyzing stroke at 21 and lived with brothers or sisters until he moved to a care centre on the West Coast in his senior years.)

When Irwin passed away, the youngest son, Scotty, inherited the original quarter-section and that is where he and Mandy raised their family.

Each of Irwin and Minnie's children had lives worthy of a biography.

People who raised families in the 20's, 30's and 40's in Canada's northwest were strong, committed individuals; men and women who were not afraid of hard work; men and women who saw opportunity in the country; men and women who took chances and created futures for their children and for their community.

Dan Pomeroy moved to Fort Nelson and became the "go-to" guy in town. He owned the saw-mill and was instrumental in getting the first school built there. Dan's communication skills and outgoing nature contributed to his political savvy and he used both these attributes in business and in the community.

Walter and Gordon remained on their farms to raise their families, earning the respect of their friends and neighbours.

It was Ralph who began the true entrepreneurial legacy of the Pomeroys. He bought an existing hotel with a liquor license in Fort St. John in 1939 and renamed it the Pomeroy Hotel. When the Alaska Highway went through in 1942, he opened a lumber business and worked on the Hart Highway. He bought and sold equipment, managed his money well and then bought 50% ownership of the local theatre. In 1952 he sold his hotel and went ranching for a few years. Missing the challenge of commerce and investment, Ralph soon left the ranch and bought his father-in-law's department store. Then he built a second theatre in town.

The Pomeroy brothers and their offspring eventually owned many interconnected businesses and properties in Fort St.John.

Scotty was the only Pomeroy brother who never became an influence in town. He was a small, quiet man, a man with no interest in acquisitions or lofty positions. Intelligent and hard-working as all the other Pomeroy boys, Scotty unfortunately had a problem with alcohol. After finishing school, he was content to spend his days at CanFor and his nights at the local bar.

Most of the Pomeroy boys shared one major trait—big personalities.

Walter alone was a churchgoing, law-abiding teetotaler. Due to his easy-going walk, his usual nickname was "Slow-come", but at the last Pomeroy family reunion, he received a moniker that more aptly reflected his status among the brothers. As the father of the most children, Walter was named "Stud of the Year."

In their younger, single days, the rest of the boys were known as guys who would do almost anything for a good time. Moderation was not a word in their vocabulary.

Dan and Scotty had the reputation of being the worst hell-raisers. Whether they were alone or they were together, most of the escapades involved a vehicle and booze.

In 1957 after receiving $25,000 from the government for expropriated land, Scotty celebrated by buying his brother-in-law Earl's new Dodge. After showing off his new car and going on a "bender", he decided it was time to head out to his farm. Scotty only knew one way to drive—fast—and he put his foot to the pedal. Unfortunately, the new Dodge was low to the ground and the railway tracks were high. Hitting the crossing at top speed was a big mistake. When the Dodge connected with the steel rails, the floor of the car was ripped right off! Undeterred, Scotty managed to get the car home and then used flattened cardboard boxes to craft a new floor.

Dan's cars didn't escape the Pomeroy touch either.

When Dan bought his first new car, he was irritated by a problem with the hood. No matter what he tried, the hood would pop open on the highway. After a particularly aggravating day of tinkering with the car and a few hours nursing a bottle of rye, Dan decided there was only one solution to his problem. He got in the car, headed out onto a long stretch of country road and opened 'er up! After reaching maximum speed and hitting a few good bumps, the hood popped up for the last time and blew off into the ditch. It stayed there.

Dan's next purchase was a new Volkswagen. Once again, he managed to buy a car with problems. After several trips to the garage, Dan was convinced that the Volkswagen was a piece of crap built by Hitler as some diabolical plot against America. He got in the despised car and picked up Scotty. The brothers got a couple of bottles of rye, a couple of sledgehammers and beat the car into a solid mass of junk.

Then there was the infamous "pig run."

Every year, Dan would butcher pigs for freezing and he usually had Scotty help him with the heavy work. It wasn't a pleasant job and the Pomeroy boys utilized quantities of alcohol to make the work more tolerable. The pigs were heavy and needed to be lifted into the scalding pot.

Dan had installed an A-frame winch on the front of his truck and they decided that this winch could be used for lifting the pig carcasses and lowering them into the water. The device worked perfectly, so Dan and Scotty rewarded themselves with a hearty toast of rye. Each finished pig brought another celebratory round of drinks. Finally, when the last pig was slaughtered and lifted onto the winch for scalding, the boys realized that they were out of rye. Not wanting to do the final scalding without some liquid fortitude, Dan and Scotty drove all the way to town with the pig's carcass still hanging from the front of the truck.

Although these anecdotes are about Scotty and Dan, they illustrate the way things were for Bob as he grew up in Fort St.John in the 40's and 50's. This was his family; his dad, his uncle. These were his role models; the men whose behavior he accepted as being normal, whose influence molded his own personality and whose hard living was Bob's example of how a man behaved.

Three

> "Children filled with rage and shame either go to super-achievement or become slobs"
>
> —DR. JOHN BRADSHAW

William Robert Pomeroy was born on the 30th of September, 1947, the only son of Ross "Scotty" and Martha "Mandy" Pomeroy. Along with sisters Judy and Joan, he is left-handed and, as his likewise left-handed friend Gerry Tucker would say, "always in his right mind."

Mandy's family, the Millsaps, were not churchgoers. Her brother, in particular, seemed to have a major dislike of organized religion and made no bones about it. A retired Pastor still remembers the day that Mandy's brother showed up at his door absolutely furious, shaking his fist at him in rage.

Millsap's wife had been attending church with their children and the woman was very insistent that her husband stop drinking, start treating her better and begin behaving like a better father. Millsap took that as a threat to his lifestyle and he threatened to do the Pastor some serious damage if he didn't stop trying to break up good marriages!

Mandy didn't take such a hard line against religion but she did not introduce her brood to any faith either. She may have believed in God but she was too busy raising chickens and selling eggs to worry about teaching her kids about the dangers of eternal damnation. Although she wanted to be a good wife and mother, she did not always succeed with the latter. When Scotty chose to spend time in the hotel pub, Mandy would go into town and drink with him.

She would drop her daughter Marie at her mother's house for hours or even days so that she could be with her husband. After their son Bob was born, she kept her focus on Scotty. Marie would be dropped off at Grandma Millsap's. Any relative that was handy would be pressed into service to stay with Bob. Mandy's brother Earl was a bachelor in those days and he was the usual sitter for the 3 month old baby boy. After Earl went to the Yukon to work, he would come to stay with Mandy and Scotty on his weeks off and still end up babysitting while Bob's parents sat in the pub. Marie, as usual, was with Grandma.

Once Judy and Joan were added to the brood, the general neglect of parenting continued. Only the size of the family changed and the Pomeroy kids grew up by the seat of their pants. With four kids at home, Mandy spent less time at the bar with Scotty but she had the majority of the duties of running the farm. She had her chickens to feed, her eggs to sell, and a sick daughter to tend. The three healthy kids learned how to take care of themselves and each other. For the most part, the kids did very well.

Then Bob fell face-first into a rose bush.

Local doctors did as much as they could to help repair Bob's injured eyes but it was obvious that he required the skill of specialists in Vancouver. Scotty could not leave as the family needed his regular paycheque. Mandy had to be at the farm to keep everything running. Bob was sent to Vancouver for treatment alone. While there, he was boarded with the Mercer family and expected to navigate his way to and from the hospital treatment centre on his own. He was barely 8 years old, had never been away from Fort St. John, and had never taken a city transit bus.

Not surprisingly, he got lost on his first attempt to return to the Mercer house and he still remembers standing on a Vancouver street, crying his eyes out and asking strangers for help.

Back in Fort St.John, the sight of Bob sitting alone on the corner outside of the hotel was a common sight. His sisters generally hung out together at the house but when Bob wasn't with his cousins Mike and Pat, he was a loner; kicking stones, watching, thinking.

It is an undeniable fact that Mandy was very courageous in deciding to keep her first baby. In the 40's, unwed mothers would automatically be banished to a convent and then be ordered to give the child up for adoption. Considering that she only had a grade two education, Mandy managed to survive. She worked as a live-in domestic for an understanding family that allowed her to keep her daughter with her.

She learned how to manage money and she finally found a man who loved her enough to accept her child. Mandy took pride in the Pomeroy name and, perhaps due to Marie's known illegitimacy, she was especially demanding of the girl. Marie had been diagnosed with a brain tumor and was a difficult child. Mandy loved her first daughter but often used violent discipline with her. Her frustration with the girl's behavior could erupt into fury when provoked.

Neither of Bob's younger sisters recalls incidents of abuse towards Marie.

In fact, both women adamantly refute stories of Mandy using physical violence towards their half-sister. This is contradictory to incidents remembered all-too-vividly by Bob and by others who were shocked witnesses.

One particularly upsetting episode occurred when Bob was perhaps ten. Marie would have been about fourteen. A cousin was outside in their yard and heard a lot of yelling coming from the house. When the cousin ran inside to investigate, the scene was chaotic. Marie had been thrown to the floor and Mandy was astride her, pounding her head against the floor. Marie was crying, saying she was sorry for whatever she had done and begging her mother to stop but Mandy kept up with the head-pounding. Bob kept trying to pull his mother off the girl but was loudly warned to stay away or he would suffer the same fate. At that age, Bob knew he wouldn't stand a chance against his powerful mother—especially if she was enraged. Both he and his cousin ran outside, not knowing what to do. Bob felt helpless and he stood by the house, tight-fisted, tight-lipped and seething with anger.

Mandy and Scotty's kids do agree that they were left to fend for themselves a lot of the time and they handled many of the farm jobs that a father would normally do.

When fall came and the weather turned, Mandy would remind Scotty to order a stock of wood. But then the wood would just sit in the yard while the children shivered in a cold house and the parents warmed their seats in the hotel downtown.

Bob became the man out of necessity and out of a protective love for his sisters. Only 11 or 12, and still a skinny little kid, Bob would grab a huge wood saw and tackle the logs.

Too lightweight to manage the job on his own, he would sit one of his sisters, usually Joan, on the log to keep it steady enough for him to work the saw. Sometimes, when a log was particularly large, he would enlist his sister Judy to grab the other end of the saw and help him get the job done.

Cousins who came over to play recall standing around watching in awe as Bob sawed logs until he was exhausted and crying, his fingers blistered and bleeding from his efforts.

About that time, Marie's tumor got worse and Mandy travelled to Edmonton to be with her while the girl underwent tests and treatments in the city hospital. Bob, Judy and Joan got farmed out to various relatives for weeks at a time and never complained. They were fed, protected and warm for these brief intervals so were quite happy with the arrangements.

Home life didn't improve when Mandy returned. If Mandy took Joan to town with her, she would leave the preteen alone to hang around while she went to the hotel to sit with Scotty. Hours would pass and Joan could only hope that her mother would remember she was outside. More often than not, Joan would be forgotten. Too tired and too hungry to wait any longer, she would call her Aunt Lottie and ask for a ride home.

In spite of absences from the house and regardless of her lack of parenting skills, Mandy was a lioness when it came to defending both the family name and her offspring. Although she disciplined her children harshly, she would not allow anyone else to criticize any one of them.

When Bob was in grade five, he was in the school choir. During one concert, all the parents had been invited and Mandy had made the effort to attend.

Things began well enough but suddenly the male teacher put his hands up, stopped a song and looked directly at Bob. With some amount of harshness, and a move that would be unacceptable in today's schools, he admonished the young boy in front of the whole crowd with "Mr. Pomeroy, you are off-key." Naturally, Bob was embarrassed but what happened next embarrassed him even more.

Mandy stood up and loudly told the teacher that her son's name was

"Bob" and that he could not speak to him like that. The inexperienced teacher then lipped back to Mandy, telling her that he could call his students anything he wished to call them.

Big mistake.

Mandy rushed forward, grabbed the teacher by his hair and slugged him. And then she walked out.

For Mandy, Mr. Pomeroy was her husband. Her son, Bob, was still a boy and, although he hadn't earned the title of "Mr." yet, he was still a Pomeroy and entitled to respect. The incident was the talk of all the parents.

From that day on, any time kids misbehaved in the schoolyard, the other kids would taunt them with "Watch out or Mrs. Pomeroy will get you!"

Bob would laugh along with them but he was cringing with embarrassment.

The Fort St. John version of the "Three Amigos" (Bob, his cousins Pat and Mike) hung around together a lot and each of them admits to instigating one bit of mischief or another. These were high-spirited young boys with no video games or non-stop television programming to fill their summer days. Left to their own imaginations, the boys resorted to playing jokes on other family members.

When the boys were ten to twelve year olds, they stole a case of beer from Pat and Mike's older brother Irwin. The kids sat in the shade beside the farm slough, watching the cows meander about in the murky water, and they chug-a-lugged the full dozen bottles of ale. Needless to say, they got very drunk. Then they started to worry about Irwin's probable reaction. No one remembers who thought up the brilliant solution to their dilemma but they all recall what they did next.

Wading in with the cows, the boys refilled all twelve bottles with the disgustingly dirty water. Then they very carefully recapped them all and placed them back in the case.

The next afternoon, a Sunday, when his buddies dropped by, Irwin brought out the case of "cold ones" he had promised. As he uncapped the bottles, he had no idea he was being watched by the three conspirators who were peering around a corner. When all the guys had beer in hand, they raised the bottles in "toast" and took a long swig. The gagging, spitting, and retching were swiftly followed by yells and curses when Irwin heard laughter coming from behind the house. He started running and the three kids high-tailed it as fast as they could. Finally feeling they were far enough away for temporary safety, the boys fell to the ground and laughed until they were physically ill.

This was also the summer that the "Three Amigos" got into the big "Chicken Slaughter."

At 11, Bob already had a 22 rifle and one afternoon the boys decided it would be fun to practice target shooting. They didn't have any money for shells so they headed into town and shoplifted a few boxes from their Uncle Ralph's Central Department Store. Back at Bob's farm, they began shooting cans off the fence. Soon bored with that, someone, most likely Bob, got the bright idea that there would be more of a challenge in shooting at some of the chickens that were scurrying about the yard.

Before long, they were out of shells and took a moment to look around their firing range. Shocked at the realization that they had killed at least a dozen of Mandy's egg producers, the sharpshooters grabbed the carcasses and threw them into the dugout.

Pat and Mike headed home hoping their Aunt wouldn't take a head count of her poultry. She didn't have to. By the time Mandy got home that evening, the dead chickens were floating on the surface of the water in the dugout, feathery witness to the afternoon's massacre.

There are two versions to what happened next. The first one is the story that Bob bragged about to pals, trying to make light of the situation and to make himself sort of a tough guy. In that version, Bob said that when his mother asked what happened to her chickens, he blithely remarked that they must have drowned.

The other version, the truer one as told by both cousins, is not as flippant.

Mandy saw her chickens floating in the dugout and immediately demanded that Bob tell her the truth. Bob was frightened and he told her that he, along with Mike and Pat, had shot the birds and were sorry.

Mandy was furious, as could be expected, but she wanted to hear the story from Mike and Pat as well. She called over to Gordie's farm and told her brother-in-law what Bob had said. Unfortunately for Bob, Mike and Pat were so scared of Mandy—even more than they feared the wrath of their father—that they lied through their teeth and said they had been nowhere near the farm that day.

Mandy chose to believe Mike and Pat.

Bob got two major beatings that day; the first, for shooting the chickens and the second for lying to his mother. In each beating, he got one "hit" for each chicken that had been killed. This physical abuse only increased Bob's antagonism towards his mother. He could tolerate the beatings and he could tolerate the hard farm chores. But he could not put up with the fact that she chose to believe other people's lies when he told the truth.

(Note: When Mike Pomeroy was in Vancouver being interviewed for this book, he became very emotional about the chicken event. The memory of Bob's bruises from the beatings and the memory of his denials had brought everything back, even after fifty years. When Mike returned to Fort St.John, he telephoned Bob to apologize again.)

Mandy's chickens became one way Bob could get some revenge. He never destroyed quantities of them at one time but chose to be smarter about his "culling of the herd." Mike and Pat, feeling remorseful about allowing Bob to take all the punishment for the "big kill", were eager to pay Mandy back for beating their cousin.

From time to time the three boys would steal one chicken from her and take it back to Gordie's farm. With the help of Irwin, the boys had built a thirty foot tree-house, complete with a trap door. When an unfortunate chicken was taken to the tree-house, the boys would hold a "kangaroo court", the bird being designated as the accused prisoner. Mike would be the prosecutor, Pat the hapless defense attorney and Bob the judge. Once the judge declared his verdict, a noose was affixed and the trap door utilized for the execution. In this court, the bird was always found guilty and always hung by the neck until dead.

The one time that Bob bent his own "one chicken" rule, he paid for it the hard way.

Needing some cash, Bob tossed a few of his mother's chickens into a burlap bag, got on his horse and headed to town to make a quick sale.

He didn't take the time to tie the birds' legs together and just tossed them into a burlap bag tied to the back of the saddle. Eventually the sharp claws were able to make some holes and the hens began to scratch wildly. Feeling the jabs, the horse retaliated by bucking hard. Bob was thrown to the ground, the chickens escaped and the young rustler got nothing but bumps and bruises for his efforts.

Bob's home remained a contradiction. There would be loud, almost violent, discipline or there would be no discipline at all. Bob was given no rules and yet he was expected to behave. He was often afraid to go home—especially when his parents were drinking or fighting—or both, which was the norm.

One afternoon, when he was perhaps 12, Bob came running over to a neighbour's house, extremely upset and fighting tears. As it would be, this was the home of the local Pastor, Bob Rogers. When Rogers calmed him down and asked what had happened, Bob told him that Scotty had come home drunk and that his furious mother had taken a hot frying pan off the stove and had hit his father over the head—hot butter and eggs included. He didn't know if his dad was dead or alive. Pastor and Mrs. Rogers let Bob stay for supper with their family and go home only when things had calmed down and they were assured that Scotty would be all right.

What the young boy didn't know was that Pastor Rogers lost a lot of sleep worrying about his young neighbour. Bob was a skinny, almost gaunt, boy and when he had turned up at the Rogers' home that afternoon, he had been shaking in fear. Rogers had not had any personal contact with either Scotty or Mandy. He had heard rumors, of course, but as a man of the cloth, he wanted no part of town gossip. He wanted to see for himself just what kind of parents could cause such turmoil in a boy.

Rogers knew that Mandy Pomeroy raised chickens for extra household income so he went to the house one afternoon to enquire about buying fresh eggs. Marie answered the door but did not welcome Rogers into the house. She yelled back over her shoulder "Ma . . . there's a man at the door who wants to buy eggs" and almost immediately Mandy appeared.

Word around town was that Scotty's wife was a fastidious housekeeper, to the point of being extreme. Everyone seemed to know that each evening, after the children were in bed, Mandy would scrub every inch of her kitchen floor and then pour boiling water over it to rinse. She would repeat the floor scalding in the morning.

Because of her reputation for cleanliness, Rogers had expected to see "June Cleaver", white apron at all. He actually hoped that he would be meeting a gentle, motherly woman- a quiet woman driven to physical violence in a rare moment.

The woman who came to the door had a cigarette in her mouth, a long ash dangling precariously at the end of it. Her booming voice and brusque manner gave him reason to believe that the frying pan incident may not have been an isolated case and he promised himself to find time for Bob whenever it was needed.

After that, it became a regular habit of Bob's to go to the Rogers home after school. It was his safe haven and young Bob became quite fond of "Pastor Bob." He began to hang out with the Rogers boys, Darryl and Darcy, and more than once instigated some group mischief. When the trio would be caught, Bob would stand in their kitchen and quizzically watch the others being reprimanded. He couldn't understand balanced family dynamics and he certainly wasn't accustomed to communication or positive reinforcement.

After one of the juvenile capers went wrong, Darryl and Darcy Rogers were tongue-lashed by their father and given some arduous chores to do as penance. The boys were really disgusted because they had been punished and nothing happened to their partner-in-crime.

They begrudged the fact that they had strict parents and told Bob he was one lucky kid. Bob told the boys that they were the lucky ones. Darryl was shocked and asked Bob why he would say such a stupid thing. With wisdom beyond his years, Bob remarked that the boys were "lucky because your parents love you." Still unconvinced, Darryl told Bob that he was ". . . nuts! You weren't punished!" to which Bob responded, "That's what I mean. My parents don't give a damn."

This keen sense of observation has served Bob well. He watched the Rogers family. He watched other Pomeroy families. And he watched his own. He soon learned to determine which adults could be trusted and he learned how to analyze people, how to sense motivation and how to protect himself from hurt.

Bob instinctively knew that one of the adults he would be able to depend on was Pastor Rogers. Pastor Bob always told Bob the truth and didn't pull any punches. Their talks were the basis for an almost father-son relationship. This kind neighbour understood Bob's need for approval and he never turned him away or was too busy to talk.

(Many years later, after Bob was married to Marj and briefly attended a local church, he invited Pastor Rogers to come and speak to the congregation. When he introduced his old mentor, Bob told the members to listen carefully and to believe every word the man said, that this was one of the few men he truly respected. Although the Pastor and his wife were a lot older than Marj and Bob, they spent a lot of time with the couple. Tim and Kim even attended Sunday School at the "People's Church" where Rogers was the Pastor.)

By the time Bob was 12, he was treated as a man. For better or worse, his childhood was gone. He knew how to handle a gun and ride a horse. He depended on no one. If he needed money, he would babysit for friends. If he needed to hang out with someone who treated him like a son, he'd go see Pastor Rogers or go moose hunting with grown men from the area.

He'd be gone for an afternoon or he'd be gone overnight. No one noticed and no one seemed to care. If he needed someone to cover for him, he'd ask his sister Judy. The siblings had an unspoken pact—neither one would ever "rat" on the other nor would either one stop from protecting the other to the end.

For some reason, perhaps due to the community's lack of respect for his parents, perhaps due to the incident with the choir teacher years prior, Bob was singled out. Teachers didn't know quite how to deal with him and some were downright cruel. Instead of finding out how to help him with classes, they labelled him as stupid. The truth was that Bob, like most of the Millsaps, had a reading problem. He is not dyslexic. He sees letters correctly but his mind seems to race too fast to concentrate and turn the letters into words. This idiosyncrasy frustrated the heck out of him when he was young.

Bob always knew he wasn't stupid. In fact, he figured he was smarter than most of the kids he saw getting smiles of approval from the teachers. When his lack of reading skills kept him from getting good grades, he simply gave up.

Many people remember him being called out for doing absolutely nothing wrong.

If several students misbehaved, it would be Bob who got the strap. If the entire class was noisy, it would be Bob who was made to stand and be chastised. If something was missing or broken, it was Bob who the principal would accuse. His best friend Viggo couldn't understand why Bob bore the brunt of the discipline.

Although Bob did stir up some of the disruption, Viggo still remembers clearly that most of the punishment piled on Bob was unfair and unwarranted. He was put back a year and the only saving grace of that embarrassment was having his sister Judy in the same classroom.

As a team, they were less vulnerable to being picked on and they became each other's support system.

During that time, Scotty had a few lucid moments and reconnected briefly with his son. Getting an especially good cheque one month, Scotty bought Bob a horse. This was a big event for Bob. When Grandpa Ross gave him a horse, it was always a stolen one and soon recovered by the owner. "Trinket" was his to keep, something that truly belonged to him. Scotty had not shown Bob affection in the past and he had never spent time with his son in the way that most dads do. Bob was entering puberty and just learning about emotions and relationships. He knew that he felt good inside when he got this gift from his father and it was an easy step for a young boy to equate love with gifts. Unfortunately, less than a year later, Trinket got into a supply of oats and died.

The summer that Bob was 13, the travelling circus arrived in Fort St. John. Bob and an older pal, Manny, worked in the booths for a couple of weeks, saved their daily pay and then took off together for Victoria, BC. They were still kids but they got jobs working at Gibson's 7-pin bowling alley for the rest of the summer. Bob only made enough money to survive but he was happy to be on his own and away from the turmoil of his home. By the end of August, though, the job ended and he used the last of his money for a bus ticket back to the farm.

Bob started school that September but the writing was on the wall for any possible success. He had barely completed grade six and for grade seven, the teachers had placed him in the dreaded "Occupational Class." He was teased mercilessly. Even Judy couldn't help him any more as she was in the regular classroom.

Bob only tolerated his days at school. The final blow came one afternoon when one teacher reached her limit. She was not equipped to handle a boy who had reading difficulties and her own frustration was often vented in sarcastic remarks towards her student.

On the day in particular, when Bob did not have the answer she had been looking for, she looked him in the eye and loudly proclaimed, "You are stupid and just warming a seat in this classroom. You'll never amount to anything."

Bob walked out of the room, went home and told Mandy that he was quitting school. She was very angry as she expected each of her children to live up to the Pomeroy name. Bob could not be moved on his decision so Mandy gave him an ultimatum. Go back to school or get out.

Bob chose to get out.

He packed up some clothes and walked over to Uncle Merle and Aunt Lottie's. They let him stay with them and gave him a job washing floors in the Frontier Hotel for $1.00 a day plus his room and board. Some days in the winter, when it was too cold to walk back to Aunt Lottie's, Bob would just curl up on the bathroom floor of the hotel and sleep there. On his days off he would go to the farm to visit his sisters, go riding with Pat and Mike or stop to visit his Grandpa Ross Millsap.

When he stopped by to see his sisters, Bob would try to time his visits so that Mandy would not be home and a confrontation could be avoided. Although his beatings were finally behind him, Bob still preferred not to deal with his mother. If they did meet, he faced her with open antagonism. The physical attacks had been one thing but the boy had been hurt deeper by his mother's refusal to believe anything he said. He had absolutely no respect for her and it showed. One afternoon, as Bob was heading out on horseback with Pat and Mike, Mandy made the mistake of asking where they were going. Without blinking, Bob responded with "None of your f**king business." Mandy just turned on her heel and walked away.

The mother-son relationship has never been repaired.

Ross Millsap was hardly the perfect role model for a young school dropout but Bob was looking for a man unlike his father. He wanted to be part of a man "with balls"; one who created his own excitement- a man who did as he wanted and who went where he wanted. He wanted to be connected to a man who didn't give a damn what others said about him.

Grandpa Ross spun stories and Bob listened in awe. He believed what he wanted to believe. Bob knew what people in town said about his grandfather but he also knew that the men who criticized Ross behind his back were the same men who would stand around listening to him recount his latest adventure.

These were the same men who would loosen up after a few drinks and announce that they wished they could have the same free lifestyle; that they could just run off when times got tough.

Ross had a wife and a farm and a bunch of kids but he managed to come and go as he pleased.

Grandpa Millsap was the original free spirit and he never hid his appreciation for the female population. Bob used him as the best "bad example" and emulated many of his flirting techniques, even after he saw the lecherous codger turn into the stereotypical "dirty old man."

He never slowed down. When Ross was in his eighties, Bob and his then wife, Marj, picked him up to drive him to the Edmonton race track. As the car rolled past an attractive young woman, Ross stuck his head out the open window to crane his neck and make sexist comments about the girl's luscious legs and "tender young thighs." Finally retired to a nursing home in Pouce Coupe, and right up to the day he died, Grandpa Ross would flirt and pat women's backsides.

Millsap was an acknowledged horse thief but no one did anything about it. He was a womanizer but no one complained. He had no job and no sense of commitment but his family survived.

He was a fabricator of stories but, because he told people what they wanted to hear, no one called him a liar. He was a big man, a rough and tumble kind of "man's man" and Bob idolized him. He knew his grandfather's faults and his reputation but he also knew that the old man loved him unconditionally and always had time to listen to him. When Ross turned up at Scotty's farm after another of his absences, he usually had a horse to turn over to his grandson. Bob was thrilled and didn't even mind when the true owner appeared in a few days to reclaim his property. What the heck! He had a great horse to ride for a little while and that was more than he got from his parents.

Riding horses gave Bob freedom and an escape from his troubles. He could get on a horse, ride for miles and not hear any yelling or see any abuse. Horses became his sanctity, his escape. He continues to find solace and security in their strength and loyalty.

What most people probably don't know about Grandpa Ross was that he didn't always steal horses for himself. In today's vernacular, he would be called a "hired gun" because, in fact, Ross earned money for his family by stealing horses under contract.

He was an employee of the "big boys" who did not want to get their own hands dirty. And, besides, there was arguably no one in the entire Peace region who could wrangle or tame horses like Ross Millsap.

Fred Cunningham clearly remembers Ross being dropped off, along with two saddles and at least four halters, just outside of the Peavine Metis Settlement by a helicopter. A few days later, a truck would appear and Ross would be riding one horse and leading three or four others.

There would be a trade-off with Ross keeping one horse and earning some cash to get supplies for his family. Everyone on the Peavine Settlement knew Ross and Ross knew every Metis and Native in the region. There was an understanding between them; he didn't steal their horses and they treated him like a friend and brother, never turning him in.

Ross Millsap was most certainly an independent character. He always did things his way. When he put his mind to something, there was nothing that would change it. He remained stubbornly single-minded, even as he approached the end of his life. When he was ninety years old, he took off for the woods and spent the winter alone in a cave in minus 30-degree weather!

Bob did have another father figure in town. After school, he sometimes walked along with a younger classmate, Nancy Broadhurst. Nancy's father George owned the car wash and he didn't mind when the local kids hung around.

George figured that, if the kids were at the car wash and talking with him, they weren't getting into trouble. He sold Coca Cola, had music playing and the boys could watch cars being washed and talk about which ones they would buy when they were older.

The car wash, like most service stations and stores in the 50's, had an old chest style cooler. It was filled with water and a compressor kept the bottles of pop nicely chilled; the coke bottles hanging by their necks on a conveyor. When a quarter was dropped into the coin slot, the conveyor would move back and release the neck of one bottle at the beginning of the row. Bob would sit on a stool beside the cooler and watch the mechanism each time someone dropped in a coin. He studied the cooler and the bottles from every angle. He had no cash but he did have a teenager's thirst for Coca Cola and he did have the ability to figure things out for himself.

Soon customers began to complain that they were receiving empty bottles for their quarters.

When George checked his cooler, sure enough, he found a few empties still hanging by their necks and, when he went to refill the cooler, he noticed that the empty bottles were at the end of the rows.

One afternoon he hid around a corner to see just what was happening. Bob arrived with the other kids and, as soon as he was alone, he reached into his pocket, pulled out a regular bottle opener, reached inside and popped a top off a bottle from the back of the row. Then he carefully joined two straws together. Leaning over the cooler and inserting the extended straw, Bob cleverly enjoyed a nice cold bottle of Coca Cola. When he straightened up, however, he found George Broadhurst at his side and George was not happy.

Bob was instructed to sit on top of the icy cooler and not to move an inch until George came back to let him go.

He sat there for much longer than planned. George got busy and then left the car wash to do some business downtown. He totally forgot about Bob sitting on the cooler until hours later. Rushing back, George was surprised to see that Bob had remained in his appointed place. He apologized for leaving and praised the boy for not taking off. In turn, Bob apologized for stealing the cola and said he deserved the punishment.

The two became close friends and George always encouraged Bob to go after what he wanted in life; he told the boy that he was as worthy as anyone else and probably a whole lot smarter.

Years later, when Nancy told her father about Bob's successes, George told her that nothing ever came easy for Bob, that people had to give him credit for his efforts because he had to work twice as hard for everything he ever got.

He didn't know just how true this was.

Four

"The only thing that overcomes hard luck is hard work"
—*HARRY GOLDEN*
SIMPSONS CONTEMPORARY QUOTATIONS

A lack of a high school education reduces the prospects for a successful future.

Dropping out of school at thirteen certainly stacks the odds against a boy even more.

Anyone who begins such a "hard luck life" without a strong will or a sharp mind usually ends up earning a meager living. Thankfully, Bob did possess both a strong will and a sharp mind. He also had a strong back and did not mind doing physical work. Whatever it took to be on his own, whatever it took to make money, he would do.

After the summer of being first a "carny" and then a bowling alley pin-boy, Bob spent a lot of his time hanging around with Uncle Ralph. He had been living with Uncle Merle and Aunt Lottie, helping at the hotel but, essentially, he just existed day to day.

With his friends in school, his pockets empty and his life in turmoil, Bob became a loose cannon. He quickly earned a reputation for being a fighter and a storyteller and many of the Pomeroys detached themselves from him, thinking he would self-destruct. He was his own worst enemy because he kept the situation at home a secret. Hardly anyone knew the basis of his anger.

The ones who did know just shook their heads and kept quiet. In those days, people did not get involved in the business of others. No one paid attention to the changes in the young boy's personality. If they had, they may have realized that it was only when Bob felt threatened or insecure that he resorted to using his fists.

Uncle Ralph had kids of his own. They were going to university or working and were giving him a great source of pride and contentment.

He liked young Bob and it hurt him to see a nephew floundering in a sea of trouble. He did not know exactly how he could help the boy but soon enough a solution walked right in his door. A couple of regular customers of Central Department Store, Cliff and Helen Innes, operated a large sheep herd outside of Fort St.John. The American couple had brought the first huge herd of sheep to northern BC and they had great difficulties in finding ranch hands who would work with anything but cattle. Their own teenagers attended school and their herd was too large for their one foreman, Hank, to handle. They mentioned their difficulties to Ralph one day when they stopped in for supplies. Without a second thought, Ralph told them he had a nephew who could ride a horse and handle a rifle.

The next day Bob was a sheepherder.

The Innes couple gave Bob a heavy lamb jacket and some warm winter clothes and drove him out to the range. They paid him $1.00 a day plus provisions and gave him a "wall tent" (tent with three-foot walls and a stove) to sleep in. He worked 14-hour days and learned to be even more self-reliant. On his horse for hours at a time in rain, sleet or snow, Bob found ways to keep warm and keep his stomach filled. Hank appreciated the company as well as an extra pair of eyes watching the sheep, and he treated the boy as an equal.

The men used a rubber-tired farm wagon called a "gutwagon" to transport their provisions. (It was called a gutwagon because it literally knocked the guts out of anyone riding it over the bumpy range.)

One afternoon, Bob was sitting on the front seat of the wagon, supposedly guarding the sheep.

It was a hot spring day and he dozed off in the sunshine.

Hank had been riding around the far perimeter of the herd and when he got in sight of the wagon, he noticed that Bob had fallen asleep on the job. The horse attached to the wagon was quietly grazing. First Hank tried to wake the boy up by waving and shouting. When he got no response, the former Green Beret sharpshooter carefully took aim and fired a single shot just over the horse's head. The horse was startled and immediately bolted, waking Bob up and knocking him off the front seat and back into the wagon. There was no time to grab the reins and Bob endured a "gutbusting" ride all around the range until the spooked horse finally calmed down and stopped.

From that day onward, Bob learned to stay awake—and to keep his hands on the reins at all times.

Spring brought new lambs and the little ones were the most vulnerable to preying wolves. Hank and Bob built a large corral for the lambs, one with strong, 4 foot high fencing. Each night the two men would take turns patrolling the corral.

They would wear gas lamps on their hats to light the dark corners and help them see unwelcome visitors.

On one of Bob's shifts, as he turned the corner to enter the corral, he came across a huge grey wolf. The size of the animal scared Bob so much that he dropped his lamp, turned on his heel and ran to get Hank. The older man was not fazed. It was his turn to sleep and he just yelled at the boy and told him to go back, get his lamp and keep guarding the sheep. Bob did as he was told, albeit shaking with fear. The next night, the wolf returned and, although Hank took a shot at it, the animal managed to get away.

The huge wolf turned up every few days that spring. He would appear suddenly and then take off when either Bob or Hank tried to shoot him. He never was caught. Everyone thought that the men were exaggerating the wolf's size but their description was validated when, months later, another rancher saw a grey wolf large enough and powerful enough to kill his cow and haul away the entire head!

Cliff and Helen took notice of their young charge in many ways.

After Bob had worked for them for a month and had received his first paycheque ($25.00), they took him into town and gave him a bonus—a brand new pair of jeans and well-fitting shirt. This gift would have equaled two week's pay and Bob was floored at their kindness.

During his time working for the Innes family, Bob spent his day off hanging out at their ranch. Cliff and Helen's kids were Bob's age and he could act like a regular teenager around them. Scotty and Lana had an unruly horse called "Penny" and the boys were determined to tame it. Bob, in particular, seemed to feel the necessity of proving his horsemanship and manhood.

Time after time, the boys would race after the horse and try to get astride her. Finally, Bob was successful and walked the animal around slowly to keep her calmed down. After a few minutes, Bob started to boast a bit to the others about just how skilled a horseman he was. Lana was impressed but Scotty thought Bob needed a dose of reality. He grabbed a pail and threw it at the horse.

Penny bucked high and hard, pitching Bob off against a tree.

When he landed, he had the wind knocked out of him but not the mischief. He lay very still and unresponsive. Minutes passed and both Lana and Scotty panicked. When they started to run back to the house screaming that they had killed their friend, Bob sat up and started to laugh.

After almost a year with the Innes sheep, Bob knew for certain that he could handle hard work.

He had spent many long nights thinking and planning and had decided that, if he used his head and applied a good work ethic to business, he could make something of his life.

The next spring he headed back to town.

There wasn't any real work available for a 15-year-old boy so Bob did whatever he wanted and dropped by the farm when he felt like seeing his sisters. People in town did not have expectations of him becoming much of anything and they tired of him just hanging around. At 16, the police picked him up for vagrancy. They dropped him off at the farm and warned him to smarten up.

Judy didn't know what "vagrancy" meant but she knew it had to be trouble enough for the police to get involved. She was frightened and urged him to find a job somehow. Mandy wasn't home and Scotty was at the local pub as usual, so Bob jumped in his dad's truck and took off back to town. Unfortunately, he backed into another vehicle and caused some damage. Bob drove the truck back to the farm and left without mentioning the accident. As Scotty was usually "in the cups", he did not realize his truck had been in an accident. When the police arrived at the farm the next day carrying a paint chip that matched the truck, Scotty knew nothing. Judy, of course, said nothing and Bob was long gone!

Once Bob had dropped the truck off, he headed back to town and asked his Uncle Merle to get him a job with Arrow Drilling right away. He took off for the rigs before Scotty or Mandy could get hold of him and he spent the next six weeks cleaning up the campsite for the drilling company.

By the time he was 17, Uncle Merle gave him a job "roughnecking." The days were long and the work hard but Bob found ways to lighten up the time in camp. After everyone had been teasing Ethel, the camp cook, about the bland food, Bob decided to take it one step further. He threw a 2-inch hammer into the pot of simmering soup one day. When the cook discovered the hammer, Bob told her that his boss, Freddie Joseph, had done it to add some flavor to the meal.

After the job ended, Bob returned to Fort St.John with some cash in his jeans and an exaggerated boast of being a "skilled motorman." His cousins knew that he hadn't worked on the rigs long enough to achieve that status but they also admitted that he probably learned more than anyone else would have done in that time. They also knew that he had a deep need to be recognized and to be appreciated for accomplishing something so they kept their mouths shut and just enjoyed his company.

Bob's run-ins with law officers in those days were numerous, as he had no respect for authority figures. His father was weak, his mother was a bully, and his teachers had been overbearing, ill-trained enforcers. Bob did what he wanted, and came very close to taunting the police to stop him. He ended up with the reputation of being a hoodlum.

In one instance, however, Bob redeemed himself and became almost a local hero.

One of the RCMP officers in Fort St.John was especially miserable to teenagers.

There were many times that he allegedly abused his authority and overstepped his boundaries. The kids hated him. Bob was 19 at the time and he had already experienced some run-ins with this particular cop. At one Legion dance, the officer seemed to be going overboard with his harassment of the teens, pushing them physically and abusing them verbally. When he reached Bob, he harshly grabbed him by the necktie and held his grasp even though it was obvious that Bob was choking. Fortunately, Bob broke free and then he used all his might to swing at the cop and punch him to the ground. Everyone who had seen the incident stood around and cheered. The embarrassed cop was now furious and he called for backup. Bob was arrested and taken to the holding cells. What people never knew is that a few of the RCMP officers got together in the cells that night and beat the teenager up badly. Bob never gave them the satisfaction of complaining.

Bob's free time was not always spent in fighting.

He had inherited an appreciation for women from his Grandpa Ross.

To call Bob a "ladies man" would be an understatement.

Puberty hit him like a plank across the back of his head and he never slowed down to check for injury.

He knew he needed to dress well to pursue the fairer sex so was always on the hunt for a way to make money.

After Bob's childhood friend, Viggo Pedersen had finished high school, the two of them headed to Slave Lake to work as "slashers" for the pipeline. They had been given a small trailer to live in but did not have the foresight to plan for food until their first payday. It was already very cold and the trailer had no heater. The boys used the gas oven to try to keep warm and they pooled together their few dollars to buy what they could afford.

They lived for days on instant puddings mixed with water.

Cold, hungry and ill prepared for working in the cold, the boys muddled along but Viggo was injured and had to go home after little more than a week. Bob managed to stay at the job longer but he could not handle the cold of the trailer alone.

After Viggo left, he would go into Slave Lake after work and sleep in the heated washroom of the hotel.

The front desk girls quickly found out what he was doing and they helped him with a pillow and a couple of "borrowed" blankets from the hotel.

Once he got a full paycheque, Bob moved into an apartment with three other pipeline guys, thinking that he would finally have a real bed. Unfortunately, his roommates partied so much that Bob soon found himself sleeping on the hotel washroom floor again just to get a solid night's sleep.

Coming back to Fort St. John with a wallet full of cash, Bob connected with Viggo again and the two decided to head off to Saskatchewan to look for greener pastures.

They picked up a pal, Darcy Rogers (son of the Pastor) and hit the road. They got as far as Mayerthorpe before they were stopped for speeding. Cash and liquor had sharpened Bob's attitude and he got into a verbal altercation with the police officer. The planned road trip was curtailed when Bob was thrown in jail for the night to cool off.

Darcy and Viggo booked into a motel and the next day the three of them began to celebrate Bob's "coming out" party. Bob finally passed out on the bed and left Viggo and Darcy alone to find something to amuse themselves. And so they did. Darcy pulled out a can of black shoe polish and the boys smeared the gooey stuff all over Bob's hands as he slept. Then they softly tickled Bob's face. Naturally, Bob kept wiping away the tickles and ended up transferring the black smudges to his face. When the guys made a lot of noise with their laughter, Bob woke up groggy and cranky. He went to the bathroom, saw his face and was furious. A knock-down, drag-out, fight ensued and the motel room took the worst of the beating.

Finally, Bob picked up the television set and threw it into the bathtub. The huge crash shocked everyone, the free-for-all stopped and the boys headed back home.

About a year later, Bob found himself working in Edmonton.

By then, and in spite of seeing his father's alcoholism, Bob was drinking on a regular basis. In spite of hating the violence he often saw at home, he used the same technique to communicate his own feelings.

Bob palled around with a young neighbour, Billy Genowich, in those days. The boys drank together and somehow Billy could always get his hands on a car.

One summer afternoon, the boys had polished off some liquor and thought it might be a good time to go for a joy ride. They were heading down 118th Avenue, not a care in the world, when they were stopped for speeding. The police officer smelled alcohol and demanded identification from Billy, who was driving.

Billy needed his license for his job and he was terrified. Bob immediately got out of the car and began a heated argument with the police officer, hoping to create a diversion.

When he reached the officer at the other side of the car, Bob suddenly stopped, turned slightly and looked at Billy. When the officer followed his glance, Bob took a swing. The police officer fell to the ground, Bob hopped back in the car and the boys sped off. No ticket had been written and subsequently no arrest was ever made.

That summer Bob tried working as an apprentice sheet metal worker in Edmonton and moved in with his Aunt Dorothy and her family for a short time.

Even there, he felt rejected and only slightly tolerated by his cousins.

In spite of all his bravado, he was insecure and always tried very hard to be as perfect as possible. He kept his room clean and his clothes immaculate but he still felt that he was not accepted as an equal to the more educated, more affluent cousins. His sister Joan thought he was exaggerating about his feeling of rejection but then, on one visit to Edmonton, she saw that he truly was ostracized. His cousin's boyfriend had a dog that was not well trained. Bob had carefully folded his pressed pants over a hanger looped around a doorknob and the young couple watched as the dog peed all over Bob's pants.

They laughed without apology at his misery.

Bob said and did nothing about the incident. He swallowed his pride and hid his hurt. He was, after all, grateful for their family's hospitality.

He took his anger and aggression to the rodeo arena.

There, with the horses, Bob could work out his frustrations. He at least had a fair chance with the rodeo stock. They would buck and kick and roll and he would hang on with everything he had. For a few seconds he would finally feel like he had total control of something in his life.

When he was not on the back of a bucking horse, he was entering the wild horse races with Mike and Pat or bulldogging steers. When the rodeo day ended, the drinking night began. As usual, Bob's mouth got him into trouble more often than not.

He did not always come off on the winning end of fights.

His uncle Les lived in Edmonton and late one Saturday night got a call from a pay phone. The weary, muffled voice managed to say that it was Bob. He had been in a fight and was badly beaten. He did not know who else to call. Les got in his truck, drove to St. Albert and rescued his nephew, no questions asked. Bob was part of his family and that was enough. Les and his wife at the time, Helen, adored Bob and the two of them patched the boy up over the next few days.

A few weeks later, when his cousins Mike and Pat got a place in Edmonton, Bob was overjoyed to move in with them. A fourth roommate, Jim, joined them and life became pretty good for while. There were pubs to drink in, girls to flirt with and regular pay cheques to spend. Pat was only 17 at the time but he carried his brother Irwin's identification in his wallet so he could go to the pubs with Bob and Mike. The ruse generally worked but one night an astute hotel manager called the police. He had taken the trouble to actually look at the photo on Pat's license and noticed that it did not match the face on the kid slurping down beer.

The police were called and the trio was hauled outside.

With the beer providing liquid courage, the boys stood up to the cops and there was a scuffle. The police had intended to toss the kids out of the pub with a warning but then Bob managed to slam a door on one police officer's foot. The furious cop was ready to press charges and he demanded information on all three of the boys.

When he discovered that, although Pat was the youngest, he was also the only one with a steady job, so he just wrote out a summons to appear. He figured that, at the very least, the city would get some money out of the situation and all the boys were allowed to leave. What the police officer never knew, of course, is that Mike was the Pomeroy who actually appeared at court. Pat's job still took precedence and he could not afford to take the day off.

Bob had another encounter with a police officer during these years. Driving to Grande Prairie from Edmonton one evening with this '59 Ford, Bob and his friend Sandy Campbell had stopped in Whitecourt. Bob had a bit too much to drink, so when they resumed the drive, he crawled into the back seat and let Sandy take the wheel.

The car was approaching a hill on the old highway when, just beyond their range of sight, an RCMP cruiser was making a U-turn. As Bob's car sped over the crest of the hill, it T-boned the cruiser. All three were taken to the hospital by ambulance. One of Bob's eyes was virtually knocked out and he needed stitches to repair his face. Sandy was badly shaken up and had cuts and bruises. The police officer was badly injured as well but thankfully, there were no fatalities. Both cars had been demolished, the police car being cut in half from the impact. Although the police officer was making an illegal u-turn on the highway, Sandy was charged with undue care and attention. Bob carried a photo of the wreckage for years!

In spite of the drinking and the narrow escapes, Bob still found the time to chase skirts.

The stories about Bob's womanizing could fill volumes. He searched women out like a heat-seeking missile and the more receptive a girl was to his charms; the more likely he was to move on to the next conquest.

To Bob, getting attention from a beautiful girl meant that he was lovable, that he could be loved.

As a young single guy living in Edmonton, he found a myriad of ways to pick up girls. He found a job selling Aristocrat's "hope chest merchandise" to girls in offices. He excelled at it. Booking home parties, Bob was the centre of attention and he could overcome any obstacle.

One of the company's touted features was the strength of their china plates.

To demonstrate, a salesman would "accidentally" drop a plate on the floor. The dishes were not supposed to break and they usually didn't. At one party, however, when Bob was surrounded by ten or twelve attentive young ladies, Bob dropped a plate and it split into six pieces. Without missing a step, Bob picked up the pieces and handed them around, asking the girls to examine the thickness of the china and see the absence of tiny fragments which, with other china, would surely be dangerous.

Bob didn't see this job as a dead-end career. He saw it as a great opportunity to make money and meet single women. When other guys remarked that selling pots and pans at home parties seemed to be a sissy occupation, Bob laughed and asked them if they knew a better way to be invited to parties as the only guy in a room of six to twenty single girls. He not only loads of phone numbers but he also got commissions.

On his days off, Bob walked around the neighborhood meeting people and getting connected. He soon became aware that there were three cute girls sharing a basement suite nearby. He wanted to meet them but, after a couple of weeks, there had not been an opportunity to "accidentally" run into any of them. One night he snuck over to their window and then loudly kicked it, breaking the glass and scaring them all. Then he ran around to their entrance door, knocked, said he was a neighbour, that he had heard a noise and asked if they were all right. When the girls opened the door, he politely introduced himself and offered to hang around to protect them from whatever hoodlum may still be lurking outside.

He never had a clue that this might have been dangerous nonetheless more than slightly illegal. His crazy idea may have turned out less than humorous if one of the girls' fathers happened to live upstairs!

Although he no longer lived with Les and Helen Collier, he often took his uncle to lunch to tell him about all his latest adventures.

On one of these lunches, he had just finished describing his skills in meeting women when he spotted four girls being seated nearby. Bob winked at Les and said, "Look. I'll show you." He swiftly hid the bottle of ketchup under a jacket. Then he walked over to the girls and asked them if they minded sharing their ketchup. Before he left with the condiment, he had introduced himself and had given his phone number to each one of them. Returning to his own table, Bob said he didn't really care if the girls called or not, he just wanted to prove that he could get friendly with any woman. Then he added, "But I'll betcha at least one will call me."

Bob had such a knack for meeting girls in Edmonton that Pat and Mike always let him lead the way. If the boys stopped for a hamburger, Bob would scope out the restaurant for prospects and would not hesitate to walk over to a table of girls on the pretext of needing ketchup or salt or napkins.

This wasn't Fort St. John, after all. It was the big city and no one in Edmonton knew he was "that loser." In Edmonton, he was just Bob the super-salesman, the guy with the big smile and smooth line.

That would probably be all any other young guy would want out of life but Bob wanted—and needed—more. When Jim decided to head north for higher wages, Bob decided to do the same thing.

He soon found himself working on the rigs outside of Red Earth. The men on the rigs are paid high wages because the work is not only hard, it is dangerous. Bob's life was changed instantly when an accident left him with two severely crushed legs. He was rushed to hospital in Peace River in the back seat of a car. There was no ambulance and certainly no Demerol or Morphine available. To help him tolerate the excruciating pain, the crew members that accompanied him kept giving him gulps of whiskey. By the time they reached Peace River, Bob was extremely drunk. So drunk, in fact, that the medical staff had to sober him up substantially before they could safely administer any prescription medication for his pain.

His legs were badly swollen and the attendants had to cut his pants off to examine him. After seeing the condition of his legs, the medical staff realized that the best they could do was to stabilize him and get him to Edmonton for surgery as soon as possible.

The surgery was just the beginning of Bob's problems. The accident happened in Red Earth, Alberta but the company was based out of BC. The paperwork had not been completed to register the project with the Workers Compensation Board in Alberta and Bob was caught in the middle. He had no money and WCB was not paying a dime until the matter was resolved. Bob went to the welfare office for some interim help but, because he owned a car, he did not qualify. Thankfully, he ran into an old neighbour from the apartment he had shared with his cousins. The man was an RCMP officer and he knew just what to do. He gave Bob a temporary place to sleep and found him a lawyer. Once the lawyer got involved, the WCB found a way to approve both Bob's entitled payments and his therapy. It took months of rehab at the Workers' Compensation facility before he could walk again.

For the next 45 years, Bob lived in constant pain, pain that would have stopped any other man in his tracks. He never let this injury slow him down and he never let it stop his ambition. He knew that pain, like the bucking horses at the rodeo, was something in his life that he could control.

It would not be until December 2008 that Bob's knees would be repaired. When he finally had surgery in Arizona, his specialists said that they did not know how he could have been walking in such a condition, that his knees were virtually smashed. They marveled at his inner strength and tolerance for pain.

Any one who knows Bob would not be surprised.

Unable to work on the rigs anymore, and just 20 years old, Bob was at the mercy of others again. He got a job working for a rental company but quickly figured out that he would not make his mark on the world in anything he would find in Edmonton.

He decided to head back to Fort St. John.

The summer of 1968, Bob felt that his life had taken a sharp turn backwards. He was back in the same town that had held few prospects for him in the past, his former friends were building families, and he was working nine to five at the local Co-Op tire shop.

To make matters worse, the "tough Pomeroy kid" was limping around on busted legs.

With his usual positive attitude and his near-legendary charm with the opposite sex, Bob made the most of his free time. He always had his pal Viggo and he usually had a steady girlfriend.

Bob and one of his girlfriends often double-dated with Viggo and his future wife. Viggo remembers one weekend the boys had some extra cash and decided to really impress the girls. They chartered a small plane to take an aerial tour of the new dam project and the beautiful countryside. Taking off, Bob and his girl settled in to the rear seats and the pilot began his descriptions of the view below. When the flight was over, Viggo turned to Bob to talk about what they had seen. Bob was very shocked that they were on the ground already. The couple had started "necking" and had missed the entire experience. Weeks later, that same girlfriend was history.

Bob had met Marjorie Dutka.

Even though Marj had attended high school with Judy, she had never met Bob. He, of course, had dropped out of sight after he turned 14 and Marj was busy enough with school and her own family to enquire about any of Judy's siblings. In 1968, her only thoughts after graduation were to work hard, save her money and then go on to University. She worked as a cashier at Marshall Wells store and shared a house with three other girls. The last thing on her mind was to get involved with anyone who would interfere with her goals.

Fate had other plans.

One specific Sunday proved to be a "comedy of errors" for both Bob and Marj.

Roughhousing with her roommates in the afternoon, Marj ended up on the floor with a misdirected knee accidentally thrust in her eye. Not only painful, the eye was also swelling shut.

Late that same afternoon, and in another part of town, Bob was in another of his infamous brawls. His eye had caught the hard side of a well-placed fist and was turning darker by the hour.

On his way to work Monday morning, Bob decided to stop by Marshall Wells and get a pair of dark glasses to hide his battle scars. He was surprised to see that the cashier was wearing sunglasses indoors and jokingly asked if she had been in a fight too. The two shared stories and laughed at the coincidence that brought them together. The laughing turned into flirting and the flirting ended in a date that week. Marj seemed too good to be true—a local girl from a good family, a girl who surely knew about his bad boy reputation in town but who cared about him anyway.

Bob fell hard. They were married months later in January 1969. Marj was expecting a baby, they had no place to live and Bob was out of work. They headed back to Edmonton.

Bob's sense of pride was his biggest motivation—that, and his yearning for a real family. No one—ever—would have to take care of his children. He promised himself that his children would always have a dad, a loving mother, and a safe house.

When the newlyweds set up housekeeping, they were renting a small furnished basement suite and sharing the bathroom with the owner's daughters. Bob started a job immediately at a nearby gas station but he really wanted to get into a big company.

Although he was able to convince Loblaw's Grocers to hire him, he was warned that his lack of education would probably hold him back.

Bob took that as an opportunity and a challenge.

He worked his 8-hour shifts to earn his pay and then he worked as many as eight hours more each day without pay, apprenticing with managers from each department, learning the ins and outs of the grocery business.

Soon he became recognized for the speed at which he acquired total comprehension of systems and procedures.

It took only a few months before Loblaw's felt confident in transferring him to Fort Nelson as Assistant Manager to help with the conversion of a local grocer into a Loblaw's subsidiary.

The couple stayed in Fort Nelson almost a year, just long enough for Bob to complete the store conversion and for Marj to give birth to their daughter Kim.

Then it was back to Edmonton where the grocery store proved to have its own hazards for Bob.

Shortly after returning to Loblaw's and resuming work in the produce department, Bob was busily chopping the ends of corn cobs when his hand slipped and he managed to hack off most of his little finger. (In Bob's way of handling things, he has always used this partial amputation to his advantage. When anyone asks him how much schooling he had, he holds up six fingers and his half-finger!)

He had a wife, a toddler and was out of work.

Determined to support his little family, Bob began selling pots and pans door to door. His Aunt Helen insisted that they live with her for a few weeks until they could get some cash together.

For Helen, it was no hardship at all because she enjoyed Marj's company during the day, looked forward to Bob's jokes and stories in the evening and was totally smitten with having sweet little Kim in her house. This was not a good situation for Marj, though. She was pregnant with their second child and she insisted that Bob move them back home.

They returned to Fort St.John in the fall of 1970, and rented a suite in a triplex in town. Bob started working for Uncle Ralph and Tim was born that December.

Five

"Whether you think you can, or think you can't, you are usually right"

—HENRY FORD

For a few years, Bob was the average young father and husband. When he wasn't working, he spent time with Marj and the kids and began to enjoy the life of the middle class. He even found time to coach the baseball team that Marj's younger brother played with.

Working for his uncle Ralph gave Bob the respectability he had always craved.

Uncle Ralph Pomeroy was the family entrepreneur. Although Ralph sent his own son Glen to university, he knew a man could still become successful through a lot of hard work and a little bit of luck. While Glen was becoming a lawyer, his cousin Bob was becoming Ralph's protégé.

Ralph figured that the other Pomeroy boys had fathers they could learn from but Bob had been shortchanged in that department. He saw a bit of himself in Bob. He recognized Bob's need for respect and his willingness to take whatever risks were needed to earn that respect. Ralph's focus on Bob was so strong that he "blew off" other nephews who asked him for advice. He knew the obstacles Bob had to overcome but he also knew that Bob had the heart of a lion. Uncle Ralph was the one person who believed that Bob would eventually end up with more money than anyone else in the family.

At Central Department Store, Ralph gave Bob the freedom to make changes and use his instincts for marketing and promotion.

The population of Fort St.John had risen to over nine thousand by the mid-seventies and a man who knew how to create interest in a business was certain to do well.

Bob set up displays, organized special events and was Ralph's "hands-on" guy whenever and wherever needed. He even modeled parkas and men's wear at a fashion show when not many other guys were willing to get on stage. Ralph, was happy to turn over responsibilities to Bob. He was still one of the few people in town who were not at all surprised at Bob's dependability.

Bob's sense of humor got good use at the store. When he started working for Uncle Ralph, he gave his friend Nancy a job as cashier. Between customers, the two of them would stock shelves and create merchandising displays. One day, after they had set up a western-themed scene using bales of hay, Bob put a saddle on a sawhorse and coaxed Nancy to sit on it and strike a pose. As soon as she was in place, he grabbed a set of "horse hobblers" and fastened her ankles together under the belly of the sawhorse. The he left her there to squirm in embarrassment while he waited on customers. Nancy was a shy seventeen year old and she thought she would never forgive him. She met him with stony silence for days afterwards. They eventually made up after Bob charmed his way back into her good books.

A few years later, after Bob returned to Fort St.John and began making a name in business, Nancy had the opportunity for what she considered justifiable payback.

Bob worked hard to overcome the social shunning he felt in his younger days. He always wore expensive, well-tailored suits; always kept himself immaculately well groomed.

He also made it a point to make daily "walk-abouts" in the community and to stop in to talk to businessmen and their employees. It was his way of keeping an ear to the ground and always knowing what was happening in town.

On his way to an important meeting, Bob stopped by to say good morning to Nancy. Expecting his arrival, she had written, "Horny and available cheap" in black marker on a large piece of paper. As Bob left, Nancy fondly rubbed his upper back, simultaneously attaching the paper sign with tape. Bob never had a clue and he walked around for hours wearing the offensive statement.

Not one person removed the sign nor did anyone tell him about it. By the time he removed his jacket and discovered the prank, hundreds of people had snickered behind his back and he was not a happy camper. It was Nancy's turn to beg forgiveness from Bob and, when she did, she reminded him about his actions years before. They made up but Bob claims that her prank is one reason he's "watched his back" more than ever.

The regular paycheque from Central Department Store and the occasional bonuses made it possible for Bob, Marj, Tim and Kim to move out of their rented house and on to an acreage right next to Scotty and Mandy's farm. The road heading out towards the airport and the land around it even became known as the Pomeroy subdivision. They lived on that acreage for about a year, Bob got some horses and they officially became an established "Fort St.John Pomeroy" family.

Under Ralph's tutelage, Bob started to branch out.

Bob was always 100% business. He treated everyone equally. If there was a job to be done or a favor to be fulfilled, there was a cost to be paid. He was upfront about any and every deal. If someone needed something and Bob could fill that need, he jumped in with an offer. If there was any urgency in the matter, his price would be set higher to reflect that urgency. He applied no pressure. It was up to the individual if the immediate help was worth the cost. Bob never made any bones about overcharging. Nothing was hidden; no arrangement was underhanded. The deal would be put on the table and, if terms were met, things were done as promised. Bob soon became the "go-to" guy in Fort St.John and he worked seven days a week to maintain that status.

He always remembered to financially thank anyone who helped him get things done and he made sure to repay special favors as soon as possible.

People wanted to be his friend—a far cry from school years—and even if they did not know him personally, some people liked to say that they did. George Martin still laughs about one afternoon when he and Bob were at a supplier and overheard a complete stranger try to get a better deal by saying he was " a good pal of Bob Pomeroy."

After little more than a year, Bob and Marj sold their acreage and the horses. There was no time for hobbies. Bob was wheeling and dealing and needed to be closer to the action The couple bought a double lot close to the arena in town and shortly afterwards had their first major upheaval.

Being in town fulltime was great for Bob but it brought the gossip to Marj's ears faster than ever. She was already unhappy with Bob's drinking but now rumors of his womanizing seemed to come on a daily basis. It hurt her deeply.

One night Bob arrived home to find his clothes packed on the front doorstep and the door locked. Begging forgiveness, he promised to slow down his drinking. He vehemently denied any liaisons.

Marj took him back.

Bob may have slowed down his interest in women but he did not slow down his adventures with his buddies. Gib Daniels was a local teacher and the two of them always seemed to find something to add excitement to their lives. Sometimes it was horses, sometimes just a drive south to visit friends. It never took much prodding to get either of them on the road.

One weekend, Bob described a particularly vicious police dog that his cousin Aletha's husband owned. Frank Long had been in the RCMP and had adopted the dog when he retired. The dog had been trained to attack and Frank always warned people to keep their distance. Gib bragged that he could handle any dog. When Bob countered that no one but Frank could handle the dog, Gib took the statement as a challenge. He told Bob he would prove his skills and he headed for his car.

Gib and Bob spent almost a full day driving to Salmon Arm. When they strode into the Long's yard, sure enough, the vicious guard dog was waiting. When the dog began growling menacingly, both men stood still. Bob was questioning the sanity of their situation and wanted to head back to the car but Gib told him to stand strong. With that, Gib reached out, firmly grabbed the dog by the head, stared him straight into the eyes and yelled "Behave." The dog cowered and crept under the porch.

After that experience, Bob never doubted Gib's prowess as a "dog whisperer." The point being made, the two men took five minutes to bid a quick "hello" to Aletha, hopped in their car and drove back to Fort St.John. Gib was back at school teaching the next day and Bob was back at the store.

The next spring, Ralph was told about a huge liquidation sale of men's wear and western wear. After Frank retired from the RCMP, he and Aletha had opened their mens' store but Salmon Arm proved to be the wrong place for western wear. The year before, Frank had asked for Bob's help in selecting merchandise for the store so Bob knew the quality of the goods. When Ralph asked Bob to go and see if he could get a few deals for the store—maybe some jackets at a discount or some work pants that they could use as an advertised special sale—Bob went willingly. He was not happy about his cousin's business failing but he certainly did not see any wisdom in letting strangers grab the bargains.

Seeing the receiver increasing discounts prices for quantity sales, Bob stepped up and offered them 10 cents on the dollar. The receiver agreed to the discount but only if Bob took everything in the place. He did just that.

When Bob returned to Fort St. John, he was hauling with him a semi-trailer full of men's clothing. Ralph was shocked. He expressed his concern for the quantity of clothing, the cash outlay and the shortage of shelf space in the store. He wondered if Bob had made a huge mistake—or perhaps lost his mind. Bob assured him that it was neither.

He also told Ralph that he did not have to worry because he had bought the stock himself. He had called his friend Al Hunt from the sale and the two had formed a partnership to operate Hunt's Western Wear and Tack. Al was a popular radio announcer and rodeo guy and he was the perfect partner to bring publicity to any business. Bob and Al had not only bought all the liquidated men's wear from Frank's store but they also bought Vern's Men's Wear across the street from Central Department Store—lock, stock and barrel.

Instead of being angry with his nephew becoming his competitor, Ralph was proud of Bob's initiative. Any concerns he may have had for Bob about making such a large inventory purchase were soon dispelled. What happened within weeks was the first example of Bob's impeccable timing.

Just as he and Al got the new store set up, the big dam project was announced. Hundreds of men got work and they all needed work clothes. Bob and Al were on their way.

Life became good and Bob found many ways to spend his new cash.

He and Viggo bought a 17 ½-foot boat together and they water-skied as often as they could. Summer days the pals could be found at the lake with their wives and children and family life seemed to agree with Bob. He and Marj bought and sold a few properties but by the time both Kim and Tim were in school, they had settled in Montney on a quarter section of land.

When they first bought the land, they lived in a small doublewide mobile home. It had two bedrooms but Marj made it clear that she wanted to raise her children in a "real house" where Tim and Kim would each have a bedroom.

Bob went into town one day and, without mentioning a word to Marj, sold the doublewide. The new owners wanted possession immediately so Bob and his little family moved into the workshop for the summer while their new house was being built.

Needing to rent a post-pounder for work on his property, Bob realized that renting was an expensive proposition. He talked to his pal Viggo and the two of them bought the equipment. Bob and Viggo each used the pounder, and then Scotty used it on his farm. When all their work was complete, Bob sold his half-interest to Viggo's family.

He had been able to get his work done with very little cost by looking at the big picture and by following his own mantra: Buy low; get maximum use; sell at a profit.

Every morning, Bob would get up early and, after grooming himself impeccably, do his drive around/walk around to see what was happening in the area. If he saw even a glimmer of opportunity, he grabbed it. When another man might take a pass on a menial job, or consider some task too small for any commitment, Bob jumped in. He knew that he would rather make a few bucks regularly on many small enterprises than go broke waiting for one big score.

When he learned that there was no one cutting the grass and weeds along the municipal roads, he bought the large piece of equipment to handle the job. He knew he could find someone to run it—his friend Gib was a teacher and available for work all summer. As the grass just needed cutting during the same months, it was a great setup. The teacher had a steady summer job; the money paid for the equipment and the salary; Bob made some money on the side. Perfect.

Soon Marj stopped trying to keep count of Bob's many ventures. They started; they stopped. They made money and they lost money. Usually, they made money.

Bob started buying horses again. By properly fencing his acreage, he could also board horses for other people. That move covered most of his own expenses. During the summer, Bob and Marj would organize small horse events on their property. Marj would make posters and Bob would put them up all over town as he made his daily "meet and greet" rounds. These events became like local community days. Marj handled the registrations and then set up concessions for food and drinks to cover their basic costs. Tim and Kim became very popular at school because of these events and because of the classroom field trips that Marj organized for their school. Bob was creating community goodwill for himself and building a reputation of influence. He was determined to have not only money but also respect.

From the Montney property, the family moved to their Airport Road property and built a house and barn there. Bob's usual focus on Arabian horses was swayed momentarily when he bought a thoroughbred racehorse with his pal Gib. The horse was a claiming horse, an eight-year-old black mare called "Princess Fabius." It was her heritage that captured Bob's interest. The mare was a daughter of the famous racehorse, Fabius; the horse that won not only the Preakness in the late 50's, but also the coveted Triple Crown and still remains as an icon in the racing annals. Bob and Gib kept Princess Fabius for over two years but had to sell when cash got tight for both of them.

Back at the Men's Wear, Al and Bob's partnership had some bumpy spots. Although the two men shared many crazy adventures in and away from the business, they also had their disagreements.

There had been an incident in Fort St.John where Bob had been involved in some questionable activity with another resident and his family. One thing led to another, and the other guy was put in jail. The details of the incident varied with the person telling the story, but one thing was certain—the family had a hate on for Bob Pomeroy, justified or not, and they made no bones about threatening Al if he continued his partnership with Bob.

Bob was furious that Al believed the accusations, perhaps a reminder of the way his own mother had not believed him as a child, and the business relationship suffered. The only feasible solution was to have Al own the store by himself. He bought out Bob's share and operated it alone for some months.

Once things died down, Bob and his friend George Martin bought back the store from Al, retaining the Hunt's Western Wear name.

Ironically, some time later Al Hunt opened his own Men's Wear store in the Mall in Fort St. John. Al is happy to remember that the biggest congratulatory floral arrangement was from his old friend Bob Pomeroy.

When Bob and George owned the store, they would have breakfast together and Viggo would drive into town for morning coffee with them.

Bob enjoyed bragging about the quality of the horses on his acreage. When he added the absolute perfection of his new bull calves to his stories, Viggo decided that it was time for a prank.

A couple of days later, Viggo disguised his voice and called Bob at 4:30 AM. He said he was Bob's neighbour, his very angry neighbour, whose garden was in the process of being trampled by Bob's calves.

Bob apologized profusely, jumped out of bed, threw on his clothes and headed over to the neighbors, not stopping to check his corral. When he did not find any calves in the man's garden, he pounded on the door to wake them up and ask what was going on. Of course, they did not know what he was talking about. Bob went home to discover his calves quietly sleeping.

Later that morning, at breakfast, when he saw Viggo's face red with laughter, Bob knew that he had been "had."

Between managing Ralph's store, owning his own Men's Wear store and buying and selling properties, Bob allowed his ego to grow ahead of him. His superior attitude towards many of the regular guys in town made him a few enemies as well as friends. His success also made him a target.

One night, Ralph's store was broken into and thieves stole a whole rack of leather jackets. A couple of days later, a guy called Bob at his own store (Hunt's) and offered to sell him some great leather jackets at a deep discount. Bob knew the merchandise, of course, notified the RCMP and they arranged a "sting" operation.

The police set up Bob with a "wire" and he arranged a meeting with the thieves, the RCMP listening in. At the appropriate time, the police rushed in and the men were arrested.

Some time later, a couple of hoodlums rushed into Central Department Store and threw acid on some clothing. It was obvious retaliation. Bob soon received a phone call from a guy who identified himself as "Bones." The thug said he was in Vancouver, had heard that Bob was having some trouble with vandalism and that he could offer him "protection" for the right price. Bob was not the guy anyone wanted to threaten. After firmly stressing the sure probability of much worse retaliation for any further damage to his property, Bob hung up. The threats did not resume and Bob even managed to sell some of the damaged merchandise at bargain prices.

Soon Bob and Marj were people of substance. They bought 10 acres of land with lake access on Lakeshore Drive and lived in a small cabin while they built Marj's dream house. Bob built a large barn and a tree fort for Kim and Tim, his reputation as an Arabian horse owner was growing, and their life seemed idyllic. By this time, of course, Bob had been long gone from coaching any baseball teams. His focus was on making money.

George and Starr Martin had bought the old acreage from Bob and Marj. In fact, that is how the two men became friends and partners. George had arrived in town to start work as a nurse in the hospital. He thought he was coming to close a deal on a house before his wife moved and, when the deal fell through, he decided to walk around town and consider his options. He happened to stop by Central Department Store and met Bob. After George mentioned that his wife would be very upset at not having a home to move into, Bob told him he had nothing to worry about.

Bob told George he could buy his house.

Of course, Bob had neglected to mention that his house actually was not for sale at that moment. He also did not take the time to mention to Marj that he was selling it.

After walking around the property, George made an offer. When Bob told her that their home was sold, Marj simply began packing. By that time, she was quite accustomed to Bob's surprises. Everything eventually worked out and the two couples became friends. Bob even gave Starr a job at Central Department Store.

Marj knew that the Martins were inexperienced "townies" and she knew that when Bob had convinced George to buy the acreage, he also promised to teach him about living a rural life.

The cold weather arrived early that year and Bob spent a lot of time helping George winterize his equipment. He spent so much time, in fact, that his own equipment froze while he was preparing the equipment at the Martin place.

When George needed the power hooked up at the house, BC Hydro told him that it would be at least two weeks before they could schedule the job. With winter hard on his heels, George knew he needed power immediately and he panicked. Bob reassured him and told him that he would handle the matter; that he knew the person to call.

Less than a half hour later, Bob told George to buy a 26 ounce bottle of Crown Royal whiskey, put it in a box and leave it at the bottom of the hydro pole in the morning. George did as instructed and before noon the next day, his power was connected. George had no hesitation in becoming a partner with Bob when the Men's Wear deal popped up. He knew that although Bob may not have been a guy who follows established procedures, he certainly knew how to get things done. There was the usual way and there was "Bob's way."

As a police officer in Fort St. John once remarked to George, "I often wish I could expedite matters like Bob does. If Bob Pomeroy were a cop, there wouldn't be any crooks in town."

In addition to maintaining his equipment, George had to learn to ride. Bob taught him how to care for a horse, how to saddle it and how to handle it. Finally, the day came when Bob said George was ready for his first ride outside of the small corral.

Late one afternoon, Bob showed up at the acreage and the two men headed out towards the hills, supposedly for an hour's ride. After some time riding in one direction, George suggested they turn back but Bob kept going.

Darkness fell and by that time, the men were miles away from the farm. George was tired and sore from the long ride but Bob seemed to be quite comfortable. Eventually they found themselves faced with an embankment too steep for the horses to climb with riders. George and Bob dismounted and began to lead the horses. George was in front and he struggled to climb the hill in the dark. Slipping and sliding as he pulled his horse along, he grumbled about the late time and his weary body. When he reached the top, he turned around to watch Bob effortlessly join him. Bob, of course, knew enough to allow the horse to climb at its own speed while he held on to the animal's strong tail.

George was tired, hungry and his stomach was acting up from the stress.

Half way home, he began to have a serious problem with cramps and gas. Each time the horse would hit a rough patch, the bouncy ride would get harder and George would pass gas.

Finally, after a particularly painful cramp, he let go with one loud, explosive fart. There was silence for a moment while Bob laughed and then George's eyes widened. "Uh oh, that was more than gas." The rest of the long ride home was very uncomfortable for George and two men finally got back to the house at 2 AM. George's bottom was burning and he was pissed off at Bob but he begrudgingly admitted that, in spite of the difficulties, he had learned how to use a horse to his advantage.

When Viggo had pulled the prank on Bob, George had thought it was hysterical and he teased Bob about it whenever he had the opportunity. The next spring, when Viggo's prank had been all but forgotten, Bob thought of the ultimate way to give George his own taste of funny business.

George was a nurse and he would be the first one to jump in to help any person or any animal in distress—no questions asked. Bob knew that George would not waste a second in hesitation if he called him for help in an emergency.

The morning of April 1st, at 5:30 AM, Bob poured a full gallon of ketchup all over his prize Arabian, "Razz" (Rababon Razz Dandy), and then called George in a near-hysterical state. He stammered out that his beloved Razz had gone through a barbwire fence, was cut up badly and was quite possibly dying.

George leapt out of bed, woke his wife Starr, and grabbed his box of medical supplies. The two of them rushed over to Bob's acreage. When they arrived, it was still dark and they thought they were seeing both Bob and his horse covered in blood. As they got closer, Bob started laughing and admitted that the blood was nothing more than ketchup. April Fools indeed!

This time, Marj was a party to Bob's prank and she invited the Martins into the house for breakfast. According to both George and Starr, it was a sumptuous feast and still ranks as the best breakfast they've ever enjoyed.

That did not stop George from plotting his own sweet revenge.

Bob had his teeth extracted under general anesthetic in the hospital in Fort St.John. One of the nurses on duty that day was George Martin. George was also a close friend of Bob's Dental Surgeon. It was a marriage made in heaven!

Step one. When Bob awoke from his deep sleep, he found a red ribbon lying by his hand. When he pulled on the ribbon, the other end pulled on a certain part of his anatomy, his male genitalia to be precise. There was a note attached to the bow. "Just think of what I might have done while you were unconscious!" Bob had a groggy laugh and settled down for another nap, fully expecting that he was safe and secure.

Step Two. When the Dental Surgeon had ordered Bob's dentures, he had also ordered a second set—the same fit but a slightly different appearance. Bob was eagerly anticipating his bright new smile and he totally relaxed as the Doctor slid the new teeth in his mouth. The fit was great. Smiling ever so innocently, the doctor handed Bob a mirror and asked, "Well, what do you think?"

Staring back in the mirror was a set of custom dentures—complete with the ugliest, most crooked overbite ever seen. Bob was shocked and, for a moment, speechless. Both the Doctor and his assistant were, by now, laughing uncontrollably. Moments later, the offensive "bubba teeth" were removed and Bob was fitted with the expensive, perfect teeth he had expected.

The "George and Bob Show" never really ended and Bob's sense of humor showed up at the most unusual times. Even when he was trying to do a good deed, he went for the overkill.

When a son of one of Bob's cousins killed the pet hamster belonging to the Martin kids, Bob felt almost as badly as the children did. He phoned George and told him to tell his children that Uncle Bob was bringing them a replacement.

The kids got their small cage ready and everyone waited for Bob's arrival. Soon there was a knock at the door and Bob walked in.

He was leading a small Shetland pony and he proudly deposited the animal right in the middle of the living room.

The live gifts did not stop there.

At Christmas, Bob gave the Martin kids two more replacement pets.

His dog had delivered an overabundant litter so Bob "thoughtfully" presented the family with not one, but two large puppies. Knowing how big the dogs would be in a few months, both George and Starr protested Bob's largesse.

They asked him why on earth he had given their kids two dogs. As

Bob theatrically explained, in front of the children of course, "Why? They're TWINS! You wouldn't want me to separate TWINS would you?"

The Martins kept both dogs.

Just after Bob and Marj had moved into their new house on Lakeshore Drive, Ryan was born. Marj thought she would be delivering the New Year's baby but Ryan arrived on December 31st. When friends commented that it was too bad his son had not waited a few hours to receive all the recognition, Bob scoffed and said it was much better the way it was—he needed the extra tax deduction.

Bob dropped by the old place from time to time to see how the Martins were managing.

They swapped stories about horses and hospitals and more often than not, a bottle of whiskey was drained in no time.

On one of these evenings, Bob had imbibed more than his share and Starr took his car keys. Bob collapsed on the sofa and promptly fell asleep. A few hours later, still in a drunken stupor, he rolled over and found himself staring directly into the wide pink eyes of a rabbit. Thinking he was hallucinating, Bob rolled over and went back to sleep. A little while later, after tossing and turning, the same thing occurred and once again, he thought he had really overdone the booze.

What he did not know was that the Martin kids had acquired a couple of large pet rabbits and that the rabbits had the run of the house at night. Bob was very relieved in the morning to know he was cold sober and still seeing the furry creatures.

During these years, Bob was finding ways to make money everywhere he looked. He bought a couple of trucks and started a trucking business.

He saw a need for a window company so he started Supreme Windows.

Usually, when Bob Pomeroy got a great idea or started a new business, it skyrocketed so people were more than happy to get involved with him.

Unfortunately, sometimes a business failed and sometimes people, even family, lost money. Bob lost money on those ventures as well but people conveniently forget about that fact.

Some people felt that, if they lost money with Bob on one project, they should still share in profits he may have made on another project. Not many people stopped to consider Bob's big picture. While they may have made the decision to invest in one project, Bob had taken many more risks to take on countless ventures.

He was a man possessed with becoming "someone"; a man determined to build a life of respect for his children.

After years of emotional and physical abuse and even more years of scrambling to make a living with only his wits and determination as tools, Bob had developed a strong inner need to be noticed as a winner. Whether it was using his fists or his mouth, he had to come out on top and be recognized for every thing he did, every word he said. He had crawled out from the cracks in the sidewalk and, despite a lack of education and in spite of the people who considered him to be sure bet for the soup kitchen lines, he pulled up his big boy trousers and started looking for opportunities.

All self-promoters become braggarts by default and Bob was no exception. Even his teachers had made no bones about proclaiming his failures to the world, so Bob felt the defensive need to announce his successes to anyone within earshot.

When he made deals, big or small, he could not resist bragging about them. It was the bragging, not the actual deals, that caused him problems in the community. It was the proud boasting that built up resentment towards him in Fort St. John and that followed him to some extent to Grande Prairie.

One year Bob sold a lot just outside of Fort St. John to a local firefighter. Unfortunately, after the deal was done, the buyer discovered that the fire department regulations demanded that all personnel reside within the city limits. Even though the property was less than a kilometer from the city, the fire chief was explicit. Get a house in town or get a new job. When the man told Bob about his predicament, Bob not only agreed to buy the land back, he paid him more than the original price.

The firefighter was happy. The fire chief was happy. Bob was happy. Nevertheless, Bob could not let things rest at that point. He mouthed around town that he actually still came out the winner because he had another ready buyer for the land and he would have paid the firefighter twenty thousand dollars more than he did just to get the ownership back in his hands.

As his friend and former partner, Grant Brooks, observes, "It always seemed more important to Bob that he had the reputation of being a "sharp businessman" than of being a "nice guy."

Fort St.John was booming and there was a serious shortage of commercial buildings and houses. The burgeoning pipeline industry had brought thousands of people to the city and they needed somewhere to live with their families. There was no time to wait for tracts of housing developments with long term planning.

These new families needed services and businesses needed a place to operate.

Bob had hired a local construction company to do the renovations to Hunts' Western Wear and Tack. Paul and Frank (the original G&F) had heard about the huge barn that Bob was building for himself. They drove out to see it and, once they saw his plans and his progress, they knew that he understood the building trade. G&F Construction had started building houses in Fort St. John but, when the long hours began to take a toll on Frank's family life, he approached Bob to take over his share.

Bob was happy to become a partner with an established house builder. Keeping the company name also worked out well. The new partners simply said that G&F now stood for "Good and Fast" and they set out to capture the market.

Bob knew of a company in Abbotsford, BC, that was building warehouses using a unique structural design. These buildings could be up in one quarter of the time that a regular structure was built and they were solid. Bob flew to Chilliwack and met with an engineer and then G&F built the first commercial pole buildings in Fort St. John.

He and Paul went together to Mossley and spoke with Bill Thornhill, the engineering specialist who had not only developed the pole house concept but who had already built over 600 of the houses in central Alberta. He was as busy as he could handle so he had no problem with G&F getting into the pole house business further north. By becoming their consultant for the engineering process as well as their supplier, Thornhill was able to share in the profits from their construction as well as growing his own business.

G&F built 147 pole buildings and houses in Fort St. John and Bob was building Nelson Homes (manufactured homes) on his own. He did not have any more time for horse meets or school events.

Although Bob had been able to find time to attend sports events while Tim and Kim were in elementary school, he was now, for the most part, an absentee dad.

He left the children's upbringing entirely in Marj's hands and rarely even had time to speak to them. Up at 5:30 and gone before 6:30, Bob sometimes did not get back to the house until after midnight.

Even with all his businesses, Bob was always strapped for money. He had a habit of using every penny of his income on his family, his home, his horses—and his social life. He did not let a lack of accessible cash stop him though. He always believed that it was possible to accomplish the impossible if he simply put his mind to work.

When Bob built anything, he used the leverage system and promises. G&F got rolling faster by using minimum cash and maximum good will.

The loans from the bank and the services from suppliers were set up on a very tight timeline. If one stage of the construction was delayed, it would affect the whole project and things would get very tense. Fortunately, things usually worked well.

The sub trades that knew Bob and Paul personally also knew that they would be paid once the house was sold. There was no secrecy about the financing. Bob would tell a plumbing company or a drywaller that he had no money but he would pay them the day a deal was closed. The subcontractor would accept the deal or move on to another developer. More times than not, the guy would stick with Bob and Paul.

There were already some copycat builders in town but G&F guaranteed that their houses were built the best. Just because G&F operated on good intentions and IOU's, the company still demanded good work from its trades and Bob was a hard taskmaster. He knew the schedules had to be met for all the promises to be kept. A house completed on time meant an early sale. Suppliers paid on time would release supplies for the next project. The balancing act could not be tampered with and no one got preferred status.

On a few occasions, due to the amount of work in town, G&F would use a new subcontractor, perhaps someone who had just arrived in Fort St.John and who was not aware of Bob's modus operandi.

When their part of a job was completed, some of the "new guys" demanded immediate payment. It was not unusual for Bob to try to use his physical prowess to settle disputes. It did not always work.

One day, a subcontractor demanded his payment in full. His work had been done but the house was not totally finished and G&F had not presold it.

At the time the guy had approached G&F for the work, he had agreed to wait for his payment until project completion and sale. When he changed his mind and then mouthed off in front of the other trades, Bob became furious. He shook his fist and the guy took off running with Bob fast behind him. Fortunately, for the tradesman, Bob's crushed knees did not support his bravado and he gave up the chase.

Bob's own company was building commercial and farm buildings now, both on speculation and under contract for others, as well as still erecting Nelson prefab homes. By 1980, he was a bona fide millionaire. When the downturn came suddenly the next year, both Bob and Paul lost their shirts—and their fortunes. Bob was broke.

Update: In 2008, a municipal inspector had the opportunity to check over several pole houses built by G&F Construction as well as some built by copycat builders. His appraisal found that, while the copycat pole houses were in bad shape, the pole houses built by Bob and Paul's company were superior in construction and, after three decades of occupation, they are still safe homes for families.

Six

"When everything seems to be going against you, remember that the airplane takes off against the wind, not with it."
—HENRY FORD

After the government implemented the National Energy Plan, the economical impact on Fort St. John was immediate.

OPEC had lost control of the worldwide markets. Oil prices had plummeted from $70 a barrel down to $14 a barrel and this was bad news for all the exploration areas. To add insult to injury, Paul Volker, head of the US Federal Reserve, raised interest rates from 6% to almost 20%, thinking that this rash move would bolster the economy. As was the "sheep mentality" of the Canadian government at the time, this country followed suit but went even further, increasing rates to 27%. It was a devastating move, one that many called "curing a hangnail by cutting off the whole arm."

The Site C Dam, the Mackenzie Valley pipeline project and the pulp mill planned for Fort St. John were all shelved.

Pipeline companies pulled out of Fort St. John and the housing market crashed. With mortgage payments suddenly doubling or even tripling, and no work in sight, families packed up and left town.

Banks could not even unload properties at fire sale prices. The recession was so deep that property became worth less than a couple of years of interest and unpaid taxes. Bob was right back to where he started. With the stroke of the pen signing the government edict, he went from being the #1 contractor in the city to being just another guy out of work.

G&F collapsed and Bob was hurting financially. He still owned a couple of houses at Charlie Lake but his renters had vacated and the houses were costing him money every week that passed by. He had lost virtually everything he had but, unlike many others, he did not panic and leave town. He started looking for a job.

There were problems at home as well. Bob and Marj were fighting continually. It was not about money. Marj could live as frugally as needed. It was, as usual, about other women. Their marriage was floundering at best.

With his financial problems compounded by the impending collapse of his marriage, Bob took off to Leduc to visit his sister Joan and her husband.

Before he arrived, Joan received a call from none other than Marj. She told Joan everything that Bob was going through. In spite of being angry with Bob, Marj still loved him. She wanted to ensure that Joan and Brian were especially responsive and kind to Bob during his visit with them; to show him as much love and support as possible.

Being with two people who were happily married and strongly committed to each other seemed to bring Bob back to his senses, at least temporarily. When he returned to Fort St.John, he tried very hard to keep his attention focused on Marj and his children.

The only people who were making money in northern Alberta and BC seemed to be the lawyers and receivers. Gerry Tucker owned a lot of real estate and had one of the few companies that were still solvent. The connection between Bob and Gerry had begun many decades earlier.

Gerry's father had been a successful fur buyer in northern BC, opening stores in Montney, Charlie Lake, Fort St.John and Baldonnel as well as in the lodges up the Alaska Highway that served highway crews.

He had two farms and a coal mining operation and this diversity made him a wealthy man by any standards. The problem was that this was in the North Country; it was the early 30's and 40's and men did not think about hiring accountants or tax consultants. They simply bought and sold, made deals and took care of their families.

The senior Tucker eventually bought both the original Fort St. John Hotel and Central Department Store from Carl Donnis. The high profile businesses not only attracted a certain amount of envy from the locals, it also brought the attention of the government.

Tucker did not have extensive records but the tax hounds knew where to look. They went to his wholesalers, saw what he had been purchasing over the most recent years and estimated the profits he made. They wanted their fair share.

When Revenue Canada finally demanded $35,000 for back income taxes in 1947, Gerry's father sold both the hotel and Central Department Store to Ralph Pomeroy and Early Donnis (Carl's son). Donnis later sold out his share to Ralph and, of course, the same Central Department Store was where Bob really started in business.

Bob had come back from Leduc with a renewed sense of purpose. He was determined to find a source of income. Feeling quite certain that Gerry still had some lucrative businesses and therefore some available work, Bob swallowed his pride and went to see him. He admitted to Gerry that he was "in the glue" and needed a job.

Gerry not only gave Bob a position at Titan Management, he bought Bob's houses and took over the mortgages. Bob became Titan's Property Manager and the initial responsibility was to manage Gerry's lease properties. It was not long before Bob began supervising the construction projects of Tucker Industries as well.

There were no qualms on Bob's part about working for someone else. He saw no shame in switching roles from boss to employee and he simply set about to do the very best job possible. He knew he had made money before so he knew he could do it again. All he needed was regular income to get him over what he saw as merely a bump in the road. He and Marj sold the big house on Lakeshore Drive and scaled down to a modest house on a smaller piece of land. Marj managed to run the household on their greatly reduced income and Bob focused on doing a good job for Gerry.

As a property manager, Bob excelled. He had endless energy and a total lack of inhibition when he needed to confront anyone over anything. He also found innovative ways to protect Gerry's investments.

Pat Tucker owned some properties and, seeing Bob's success at collecting rents for her husband, she turned those over to Bob's capable hands, starting with one deadbeat in particular. In spite of having a regular income, this one man just did not pay his rent. He had found it easy to give Pat one sob story after another and soon he had fallen more than three months behind.

Bob did not waste his time on telephone calls. He jumped in his truck and drove over to see the guy for a face-to-face. When no one answered the door, Bob was a bit suspicious. He thought he had heard a noise and he had noticed a vehicle parked in the yard.

Nonetheless, he left a notice in the mailbox with his name and phone number and started to leave. That's when he spotted the spanking new snowmobile.

Backing up his truck, Bob loaded the snowmobile and drove off. He dropped the expensive toy at an empty warehouse and headed back to the office. Sure enough, a short time later, the renter called Bob and asked if "anyone at the office" had happened to remove a snowmobile from his yard. Bob calmly stated that he was a property manager and it was not part of his business to talk about snowmobiles. His business was to talk about rent money.

The man knew with absolute certainty that Bob had taken the snowmobile but he was not about to admit that he had been home when Bob stopped by. The banter continued for a few moments until finally Bob coolly suggested that IF the guy could come in and pay at least his back rent, then Bob might POSSIBLY be able to help him locate the missing snowmobile. There was a click and the phone went dead.

A couple of hours later, the back rent was at the office. Along with the receipt for payment, the person at the counter gave the tenant the address where he could find the missing snowmobile.

Perhaps out of the frustration of losing almost everything he had, Bob often used brute force to assert his position. If a worker did not show him respect, he used his fists to show authority.

As Gerry Tucker's property manager, he would stop by sites to ensure that work was progressing.

One afternoon an operator was doing some backfill and getting too close to a house. Bob saw that the soil was not being packed properly so he told the man to stop and do it over properly. The guy paid no attention and kept doing the job in the same manner. Bob yelled at him and repeated his orders. This time the guy lipped back at Bob, told him he did not know what he was talking about and added, "You're not my boss."

In retrospect, the fellow probably figured that was not a good thing to say. Bob stomped over to the backhoe, hauled the man out of the machine, threw him to the ground and punched hm. Then he looked directly in his face and stated, "I am Gerry's right hand man so I AM your boss. Do it right or get out of here." Bob left and the man did the job as instructed.

His family did not appreciate Bob's occasional use of physical force but it did impress one of Kim's teenage friends. When she was 14, Kim and a girlfriend, Tammy Martin, both worked at the Cleanery, a Laundromat and cleaning place that George Martin was managing.

One evening after the two girls had closed the Cleanery, Bob picked them up to drive them home. On the way to the Martin house, Bob stopped at a warehouse as a security measure. He had just begun to check the locks when a truck drove up, screeched to a stop and a slightly inebriated man stepped out. As the two girls watched, the man strode over to Bob and began swearing at him and accusing him of ruining his life. Apparently, the man had owed Gerry Tucker a lot of money and Gerry had obtained a lien. As Gerry's bailiff, Bob had put a lock on the man's place of business.

Bob told the guy to calm down; to stop swearing in front of the young girls. When he added that there was nothing he could do, the man swore even more loudly. He started poking Bob in the chest to make his point. Twice Bob asked him to stop poking him and twice the man continued.

Finally, the guy grabbed Bob's tie and flicked it at his face with a final expletive. Bob took one arm back and punched the man out cold.

It was January and there was a lot of snow on the ground. When the guy fell back, he slid across the snow and stayed there. Bob checked to be certain he was okay and then, not wanting him to get hypothermia, Bob picked the man up and placed him safely in his truck.

Kim thought she would die of embarrassment but Tammy thought Bob was sooooo cooooool!

About this time, Bob had to go to Edmonton on business for Gerry. His friend Jerry Doell was with him and, after finishing with business, the two of them began visiting the local bars. They were at the Coast Terrace Inn and Jerry decided he needed a haircut.

The guys stopped by the hair salon at the hotel but it was just before closing. The two men flirted with the stylists and used a few bottles of wine to convince them to work a little later than usual.

Bob was always impeccably dressed and well groomed; his style being business-like and bordering on conservative, never too trendy.

When Jerry's stylist convinced him that a perm was the only way to go, Bob was also invited to try the new look.

With powers of reasoning diminished by the booze, he agreed. Bob's hair was particularly long that year and, unfortunately, the wine clouded the stylist's usual attention to timing. Marj almost choked when Bob returned home with two chemically burned ears and a big halo of dry, frizzy hair. Bob thought he could just wash the curls out but it took months of growth and many haircuts to erase the fashion mistake.

Bob became virtually indispensable to Gerry and he took over more and more duties. Gerry had his finger in many pies during those years. Some businesses he started when he saw a need, others he acquired through repossession. He soon owned all the properties alongside the Pioneer Inn, including the dry cleaners. Then, when the Co-Op needed to expand, Gerry traded them the 17 adjoining lots for one large property downtown.

He decided to keep the lucrative dry cleaning business going by moving it to the downtown property and he bought the A&W nearby.

Bob was busy with collecting rents and supervising construction so Gerry hired another man to manage the A&W and the Dry Cleaning Shop. The guy was a flashy individual who drove a big white Lincoln Continental and put Bob to shame when it came to pompously flaunting his position with Tucker. In his eyes, he could do no wrong and, for the most part, Gerry left him on his own to operate the businesses, so long as the cash kept coming in and there were no problems.

Unfortunately, there were problems and the cash flow was part of it. Deposits were not being made regularly and the reports were making Gerry's accountant, Don Blonke, nervous.

Things came to a head and became clear one afternoon when the guy dropped his Lincoln off at the garage to have his tires changed. When the mechanics opened the trunk to put in the old winter tires, they found a bag holding over $4,000 in cash—Gerry's cash.

Gerry added the supervision of the A&W to Bob's list of duties and it did not take him too long to learn everything there was to know about dry cleaning as well.

At the time Bob came looking for work, Gerry and Don were both warned not to hire him.

Many locals were glad to see Bob's fall from grace and they were happy to bring up old stories from years long passed. Some were just fed up with Bob's bragging and they were not about to see him get a break.

Fortunately, both Gerry and Don also spoke with people who had actually done solid business with Bob and they heard enough of the positive stories to take a chance.

It had seemed to Gerry that the worst TRUE thing that he heard was that Bob had no education or formal training. Although he had attended university himself, Gerry did not see a degree as the ultimate measure of a man. He recognized that hard work, loyalty and a hunger for excellence could also take a man far and he put his money on Bob Pomeroy.

At Tucker Industries, Gerry gave his employees cash bonuses for good performance. For his top achievers, men who had been with him for five years or more, Gerry had rings custom-made at Birks Jewelers. Throughout the years, Gerry had only awarded ten of the special rings. He gave Bob one of these special rings after just two years.

Crafted in solid gold, the ring was designed to represent a traditional graduation ring from college. Around the circumference of the seal is engraved "School of Hard Knocks." Bob treasured his ring more than any paycheque he had every earned. He keeps it nearby and he still considers Gerry a good friend. The feeling is mutual.

Not interested in building hotels, Gerry nonetheless carried a $550,000 second mortgage on the new hotel in Fort St.John. Ralph Jordan had the first mortgage of $7.5 Million.

The original owners had invested in a Holiday Inn franchise and, unfortunately, they opened just at the time of the economic downturn. The hotel lost money from the day it opened. Ralph foreclosed on the first mortgage and the owners had no choice but to write off their investment. Gerry did not want to assume any legal costs or financial burdens so he did not participate in the foreclosure proceedings, leaving the full ownership of the hotel with Ralph. Ralph was an investor, not a hotel man so he promptly turned over the day-to-day management to Titan. That, in turn, meant that the mess was handed to Bob.

Ralph prudently sent his novice hotel manager to Vancouver for a few weeks to work at the West Georgia Holiday Inn. While there, Bob not only got a crash course in hotel management but he also discovered his new passion. He loved the hotel business and he knew that one day this would be his only career.

Returning to Fort St.John, Bob advised Ralph to get out of the Holiday Inn franchise, that the fees were too prohibitive in that market. He convinced Ralph that he could turn an independent hotel around.

Ralph agreed and, as he was a new owner through foreclosure proceedings, he was able to break the franchise contract. After he took that step, he challenged Bob to do the impossible: to get the hotel operating in the black within a year.

Bob set to work immediately. First, they needed a name.

To curry favor with the local residents, Gerry suggested a change to "Pioneer Inn" as a tribute to the original families who settled in the area. Their advertising and marketing could focus on offering the best service to the best people around—their neighbours and friends, their nearby business associates and their community.

The next thing Bob did was to hire Clark Gainer & Associates (Vera Clark and Doug Gainer) out of Vancouver to help him set up his operations and build his first Operating Manual. Vera and Doug would check back monthly to see what was working and to modify the manual where necessary.

("Bob's Bible" as it came to be known, is still in the Pomeroy Hospitality head office. It is the backbone of their current operating guidelines!)

As manager of the hotel, Bob took tight control of inventory.

He had an uncanny ability with numbers and projections and Gerry had a hard time believing that Bob had completed only grade six at school. He had already seen Bob's capabilities in property management but that was to be expected. Hotel management was an entirely new direction for Bob. The business was not only very competitive, but it had many areas where mistakes could be made and profits lost.

The speed at which Bob mastered total comprehension of the systems took both Gerry and Ralph by complete surprise. By the end of the first year, it was obvious that Bob had an inborn ability, almost a savant skill, of seeing something done once and then being able to do it himself—only far better.

Bob's business life changed quickly and so did his home life.

He and Marj bought two more properties across from their acreage and put up a larger Nelson house on one of them. They kept the other for an expansive lawn, a tree fort and a large trampoline. The three kids had loads of room to play and Bob moved horses on to the original property. Tim and Kim were going to school and Ryan was just four.

The family became close friends with their neighbours. Both Harley and Toots adored the bright little Ryan and he had the freedom to drop in on them any time he wanted. Toots always had cookies and milk waiting along with a warm hug.

Bob was back to spending money freely and he tried to buy his children anything he felt they should have. Bob remembered only too well not having anything like his cousins had, not having a dad or mom who bothered about if he was having fun or not. He may have been overcompensating with his own kids and he did not always think before he brought home expensive presents, often things better suited to older children.

By the time Tim and Kim were just 7 or 8 years old, they already had "Kitty-Cat" junior size snowmobiles. Mastering them quickly, they tore all over the acreage in them as soon as snow fell.

The winter before Ryan turned five, Bob handed him the key to his very own 3-wheel terrain vehicle.

The excited child pulled on a snowsuit, jumped on the powerful machine and headed across the field to show Harley and Toots. Unfortunately, either due to his inexperience or to a child's lack of dexterity, Ryan managed to hit the throttle instead of slamming on the brake as he got to the neighbours'. When he crashed into their house, he was thrown off the machine, face first into their screen door. The vehicle went on through to their living room. The impact was so hard that Ryan had the mesh pattern of the screen imprinted on his face for hours.

It probably is not necessary to point out that Bob's second son was always the "firecracker" of the family. His energy level could not be contained.

Gerry Tucker remembers storing an antique potbelly cast iron furnace on Bob's property only to discover that Ryan had taken a stick and poked out all the mica inserts for something to do one day. As a child, Ryan's mischief was unstoppable and, as a teenager, he continued to be a source of anxiety for both his parents. Wrecking cars, speeding, partying: it was never anything terribly wrong, just a constant requirement for reining him in. Bob was too busy to supervise his kids on a daily basis, though, so

Marj had the job of keeping her boys in line. Kim, much to Marj's relief, was never a problem.

While the rest of Fort St.John was suffering, Bob was still a half owner of Hunts Western Wear and Tack, hotel manager of the Pioneer Inn and he had his finger on the pulse of anything that was happening.

Eventually the Men's Wear business started dying off and George and Bob mutually decided to shut it down.

They started lowering prices by ten percent each week and finally, around the first week of December, they advertised seventy percent discounts. With the stock being "high end" and the discounts being ridiculously deep, the gift-giving season just added stimulus to shoppers. People clamored for the bargains and the store operated on fourteen- hour days.

Both Starr and Marj worked the cash register during peak times and on weekends, the foursome worked until 10 pm, then donned white Stetson hats and headed out for a late dinner and dancing at the Pioneer Inn. These evenings temporarily restored some of the romance for Bob and Marj as they were spending more time together than ever.

They managed to sell most of their stock that season and made enough to pay off every one of their suppliers.

After splitting the few remaining dollars, Bob and George took their payout in the last bit of stock. George Martin still wears his cowboy boots from the store.

Bob decided to branch out and he started his own property management firm, Manta Management. Soon after, he sold half ownership to Mike Conway. Marj worked at the bank as well as handling the books for the Men's Wear store. When Manta Management started, the workload became heavier so she left the bank to do that company's books as well as those of Bob's other business interests. This was about the time that George Martin left his nursing position at the hospital. A highly principled man, he was not able to participate in one of the hospital's new procedures. Although abortions were now legal in Canada, they did not fit with George's beliefs. He felt he could not morally remain on staff. Bob invited him to join the Manta partnership.

In addition to managing properties, Bob had been buying and selling properties for himself. He was working closely with the banks and would often get first refusal on foreclosure deals. Mortgages were worthless to a bank without regular interest payments so, once the property's deed was transferred to the bank, the loans department acted quickly to find a new owner. Bob Pomeroy was one of the few men in town with regular income and he was always receptive to a good deal.

In those years, banks foreclosed houses on a daily basis. For just a thousand dollars down, an investor could pick up a solid family home and then rent it the next day, sometimes even to the former owners. Making mortgage payments was not a problem.

Bob snapped up a few of these bargains, as many as he could handle, and he made a point of telling his friends and relatives about the investment opportunity. Uncle Les Collier remembers Bob phoning him in Edmonton and advising him to invest ten thousand dollars and buy ten houses. Les and his wife talked it over and passed up on the deal. They did not have the same confidence in northern BC that Bob did and they just could not risk their savings. Today Les kicks himself in the pants for not jumping at the offer. He would make the same decision today if he had the same information as he had back then, but he also knows just how much money Bob's other friends made.

Bob was handling all his real estate transactions by himself to avoid paying any fees or commissions.

Then he started handling other deals for himself and others, both homes and businesses. If a pal said he wanted to sell his property, Bob would sniff around, find a buyer and tack on a fee.

The problem was that he was not a licensed real estate agent and it was not legal to receive commissions for any of these transactions. To be honest, Bob had not planned to be doing these types of real estate deals. They had just materialized and Bob, being his usual "Johnny on the spot" had just followed through on opportunities that had arisen. When the local real estate board finally called him on the carpet, the executives realized that, although he had no training, he had probably closed more deals than any of their licensed brokers had closed that year and he had not made any errors doing the paperwork.

As he had not only almost single-handedly kept the market afloat for a couple of desperate years and had not really hurt anyone in doing so, they did not force any issues. However, they did insist that Manta Management take on a fully licensed realtor immediately.

Enter Grant Brooks. Grant processed all the future deals while he taught Bob the legalities of the real estate profession.

Bob learned quickly but his impatience got the best of him and he resumed doing deals the "fast way" as opposed to the "proper way." Grant left Manta Management before any problems arose with the real estate board but he never cut his ties with Bob. Two decades later, he still refers to him as being a great guy, an honest man and a friend.

During this time, Bob met two other men who would also become longtime friends: Charlie Grubisich, a fellow entrepreneur who Bob respected greatly, and Ray Yenkana, a commercial realtor whose family values and business integrity had a great impact on his life and his future.

Over the next twenty-five years, Bob would call on Ray for emotional support in times of crisis. People are often surprised when they meet the man that Bob affectionately calls his "twin brother." Born in Aruba, Ray has a dark complexion. Even the most gullible person would quickly realize that the "twin" aspect of the two men is in jest. The fact is that these men are brothers at heart. As both have often said, "Ray may be black on the outside but Bob is black on the inside."

Charlie Grubisich and some partners owned the local Mack Truck dealership. When the economy tanked, the trucking business went flat and the company had more trucks than money. Like most businesses in Fort St. John, the dealership had trouble paying the rent and the owners tried breaking the lease with Titan Management. Bob and the managing partner, Scotty Gardiner, had been fighting tooth and nail for months.

Charlie's lawyer at the time, Bob Lewis, had gone over the lease contract and told him that it was ironclad. His advice was to find some way to raise some working capitol.

Fortunately for them, a truck auction came up in Prince George, and Charlie and another one of his partners, Richard Dufour, drove down to sell a couple of their extra trucks. Shortly after arriving, Charlie got a panicked phone call from Scotty, saying that Bob Pomeroy was at their office and he was putting a padlock on their door. Charlie asked to speak to Bob and he convinced him that he was not skipping out.

He said that he would be back in Fort St. John late that night and he would use the cash from the truck sale to pay as much of the rent as possible. Bob agreed and told Charlie to check in to the hotel when he got back.

It was very late when Charlie finally got back to the city and he did not really want to pay for a night in the hotel but he had made a promise to Bob and he was a man of his word.

When he stopped at the front desk of the Pioneer Inn, the clerk was expecting him. In spite of Charlie's outstanding debt to Titan Management, Bob had arranged a complimentary room for him.

In the room was a fresh fruit basket, two bottles of wine and Bob's phone number. There was also a note to call Bob no matter what time he got in. It was after midnight but Charlie picked up the phone and called.

A short time later, Bob turned up at the hotel. The men talked, shared the wine and Charlie paid most of the back rent as promised. They began a friendship based on honor and it has endured based on mutual respect. In fact, in spite of those many weeks of bitter wrangling over rent, four years later Bob and Charlie walked into Bob Lewis' office together as partners in the purchase of a hotel.

Ray Yenkana met Bob through real estate transactions with Manta Management. Their relationship compares to the "odd couple" on many levels and the friendship has endured. Ray is a deeply spiritual person whose time is equally balanced between business, family and faith. Bob is, well, he is BOB.

They have been investment partners in many projects over the years and each man knows with absolute certainty that, in spite of their differences in lifestyle, he can depend on the other for whatever may be needed—any time, any place, any where.

1982 to 1987 were dark years for Fort St.John and, while many hotels went broke, under Bob's management, the Pioneer Inn flourished.

Manta Management was doing well, Bob's own properties were doing well and his other sidelines were keeping him busy. He and Marj had even bought a fifty percent share of a home in Phoenix.

Bob saw a lot of potential in the Arizona city and he had hopes to expand there. His ultimate goal was to some day retire to a life of breeding Arabian horses in the genteel Scottsdale horse community. The agreement was that the partners would share the use of the house as well as the costs. Marj liked the idea of a vacation home in the sun and Bob wanted to use the house as his satellite office while he searched for acreages and other properties. With Bob's busy work schedule keeping him in Fort St.John for most of the time, the other partner used the house more and more. Eventually, and without telling Bob, he simply moved in permanently.

When Bob and Marj finally drove down for a few weeks holiday, the partner greeted them by telling them that they had to stay somewhere else.

Naturally, a heated argument ensued and Bob demanded that the other partner pay rent for his portion of the time used. The demand was met with a definite "No", a few expletives and a slammed door.

Bob and Marj left and settled in to a nearby motel to think about their options. The more Bob thought about how badly he had been duped, the more furious he became.

He told Marj to get in the car, they drove back to the house with Ron Barker (a cousin by marriage) and, with one well-placed punch, Bob knocked the jerk flat on his ass. Ron stood over the guy and counted him out like a boxing referee. "One. Two. Three. Yer OUT!" The partnership was officially dissolved.

Back in Fort St. John, Bob was still in control. He had done well acting as the Receiver for both Gerry Tucker and some of the local banks and he had spread his goodwill over a wide area. He frequented restaurants that had been struggling, brought in new customers for them and those owners remembered his largesse. Just like in past years, he was the "go-to" guy in the city except now he was trading favors with bankers and lawyers.

Although Fort St.John was a city, it still was "small town" in many ways. Everyone knew each other and a great deal of business was still done on handshakes, personal bartering and favors.

Bob excelled at personal bartering and favors.

A couple of years earlier, Les Collier had gone up to the Yukon for a visit. On his way back to Edmonton, he dropped in on Bob and Marj. Bob had needed Les' help many times when he was younger and he was eager to show his uncle how much his life had changed for the better.

He drove him to his property and proudly showed off his big house and the new barn. It was November and there were banks of snow everywhere. Even the main roads were messy. Bob's property was the exception.

As the pickup approached the farm, Les was not surprised to see that Bob's driveway had been cleared from end to end. He knew that Bob was a "neat freak" and his near-obsession with cleanliness did not end with his own appearance. His land, homes and businesses all had to be pristine at all times. Even his wife and children reflected his need for a picture-perfect life; each of them good-looking, well mannered and well dressed at all times.

With family, perhaps because he thought they still considered him as being an uneducated, worthless kid, Bob always tried to make a show of his "top dog" status. He would seize any opportunity to show a relative that he had some power or influence.

On this occasion, after showing Les the inside of the house, Bob invited Les to go out to the barns and see his Arabian horses. As soon as they walked out the door, he picked up a rock and threw it hard against the wall of the bunkhouse. Immediately a farm hand ran out of the building and Bob told him to get the horses ready to show. It seemed to Les that his nephew needed to impress him; that he was now the person who was in control of others. In spite of Bob's money and position, he still felt the stigma of being the loser son of the loser Pomeroy.

After Bob showed off one horse after another, he popped his head into the house and told Marj he was taking Les to town for a steak dinner.

Before they headed to the restaurant, Bob took Les to see Hunt's Western Wear and Tack.

He knew his uncle had owned a western wear store a decade earlier and he was eager to show him that he owned one now as well.

While they were walking around the place, a local bank manager came in looking for Bob. The manager was having a party at his home and had forgotten that, as it was an election day in BC, all the liquor stores were closed. He knew that if anyone could help him out, it was Bob Pomeroy.

Bob told the banker to wait in the store, took Les with him and they headed around to the back door of a restaurant that Bob frequented.

Bob hammered at the door and told the owner that he needed to borrow a case of alcohol. The man protested at first but then relented when Bob reminded him of the many favors he had done for the business in the past.

The door closed, a few minutes later reopened, and a box of a dozen assorted bottles appeared. The booze was delivered to the banker. When the banker asked how much he owed, Bob just waved him off and said, "Ask me tomorrow. I'm taking my uncle for a steak."

As the two men walked into the restaurant, Les recognized the owner from the back-door deal but said nothing. Bob told the server he did not need a menu, just a couple of the biggest T-bones they had in the kitchen. After they finished, Les asked for the bill but Bob just laughed and told him to keep his wallet in his pocket, that "there's no bill for me in this place" and they left.

Over their dinner, Bob had told Les about the opportunities to make money in Fort St. John. He told him that, although the loss of the pipeline had devastated the city, he believed that it would rebound and that anyone who could buy land or houses for bargain basement prices would see a huge profit.

When they left the restaurant, it was dark but Bob wanted to show a few potential properties to Les.

They drove out and parked by the Case agency. As Bob was outlining the possibilities for the 20-acre parcel adjacent to the building, an RCMP car drove alongside and stopped.

The officer got out, motioned for Bob to roll down his window, and then shone his flashlight into Bob's face. Bob remained very calm and asked for his name and badge number. When the officer asked why he wanted the information, Bob simply stated "You must be new in town. No one shines a flashlight in Bob Pomeroy's face any more."

After a short exchange of information, the police officer returned to his car and drove off. Bob had no show of emotion. He simply started his truck and drove home, resuming his conversation about investments along the way.

Bob was "cock of the walk" in the city—in more ways than one.

He had money, he had charm and he had the type of work that gave him the freedom to get lost for hours at a time. He also had the run of the hotel and the access to the type of women who hung out there. It was just a matter of time before his philandering resumed.

His former attorney says, "Although Bob is a genius at business; his decisions regarding women have often been less than stellar." Even his son Ryan wryly admits, "Monogamy has not always been one of father's strongest suits."

It did not matter that he was married; Bob would still cast his net for women. He seemed to have been blessed—or cursed—with fisherman's luck. He has always attracted women, usually without even trying, and his relationships have not always been good for his personal safety.

At one time in Fort St. John, for example, Bob began a dalliance with a married woman. She wanted her time with Bob to be just an extra-curricular activity so she insisted on meeting with him discreetly. Unfortunately, she had no idea that her husband had heard rumors about her flirting and he was already suspicious about Bob.

The two paramours arranged an idyllic picnic on the banks of the Peace River one afternoon and, after a light lunch and some wine, they began some more amorous activity. Suddenly a gunshot rang out and a bullet whizzed past Bob's head. The scare tactic of the woman's husband did not have to be repeated.

That affair ended that very afternoon.

Most of Bob's philandering was done on a short-term basis—flirting, some heavy "necking", the occasional one-night stand. Like most men who stray, he justified his actions by telling the women that he was not appreciated enough at home. To Bob, it was nothing serious.

Marj, on the other hand, did think it was serious. The gossip became too much to ignore and she was getting tired of denying the obvious.

Seven

"The price of success is dedication, hard work and an unrelenting devotion to the things you want to see happen"
—FRANK LLOYD WRIGHT

The success of the Pioneer Inn was arguably due to Bob's personality, his hard work and his insistence on top quality. He overlooked nothing. The rooms were immaculate, the service was excellent and the food in the restaurant was first class. Nowadays he would be labeled as being politically incorrect and even sued for discrimination, but in the mid-80's, a manager could hire women based solely on their appearance. Bob hired his restaurant and cocktail waitresses on looks alone. He knew he could train them to be good servers and, even if they were not the most skilled, his customers would appreciate the scenery.

Bob was extremely proud of the hotel and he wanted his children to know the business. By the time Tim was 12 or 13, he was bussing tables in black pants and crisp white shirts. Kim often worked longer and harder than Tim did but, being a girl, Kim was a mystery to Bob. He did not know how to interact with her so, for the most part, he simply ignored her.

When she was not helping Bob at the Pioneer Inn, she worked part-time at the dry cleaners or the A&W. Ryan was learning about cleaning rooms properly and looking out for dust or burnt out bulbs before he was six. When Bob did have time to be with his children, he spent that time with them at the hotel. On a few occasions in their teens, both Tim and Ryan got fed up and insisted on having free time to just "hang" with their friends. Kim found it more difficult to go against her father's wishes.

If Bob picked Ryan up from grandma's house, he would take him to the Pioneer while he checked up on things. If he had a few extra minutes, he would explain what he was doing and then ask his son if he understood. If he were busy, he would send Ryan to the gift shop to buy him some wine gums, or to the restaurant to watch his big brother Tim work. Marj could not swim so she was adamant that all her children take Red Cross lessons. Bob made certain that the kids made good use of the pool in the hotel to get even more water-wise. The Pioneer was such a part of their father, that the kids loved the hotel. It was a treat to be at "dad's hotel" and they took advantage of any occasion to be there with him. On Ryan's fifth birthday, for example, instead of a children's party, he requested a grown-up dinner at the hotel with Bob and Marj. They agreed and, after dressing him like a little gentleman in a suit and tie, they marched him into the dining room and invited him to order anything he wanted. Ryan ordered a lobster tail—and a hot dog. And that is what he got.

The Pioneer Inn became the centre of the northern Alberta social scene. Bob worked tirelessly with the Chamber of Commerce, the Civic Government, the Provincial Government, and any service group he could contact. If anyone needed meeting space or convention space, that person booked it through Bob Pomeroy. Organizers knew that they would be well cared for and that their function would be a success because Bob would personally see to every detail. Thanks to the new reputation and all the networking that Bob was doing, the Pioneer Inn was the immediate choice for any special events that occurred through the province's film or tourism agencies.

During the early 80's a television series called "Dallas" dominated the ratings. Set in the southern U.S. state of Texas, the story covered the fictional lives of a rich ranching family. The male stars were macho, good-looking actors who spent a lot of time on horseback in the great outdoors.

Two of the stars of the show were Patrick Duffy and Steve Kanaly. Women swooned over them and men envied their lives—both onscreen and off.

During this time, there was an overpopulation of wolves in Northern

B.C. These predators roamed in packs and they were becoming a serious threat to both the cattle and sheep ranching communities. After much consideration, the provincial government approved a one-time hunting season to reduce the wolf population by eight percent.

Even with the wildlife officers controlling the culling, hunters were ecstatic. As the start of the wolf hunt coincided with the opening of goose hunting seasn, applications for licenses poured in from both Canada and the U.S.

The cost of having government officers supervising such a large mission exceeded the Ministry's budget for the year so the BC Wildlife Association was given approval to launch a fundraising campaign. One of their events was a heavily publicized dinner and charity auction at the Pioneer Inn in Fort St. John, BC.

Bob had managed to get both the hotel and the city of Fort St.John some international attention and he was ecstatic. His ballroom and catering department would make money, his wait staff would make money, and every room in the place would be reserved at full price—all for the donation of accommodation for the main participants. The cocktail lounge and restaurant would also be running at full capacity thanks to the swarms of media people in town. The avid fans of "Dallas" would spend hours hanging around the hotel hoping for a glimpse of the television stars or a photo opportunity and they spent money there as well.

Duffy and Kanaly had waived their usual appearance fees as they were both keen hunters and looked on the event as a paid holiday. Only their actual expenses had to be covered so everyone connected with the event pitched in to make certain that they both had a great time. During the day before the actual dinner, the RCMP Public Relations Officer, Mark Dibley, took them to hunt geese. Local farmers were only too happy to give them permission to hunt on their property in exchange for a coveted photo with the celebrities.

Both of the actors were crack shots and could use many types of weapons with confidence. When the locals expressed their surprise at their expertise with rifles, they explained that they both trained for many years at the movie and television studios. Needless to say, they both bagged their limits that afternoon and celebrated with a few rounds of drinks. Ron Barker had provided his new Suburban as transportation and he had the foresight to stock a hospitality mini-bar in the back.

While Bob and Ron sat in the back seats and swapped stories with the actors, the RCMP Officer did the driving back to Fort St. John. Anxious to get back in time to freshen up before the evening's events, he began to drive faster than the posted speed limit. Radar detectors were illegal in the province but Ron had installed one in his vehicle anyway. It was mounted inconspicuously just below the huge 80's-style mobile phone unit. Suddenly, the detector started to beep. Trying to cover up, Ron reached over and pretended to answer his mobile phone. At the same time, he smoothly shut off the detector. His theatrics did not fool anyone but no one said a word.

When the hunting group reached the hotel, there was another surprise waiting. Hundreds of fans were milling around the lobby and in front of the hotel. Because the event had been so well publicized, people knew every detail of the hunt and the dinner, even the hourly schedules of Duffy and Kanaly. One very amorous stalker had even flown to Fort St. John from the U.S. Bob had to scramble to find a couple of security guards to protect both the elevators and the doors to Duffy's room to thwart her persistent efforts.

It was an exhilarating time for Bob but the hotel's success took all his attention. He ignored both his marriage and his family more as every month passed.

Some time after the Celebrity Hunt, Bob was able to book another very prestigious function for the Pioneer Inn—the BC Chamber of Commerce Annual Meeting. Newspapers from all over the province were covering the event and the visiting reporters were filing reports about the "northern City of Fort St.John, way up on the highway to Alaska."

The big city journalists were unanimous in their impression of the city. They considered the place to be a rough, backwoods town devoid of any culture or refinement. One writer went so far as to say that it was ". . . so dirty the cafes have to keep the coffee cups upside down to keep the dust from settling." (sic)

One wrote that there was not one decent place to stay or eat.

Bob took that remark personally and he worked more diligently than ever to ensure that employees took extra special care that week. The Pioneer Inn lobby, hotel rooms, lounge and restaurant had to be immaculate. The food served had to be comparable to anything found in any of the better hotel dining rooms in Vancouver. There were fresh flowers everywhere and the staff members were cautioned to take special pains with their appearance. Bob was the perfect host. He was always on duty, always on hand to attend to the smallest detail and the largest request.

Ron Barker happened to stop by the lounge one evening during the Chamber event and he was amused to see Bob dressed in a tuxedo, pandering to his well-connected, affluent guests. It seemed the perfect time for a little excitement—Fort St.John style.

Ron owned a motorcycle—a big, loud motorcycle. He went home, put on his full leather riding gear and face helmet and drove back to the hotel. When he arrived, he coasted quietly up to the back door and looked for some help. He persuaded a local teacher, Andre Kaufman, and a car dealership owner, Roy Snippa, to hold the double doors open while he quietly pushed his bike through the kitchen and up to the entrance to the lounge. Seeing Bob elegantly serving coffee to a table of delegates, Ron started the bike, revved the powerful engine and then proceeded to drive in and out of the spaces between the tables. Women were screaming in alarm and people were jumping up on chairs and tables. The incident took only a few seconds. Ron exited through the lobby and out the front door leaving behind a cloud of fumes—and a furious Bob Pomeroy.

Heading straight home, Ron parked his bike in his garage and changed quickly.

He drove back to the hotel in his car and strolled in as if he did not know a thing. Donna Spears was working at the car rental counter and she was not fooled for a minute. She knew Ron's bike and his "leathers." As he passed by her booth, she loudly hissed," If Bob doesn't kick your sorry ass for that prank, I sure as hell will."

Bob was pissed about the incident, plenty pissed, but Ron was married to one of Bob's favorite cousins, Gail, and he was not about to start a family brouhaha over the incident. Instead, he plotted revenge.

Ron's partner, Dwight, happened to share Bob's wicked sense of humor.

Bob and Dwight went to the local radio station and bought airtime for a special public announcement. The radio station manager became a co-conspirator and he produced an official sounding spot that asked for the public's help in apprehending the person responsible for public mischief and hotel damages over the weekend. The message offered a reward to anyone who could help the police with an arrest and conviction.

Of course, there had been no complaint filed so there was no actual warrant out. This seemed a great way to "scare the bejeezuz" out of Ron Barker.

The prank got out of hand. So many phone calls flooded into both the radio station and the police station that the RCMP did start to ask questions. They stopped by the car dealership to have a serious chat with Roy. He pled innocence but suggested they talk to Bob.

When the police showed up at the hotel, both Bob and Dwight decided to come clean about the prank. They explained the whole matter to the police; the fact that they thought a stupid stunt like that deserved a big scare. And, surprisingly, the police agreed. They got in on the action. That afternoon, a police car pulled up at Ron's house and two uniforms got out questioning him about the "messy business" at the Pioneer Inn. Ron spent several minutes wondering if perhaps he had gone too far.

When the police finally admitted that they were working with Bob and Dwight, Ron was relieved. Everyone involved seemed to think it was a big laugh; everyone except the schoolteacher. After hearing the phony radio announcements, learning about the police becoming involved and knowing that he had taken part in the "motorbike invasion", Kaufman spent a couple of days in absolute terror, fearful of marring his reputation and losing his job.

Score one more point for Bob.

Ron Barker and Bob have had many escapades together. They have shared many great times and they know each other's strengths and weaknesses. They also know each other's temper and, on one occasion, Ron thought he might have gone too far.

Bob had found himself in a personal predicament one summer and he devised a particularly mean-spirited scheme to try to get out of it. His plan, unfortunately, included using Ron's best friend as scapegoat.

During all of Bob's scheming, he and Ron were getting in shape for a big sheep hunting expedition in the mountains. They were hiking and working out at every opportunity to be certain they could follow the sheep aggressively. Bob never spoke of the predicament he had been in or about the way he got out of it.

Just before Ron and Bob's big hunt, however, Ron's friend told him about being "set up." Ron was furious. At first he said nothing and he left on the trip with Bob as planned. While they travelled, though, he thought more and more about the underhanded treatment his friend had received and he got even angrier. When they finally arrived at their first campsite, Ron confronted Bob and told him that no one, not even Bob, pulled a stunt like that against his friend. He said he was going to "rat him out" to everyone involved in the sorry mess as soon as they returned and Bob would have to clean up whatever fallout there might be after the truth came out.

Bob, of course, became defensive and the ensuing argument got very heated. Finally, each man threatened to shoot the other. They each had a gun and believed that each had the guts to pull the trigger so it was a serious confrontation. They went to their individual sleeping bags in silence.

Ron stayed awake all night both out of seething anger and genuine fear that he may have gone too far. He knew that Bob was furious about being threatened with exposure and he knew Bob's temper. He figured that they needed some distance between each other.

The next morning, the two men climbed into the jet boat without saying a word.

After driving downstream for a while, Ron decided he had to take a pro-active stance. He pulled into a campsite dock and told Bob, in no uncertain terms, to get the "bleep" out of his boat. Bob understood the situation clearly. As soon as he stepped out of the boat, Ron took off. He left Bob on the dock with his only option being to call Watson Lake and charter a floatplane to return to Fort St.John. Ron went back to their campsite and spent the next ten days hunting as planned, using the time to cool off his own anger.

When Bob got home, he picked up Marj and headed to Kelowna for a week's holiday. Gail Barker saw Bob when he got back to town. When Ron did not show up at the same time, she was sure that the hunting trip was just a story to cover up an affair. She got angrier with her husband as each day passed.

Thankfully, when Ron did show up, he had a sheep carcass strapped over his truck and a credible story about his quarrel with Bob.

It took a few months but eventually both men cooled down and their friendship resumed right where it left off. Bob had more important things to worry about.

His finances had become lean again.

The high interest rates on mortgages were hurting him badly. Even with the salary from the hotel and the management fees from Gerry, Bob and Marj could not continue with their own investment properties.

They sold their acreages and bought a house by the water tower in town. When things tightened even more, they sold that house and bought a condominium in Cedar Village.

Things were bad. Then they got worse.

By early 1986, the Pioneer was the most popular hotel in the whole region. Then, in spite of his excellent management, the owner drastically reduced Bob's salary. Apparently, the owner's daughter needed a job and she had asked her father to appoint her as manager. There was no legal cause to fire Bob but the man felt his loyalty had to be to the needs of his daughter. The owner knew that, if he cut Bob's salary, Bob would have no alternative but to quit. The plan worked. It was a hard pill to swallow, though, and Bob was very angry.

To help clear his mind and to distance himself from the hotel fiasco, Bob packed up the car and took Marj and the kids to visit Uncle Earl Millsap in the Lower Mainland. The bachelor uncle had a house, the beaches were close by and everyone wanted to participate in Expo '86 in Vancouver. A month later, and with his confidence restored, Bob headed back to Fort St. John.

With his job at the Pioneer Inn gone, Bob decided to concentrate on property management. He had a family to feed and a financial mess to clean up. He and Marj still owned a few rental houses but the rental income was not enough to pay the full amount of the mortgage payments. One by one, they had to be sold. Although he did not lose money on them, he certainly did not make the profits he had anticipated—or the profits he could have made if he had been able to hold on to them for a few more years.

Gerry had bought the A&W franchise in Fort St. John but both Bob and Gerry had owned the restaurant property.

The economy had shifted even more, interest rates skyrocketed and Gerry could not meet his obligations. The bank would not let him start over so Gerry took all his building keys, handed them to the bank manager and suggested that the best thing the bank could do to protect their interests was to hire Bob. Neither Bob nor Gerry had any more ownership in the A&W. As there was no one else in the city with the experience in property management of Bob Pomeroy and as, of course, he knew every aspect of each of the properties that the bank now possessed, the decision was easy to make.

Gerry, meanwhile, packed up his truck and moved to Carefree, Arizona. He and his wife found the American bankers to be more cooperative and Gerry began rebuilding his property portfolio. It took eight years, but he eventually settled payments with the Canadian banks and avoided bankruptcy.

Now the whole business was in the bank's portfolio and it was hemorrhaging money.

About the time that Bob found himself without a job, the fulltime management of the restaurant became available.

Thanks to the latest manager who "passed more food out the back door than across the counter" (according to the cook) the restaurant was in trouble again. Fed up with bad managers and staffing problems, Ethel called Bob and said she was leaving immediately. The first thing that Bob did was to find her and convince her to return to her kitchen. Then he fired the old manager and told the bank that he was taking over as general manager as well.

Bob took a hard look at the prices charged by the franchise supplier and he started buying from other sources.

Soon the A&W legal beagles were waving papers and demanding compliance. As the restaurant was now in the hands of the bank's receivers and not the original franchisee, their efforts were futile. Bob repainted the restaurant, changed the name to "Buffalo Bob's" and started to regain customers. He solicited material donations from local merchants and built a "kids' party room" onto the building with the aim of attracting birthday parties and other groups. For a while, the restaurant seemed to be heading in the right direction. It was actually making money. Unfortunately, Bob was just the manager now and any money the restaurant generated was made for the bank.

The next thing Bob did was to hire local teenagers. He knew that other kids would stop in for burgers if they knew that their friends were on staff. Bob was good to the teens he employed but he also demanded hard work and respect for both himself and for Ethel.

One young fry cook insisted on playing his ghetto blaster as loud as possible. This was irritating Ethel and he would not listen to her requests for a lower volume. She asked Bob to intervene so he stopped by the kitchen and laid out the "Less noise rule" to the boy. Then he left. A half hour later, he paid a return visit and found that the boy had cranked up the volume as soon as Bob had left. Bob shut the machine off, unplugged it and told the kid that the blaster had to go for good.

As the boy started to leave the kitchen, Bob added "And you need to go with it." Bob knew that his own son Tim worked in a restaurant and would never behave so badly towards his supervisors. Moreover, he knew that many other kids in town needed the job.

After Carnival that year, when business slowed down again, Bob had no choice but to lay off many of his young servers and kitchen help. At Ethel's request, he kept the farm kids. Both he and Ethel recognized that, for the most part, they appreciated the jobs more and worked harder.

Christmas Day, 1986, at about six AM, the telephone rang at the house and Kim answered. It was the answering service telling her that there was a huge fire at "Buffalo Bob's" and that Bob needed to go down there right away.

Kim woke Bob and he quickly drove to the restaurant. The place suffered $15,000 in damage, too much to be re-opened quickly. The only tangible thing left of "Buffalo Bob's" was the buffalo costume they had used for publicity at events. It had been stored away for the season.

Early in the New Year, 1987, Bob Pomeroy was charged with arson.

Eight

"When you soar like an eagle, you attract the hunters"
            MILTON S. GOULD, TIME, 8 DEC 1967

After the fire at the restaurant, people around town referred to Bob as "Barbecue Bob." Never to his face, though. Even when he was broke, he could command respect. Behind his back was another matter. He had been the local Bailiff, had padlocked properties and had repossessed equipment. He had swaggered around town in expensive suits when others were collecting unemployment cheques. If they snickered when he was replaced at the Pioneer Hotel, they practically danced for joy when he was charged with arson. Misery loves company and "les miserables" of Fort St. John wanted to believe the very worst of Bob Pomeroy. They all seemed to forget that he had a young family and that his wife and children were the ones who were most affected by the cruel gossip.

In spite of employees at the restaurant who swore that Bob was nowhere around the place that night and in spite of the bank's positive statements about his efforts in making "Buffalo Bob's" a success, the police kept building their file.

The local RCMP officers seemed to forget their usual boundaries when it came to their mandate of working within the law. Even today, many people question if Bob's history of physical encounters with the police affected the way his case was handled.

Some of the officers had tangled with Bob personally in prior years and they seemed to be especially aggressive in their search for evidence against him. Even to the point of conducting a questionable interrogation of Bob's seventeen-year-old daughter.

Bob and Marj were notified that, because it was Kim who received the original telephone call about the fire, the RCMP wanted to speak to her. It was their intention, according to the call, to get a short statement from her in order to clarify the exact order and timelines of events the morning of the fire. When Kim arrived at the police station with Bob and Marj, the parents were told to wait in the outer office and Kim was ushered into the investigating officer's room. She had no counsel. Her interview was not videotaped. Her parents were not allowed to be present. What followed next was an intensive forty-five minutes of badgering, repetitive questioning by the officer. Time after time, he asked Kim to tell him exactly when the call was received, exactly how her father reacted, exactly how long it took him to get dressed and exactly why she answered the telephone that morning instead of her father.

Time after time, Kim quietly responded exactly as she remembered but the officer continued his harangue, often accusing her of trying to hide something. Eventually Kim began to weep. She asked the man to stop, that she'd told him the truth and that's all she knew. She told him over and over again that her father had been home all night, that it was Christmas so she answered the phone thinking it was a friend or relative and that her father wasted no time in heading out the door. When the officer leaned over his desk and loudly demanded that she stop trying to protect her father and tell him the truth, Kim finally burst out into loud, gulping tears.

Hearing Kim crying, Bob and Marj both became concerned. Bob sprung to his feet and angrily walked into the office. He put his arm around Kim and informed the officer that the interview was over. He added that, if they had any questions about the fire or anything else, any future questioning would be with him and not any of his children.

Kim was not approached again about the matter.

After the fire, it was virtually impossible for Bob to do any business in that city. None of the banks would use his services while the court case was still active and no one would give him a job. He had become a pariah even to the businessmen he had helped and supported.

In Fort St. John, the residents had decided that he was guilty of arson and they would have no part of him.

Some of the "city's brightest" even resorted to childish stunts to make a point of their belief in the gossip.

One morning, when Bob was having coffee with his friend Brian, one of these local yokels casually dropped a lit match in Bob's lap as he walked by their table. Brian wanted to go after the idiot but Bob just shrugged it off.

The rumor mills continued to work overtime. Within months, people were convinced that Bob had set the fire; that he had run into the flames and rescued a fictional buffalo head stuffed with money; that Bob had insured the place to get a large cash settlement.

It could not have been further from the truth because, of course, the place wasn't Bob's property. It now belonged to the bank, and, with the closing of the restaurant, Bob had been deprived of a steady paycheque.

His family was impacted even further. Because of the allegations of arson, all the insurance coverage on his house and possessions was cancelled.

In early spring of 1987, the family moved.

Nine

"Being poor is a frame of mind. Being broke is only a temporary situation."

MIKE TODD, NEWSWEEK, 31 MAR 1958

Marj and Bob moved to Grande Prairie with Ryan. The trouble with the fire had forced them to work together as a strong family unit. Marj had a renewed determination to do whatever it took to get her marriage back on track. She hoped her fierce loyalty to Bob would change the way he had been living his life. They both hoped that a move to a new city would be a fresh start.

Tim wanted to finish his high school and graduate with his friends in Fort St. John. Kim also wanted to finish out her school year so they both decided to live with Mandy and Scotty until June. Tim continued working part-time at the Pioneer Inn.

Marj grew up in a close-knit, loving family and she remembered a happy, secure childhood. She quickly realized that the dynamics of Bob's family was far different from that of her own family. In spite of, or because of, Bob's lack of affection for his mother, Marj made extra efforts to form a relationship with her. She wanted Tim, Kim and Ryan to be close to their grandparents. Because of her efforts, the children were always shown genuine affection from both Mandy and Scotty.

By the time Bob's parents reached their senior years, Scotty retired from his job at CanFor and Mandy, for her part, became a far better grandmother than she had been as a mother. Although Bob remained emotionally estranged from her, his children were arguably her favorites. When

Marj and Bob travelled, they were very comfortable leaving their kids with Grandma Mandy. She was still compulsive about keeping her house clean but Bob's kids knew about her quirks and they easily adjusted in her home. Besides, Grandma Mandy had more time now and she kept track of the kids' special events, school programs and organized sports. She followed their progress closely and was always on hand to cheer them on.

Ryan enrolled in a hockey program by the time he was six but Bob rarely, if ever, attended his games. Marj was working alongside Bob during this time and they were both putting in long hours. It was Grandma Mandy who took Ryan to his games and proudly cheered him on.

She was so proud, in fact, that when he scored his first goal, she offered him a dollar for every goal he scored that season. By spring, Grandma Mandy had to cough up one hundred and fifty six dollars and she did it gladly.

Although he was living in Grande Prairie now, Bob still believed in Fort St.John. When Ray Yenkana turned up one day with information about a townhouse complex being up for grabs, Bob knew it was a good deal. Neither Bob nor Ray had any money. They did have "chutzpah"—the gift of the gab combined with boldness. They drew up a financial plan and went to two banks on the same day. With only their signatures and a financial forecast, they managed to borrow the down payment from one bank and the mortgage from the other. They had shown that they had already pre-sold two of the units as well—one, albeit to Bob's son, Tim, and the other to themselves for a rental property. Tim was still in high school, but had enough savings for his own down payment.

He was just 17, but Tim already had his father's business sense and he got roommates for enough income to cover his mortgage payments. Tim finished school in June and began working fulltime at the hotel. Like his father, he also loved the hospitality business and he was good at his job. So good, in fact, that one tourist visiting from Texas not only left him a one hundred dollar tip but also wrote a letter to the owner of the Pioneer Inn raving about his service.

Bob had redecorated the rental unit and used it as the show home for the first weeks. Then Janice McKinnon, the hostess from the lounge at the Pioneer Inn, moved in as his tenant.

Living next to Janice, Tim knew much more than he wanted to know, certainly much more than Marj ever really suspected, and he tried very hard to keep the gossip away from Kim's ears. He argued with his father a great deal and did not like being placed in the awkward situation.

Even after Bob had moved to Grande Prairie with Marj and Ryan, he still made frequent trips to Fort St. John and he wasn't very discreet about his visits with Janice. As far as business was concerned, Bob immediately recognized the huge potential of Grande Prairie. There was a huge demand for services. He and a partner, Herb Millar, started their own commercial cleaning and linen supply business to tap into some of the new money.

After checking with Corporate Registry, he discovered that Northern Linen, an established commercial laundry and supply firm in B.C., had not registered the name or company outside of that province. Bob grabbed the name and was able to capitalize on Northern Linen's advertising and reputation to get a head start in Alberta. As usual, Marj did the books and managed the office.

Bob's friend, Willie Kempin, joined in the actual physical operations and the two of them worked eighteen-hour days, usually more. Bob knew this was not the career he wanted for the rest of his life. He also knew that a couple of years slogging away in a laundry room would help him get on his way up again. Willie Kempin was the perfect work partner. He was actually a professional drywaller and so was accustomed to long hours and hard work. The drop in the housing business had drastically cut into his income as well and he was glad for any opportunity to support his family.

With just 3 or 4 hours sleep most nights, Bob and Willie still looked forward to going to work. Bob's energy is contagious. He not only enjoys work, he makes other people enjoy working with him. If there is a problem, he jokes about it. If there is a lull in activity, he pulls a prank or comes up with something new to try. If Bob and Willie were just pals before they operated Northern Linen, they surely became lifelong friends after the experience.

Starting their day at 3 AM, Bob and Willie would drive around to the businesses to pick up dirty laundry and replace with the clean supplies. They would stop for breakfast and then put in the first loads of floor mats to wash.

For the balance of the morning, both Bob and Willie would visit businesses and try to open new accounts, stopping occasionally to go back to the office and put in another load of mats.

After a quick lunch, it was back to the grind. They knew if they kept everything "in house", they could minimize their overhead so Bob and Willie tried to do as much as they could inside their office. They sent the actual laundry and embroidery orders out to Northern Linen's BC operations in Prince George.

To keep things interesting, they would challenge each other to see who could get the most new clients. One week, between the two of them, they opened eighty new accounts.

In spite of the friendly competition, both men knew they could count on each other whenever needed to close a deal. Even then, Bob managed to make it fun.

Dar's Pizza was one business that kept eluding them. Willie had been chasing after the account but the owner, Dar, kept stalling and Willie had run out of ways to convince her to sign on the dotted line.

He had shown her glowing references and promised better service with lower costs but Dar would not sign a contract. Willie expressed his frustration and Bob told him to call Dar to ask for one more appointment.

The next day, both Bob and Willie showed up at the pizza joint. After the introductions were over, Bob asked Dar to tell him exactly what she wanted. After she listed the numbers of uniforms and stressed the importance of quality embroidery work, Bob turned to look at Willie and said, very seriously, "Hell, Willie. I don't see any problems with that. She's not at all bitchy like you said she was."

Willie's shocked face made Dar burst out laughing and they got the account.

Early that spring, Bob's court case came up in Fort St.John. Bob was found not guilty. The judge made it clear that the police had not been able to provide solid evidence of arson.

The general assumption was that the fire was started by spontaneous combustion in the kitchen. Bob had no motivation to start it. Any financial benefit from the loss of the restaurant building would go directly to the bank and, in fact, Bob Pomeroy took a financial "hit" from the fire as he lost his steady income. The unfortunate outcome of the sorry mess was far greater, of course. Bob had lost the bailiff work from the bank, his financial connections in the city, and, more important to him, his reputation.

Although the arson charge had made headlines, the not guilty verdict made hardly a mention.

Charlie Grubisich had sold most of his trucks during the downturn, but he still had a strong commercial enterprise providing him with income. He was the distributor for Northern Alberta Dairy Pool and his route included most of the restaurants in the area. One of his customers had been Buffalo Bob's. After the fire had wiped out the business, Charlie did not bother sending out any invoices for past due accounts. He had been acquiring other businesses in Grande Prairie and just wrote the Buffalo Bob's account off as a loss. Six months after the court case, though, Charlie received a surprise.

Bob had given his personal guarantee to Charlie for the dairy orders for Buffalo Bob's just as Charlie had given his guarantee for back rent for the truck company years before. Although he was short of cash himself, Bob was determined to repay Charlie.

One afternoon he turned up in the yard of Leisureland Camper Village with a brand new motorbike worth about twenty three hundred dollars. Bob told Charlie he did not have cash but he wanted to give the bike to Charlie as a full settlement of the one thousand dollar account. Charlie was impressed but he did not want to accept the bike or the responsibility of selling it. He handed it back to Bob and told him to sell it and just pay him the thousand dollars. Bob did sell the bike and was able to pocket the thirteen hundred dollar difference.

This money was a like a windfall. Once again, Bob and Charlie had proven their trust of each other and their value in each other's handshake.

Bob and Marj bought a house in the Mission Heights area. Kim began her classes at Grande Prairie College that September and lived in the basement suite with one of her basketball teammates. Ryan was enrolled in elementary school and Marj continued to work for Northern Linen over the winter of 1987-88.

Their marriage was strained but they decided to take a trip to Florida as one last attempt to recapture what they had once shared. Willie and his wife, Marla, had an enviable family life and a warm, happy home so Bob and Marj had no reservations at all about leaving Ryan in their care for two weeks.

The holiday was a fiasco. Bob kept slipping away to make phone calls and Marj was convinced that his mind was more on someone else than on her. By the time they flew back to Edmonton, Marj left the airport and went to visit a girlfriend. Bob returned to Grande Prairie by himself.

Marj continued working with Bob early into summer but by August, she reached her limit. The rumors about Bob's womanizing had spread from Fort St. John to Grande Prairie and she was finished. She stopped working at Northern Linen, started working at the bank and asked for a divorce.

Bob had become involved with Janice McKinnon while he was still managing the Pioneer Inn, and Marj's suspicions about a continuing affair between the two had been well founded. It had been Janice that Bob had been phoning during their trip to Florida. All the while, he was professing his desire to work at his marriage.

Bob actually wanted to save his marriage. He does not like to fail and a divorce represents a huge failure for him. He refused the divorce request.

When Bob would only agree to a legal separation, Marj moved into another house with Kim and Ryan.

Kim was shocked about her parent's split-up. She adored her father; Marj had never said a negative word about Bob and Kim only remembers happy childhood and teen years. She had no reason to think that the family life was anything less than perfect. After the separation became public knowledge, she visited a friend in Fort St.John who told her "every one at school knew, Kim, but we loved you so much we kept our mouths shut so we wouldn't hurt you."

Bob stayed in the Mission Hills house and made the best of the new arrangements. A housekeeper kept his laundry done exactly the way he wanted, the house was clean and, if he dropped in during the day, he could joke around with her. As for the daily banter, Bob felt he was just being friendly. The housekeeper felt more. If she had her way, there would have been another woman added to the Pomeroy harem.

Coming home for lunch one afternoon, Bob walked in to his house to be greeted by an amorous and willing Mimi*. *(*Not her real name)* She was wearing one of his shirts and suggested that, if he wanted, the lunch menu could include a very "happy ending." Bob turned on his heels and headed back to the office. He also made a mental note that he had to start discriminating where and when to turn on his charm with women.

The housekeeper never brought the incident up again and neither did Bob. On her birthday, Bob decided to take her out to lunch in Clairmont just to show her that there were no hard feelings and that she was still valued as an employee. Mimi read this the wrong way and felt that perhaps Bob had thought it over and decided she was what he wanted after all.

The lunch went well but by dessert, Mimi was back to her flirting. Finally, she came right out and said what she was thinking: "You know you want to have sex with me so why don't you just do it?"

For some reason, Bob was not practicing his usual womanizing. He had been taking a couple of months to focus on nothing but work and even Mimi's brazen offer did not change his mind. He told her how flattered he was but that he had no such thing in mind. He mildly chastised her for being so loose with her affections. He told her what a nice woman she was and how much he respected her.

She kept pressing.

Finally, Bob tired of the awkward exchange. He asked her if she thought she was still a good-looking woman (She was.) The he asked her if she thought she could get any man in the place to give her a ride if she asked. (She could.) With that, Bob got up, paid the bill and, as he walked away, said "Good. You're on your own."

Bob was involved in another new business in Grande Prairie, this time with his friend Brian Surerus. Brian had devised an ingenious new piece of equipment for pile driving and Bob had helped him with the marketing and business. (When they wanted a specific phone number, they got nowhere with AGT as the number 539-7453 (KEY PILE) was already taken. That did not stop Bob. He called the number daily, sometimes more than daily, and pestered the people until they finally relented and gave up the number!)

Brian owned an International Tandem truck and a Drott excavator and he had reconfigured the equipment into a truck-mounted pile driver. The system was both convenient and efficient. The partners also had a second tandem truck with a boom and they worked out of Grande Prairie for just under two years. Eventually Brian bought out Bob's fifty percent and kept ownership of the company name. Later, when he built a hundred-man camp out of Fort Nelson, he used the name for that enterprise.

At Northern Linen, although the business was continually growing, Willie started to get complaints from customers over invoices and prices. In spite of delivering superior service, Northern Linen started losing their old customers. Willie did not like the way things were going so he went back to dry walling. Bob sold out his share to Herb Millar.

Charlie Grubisich, meanwhile, had purchased Northgate Honda in Grande Prairie. The place needing renovating and Bob said that he could handle the job. In spite of the fact that he had no training in architectural principles, Bob created the entire conceptual design. He worked tirelessly and even rolled up his sleeves to help with construction labor to make sure that he would meet Charlie's schedule.

After the Northgate Honda job was finished, Charlie hired Bob to manage Leisureland Camper Village for him.

Carrie Langstroth worked for Charlie Grubisich. Charlie's accounting partner was not a big fan of Bob Pomeroy so whenever anything to do with Bob's end of the operations came into the office, it was hastily put on Carrie's desk. She became, for all intents and purposes, Bob's supervisor.

Although Bob was busy with his job, he never stopped looking for a new opportunity to start his own business again.

Whenever he got an idea, he would stop at the office and run it by Carrie. She knew that Bob had been successful in the past and she enjoyed his company. Although she was married, she had no family and no demands to rush home. She found it easy to spend extra time at the office listening to his plans and then doing budgets and forecasts for him.

Business grew quickly and soon Charlie bought out a second RV dealership from Kevin Hanson, making his RV business one of the largest in northern Alberta.

With the expansion came more managerial requirements and, taking some misguided advice from someone else in the business, Charlie replaced Bob with the local "RV guru." This decision proved to be costly and Charlie regrets it to this very day. Not only was Bob out of work again but Charlie's business suffered from his departure.

There were still some business debts outstanding from Fort St. John and one particularly aggressive creditor had managed to get a judgment against Bob. Unfortunately, the judgment had extensive powers for collection.

Not only were Bob's bank accounts frozen, but also, without Bob's knowledge, they were able to put a "hold" on Marj's account at the branch she worked. It was a huge embarrassment for her on top of the inconvenience. She had to supply proof to her employer as well as the court that she was legally separated and had not been hiding money for Bob. Once Marj started working at the bank, she supported herself. Tim was in Fort St.John and was financially independent; Kim was attending college on student loans and her savings. They were all managing quite well.

Bob, on the other hand, was feeling a lot of pressure.

After the separation, Bob's only legal obligation was to pay child support for Ryan. On occasion, he deviated from the monthly cheque form of payment. It should be noted here that memory can be very selective. Both Bob and Marj acknowledge that Bob provided the house for Marj and Ryan. While Bob insists that he never missed a support payment, Marj recalls one month when he just showed up on the doorstep with a flashy new bike for his son. Whichever version is more accurate, the fact is that, after twenty years with Bob, Marj was never surprised.

She loved Bob with all his quirks and flaws since they were teenagers. Their attraction to each other had been immediate and strong. Looking back, Marj realizes that neither of them had been ready for marriage.

They were young and they had dreams of a wonderful life. Marj wanted happy, healthy children and Bob wanted the secure, loving home that he never had. They both worked towards building a good life for their children.

Over the years, Bob's focus shifted solely to accumulating wealth and power. He treated Marj very well and his family was never without the very best of material possessions but he began to forget about providing the very thing that he said he did not have when he was growing up—the warm and constant presence of a loving, nurturing father.

Bob always met his financial responsibilities to his family, even through the toughest times. He would work three different jobs to fulfill his commitment to ensure that they had a roof over their heads, vehicles to drive, food to eat and clothing to wear.

Unfortunately, his personal commitment to his wife was not as strong.

There were usually other women coming in and out of the relationship and, although Bob did not want to lose Marj, he could never seem to have the self-control to stay faithful to her. He always seemed to feel the need for the extra attention, for the extra assurance that he was a hot commodity. It was never a case of Marj not fulfilling her role of partner, wife and mother. It was simply a case of Bob always wanting, needing more.

As much as Marj loved Bob and as much as she hated the very thought of a divorce, she knew that it was inevitable. If they stayed together, she would not only lose her "self", she would be setting a bad example for her daughter. By separating, she and Bob could continue to care deeply for each other and remain as friends. Marj knew that Bob loved her.

He wanted to be married; he just did not know how to be married.

Marj also knew whatever happened in his life, however many years passed, that Bob would always love his children above all and that he would always choose his children over any woman; that no woman would—or could—ever come between them and their father's love.

Ten

"The tragedy of life is what dies inside a man while he lives."
—ALBERT SCHWEITZER

In late summer of 1988, Bob got a job managing the hotel in Beaverlodge. Alex and Vi Lojczyc needed someone who could take care of their three properties (Beaverlodge Hotel, Beaverlodge Motor Inn and the Beaver Inn) plus the restaurant and Bob convinced them that he could do it.

Marj and Bob were living apart and Bob arrived in Beaverlodge with virtually nothing. Tim had enrolled in college in Grande Prairie and was living in Bob's house there. He had three or four roommates to share costs and Bob subsidized them. It was Bob's last bit of property and this not only gave Tim a place to live, it also maintained the mortgage. Kim was also attending college in Grande Prairie, living with her mother and Ryan in the house Bob had bought for Marj.

Bob stayed in a room at the hotel. His only possessions were his clothes, an old GMC long box truck, a ghetto blaster and, for some inexplicable reason, a gas lawnmower. He lived like a bachelor and worked like a man possessed.

Within months, he had whipped the hotel into shape and then he tackled the dining room. Bob knew there were a lot of hotels and motels up and down the highway and there had to be a reason for travelers to stop there at Beaverlodge instead of pushing on to Grande Prairie or Dawson Creek. He made the dining room their drawing card and Bob's newly implemented Sunday brunch became legendary. The locals were not accustomed to having tuxedoed waiters pouring ice water at tables dressed with fresh linens. They were amazed at the array of breakfast and lunch entrees and the pyramids of fresh fruit.

Everyone raved about the quality and the quantity of waffles, pancakes, omelets, salads and sliced meats. Before long, people were making the half hour drive from the city just to enjoy the Sunday brunch in Beaverlodge. Ryan spent every weekend with Bob and he worked as a busboy for the brunches.

Over the next year, Bob made a high profile for himself in the hotel industry throughout the area.

It wasn't all work. Bob's friend Brian Surerus had been divorced for years and the two men spent most of their free time together. That is, when Bob was not with a woman. Once he and Marj were legally separated, he stopped making any effort to hide his womanizing. And there were many women in his life, often several at the same time. Sometimes they knew of the others, sometimes they did not. Bob made no promises. He was like a sailor in those days, with a girl in every port. In Bob's case, it was a woman in every town.

Some of the women had more staying power than others. Each had her own particular attraction.

In Beaverlodge, there was Wendy. Wendy with the friendly dog and the house. Wendy who was nice to Ryan and who let him sleep at her house when he was in town. In Grande Prairie, there was Lon. She had kids and Ryan became pals with one of her sons. Tim and Ryan knew all of Bob's women and they had their favorites. One woman that Ryan did not know was Janice McKinnon and she was still Bob's "regular" in Fort St.John. Although she had the longest relationship with his father, he did not know about her until more than two years later. Only Tim carried that secret.

Having to juggle all the names in his little black book did not seem to faze Bob at all. That is, not until his birthday in September 1988.

Brian thought it would be a great idea to use Bob's birthday as an excuse for the perfect prank. He called Bob and told him to drive to Fort St.John and join him for an early birthday lunch. Then, one by one, he called each woman that he knew Bob had been involved with and invited her to join Bob for a nice surprise. He made sure that each woman would arrive about the same time and a half hour before Bob walked in.

Sure enough, September 30 arrived and the restaurant started seating several women at different tables. Brian sat back and watched as a few of them began to recognize each other. By the time Bob walked in, the atmosphere in the room was electric. The morning was very sunny and, when Bob removed his sunglasses, it took a few seconds for his eyes to adjust. He started walking over to Brian with a big smile on his face but, as he made his way through the tables, everyone yelled "Surprise", and he recognized the other guests. Absolutely flustered, and after directing one strong expletive at Brian, Bob turned on his heel and walked out. He drove right back to Beaverlodge.

If Bob was angry with Brian for the birthday prank, he did not stay that way for long. They were soon back at their regular haunts, best pals. In Fort St. John, the nights of partying continued. Brian had a hot tub in his place and it became the centre of a lot of debauchery over that winter. They were two attractive, newly minted bachelors and, although old enough to know better, they were both behaving like testosterone-loaded teenagers.

In Beaverlodge, Bob was a businessman. In Fort St. John, he was a party animal. If Bob didn't happen to meet a new woman through his connections, he always could depend on Janice. Her marriage had ended as well so she was more than happy to be with Bob whenever he wanted her. Neither of them had a problem with affairs outside of their own relationship.

Bob's reputation continued to precede him. If anyone didn't know Bob Pomeroy, then he pretended he did—even the women wanted to be part of his circle of friends. Case in point: one "lost weekend", Bob and Brian had found a couple of cooperative gals to spend a couple of nights with them at the condominium.

It was a first-name-only basis with no strings attached. By the second night, when the foursome was playing a game of strip poker, Bob Pomeroy's name came up in conversation. The woman who had been sleeping with him all weekend exclaimed "Bob Pomeroy? Gawd, I don't have the time of day for that guy."

By spring break, Bob and Brian were both ready for a holiday in the sun and they took their kids to Hawaii. Brian's son Sean was just 16, his daughter Julia was 14 and Ryan was just nine. If their mothers had known what kind of supervision the kids would have on the holiday, they might have kept their children at home!

In spite of having their kids along, Brian and Bob turned the tropical holiday into a week of drinking and chasing skirts. Brian's kids were just teenagers but they were completely responsible for Ryan. They were given money to spend and freedom of the island while Bob and Brian did their carousing. During meals, their fathers flirted unabashedly and even gave the boys pointers on how to pick up women. Julia was mortified.

The goal for Brian and Bob was to meet a different woman each night of their vacation and they worked hard to meet their goal.

One evening, everyone was to meet at seven at a restaurant. Although the kids had been warned not to be late, Bob and Brian didn't show up until a quarter past eight. They had been drinking all afternoon and were in a rowdy mood. Waving bamboo backscratchers, they loudly ordered their meals and more drinks and then proceeded to use the backscratchers to tickle nearby diners. Or waiters. Or the kids. Or each other. After dinner, and many more drinks, the guys decided it was time to go back to their hotel.

Fortunately, they both recognized the fact that they were not fit to drive. (How they had managed to reach the restaurant is another matter!) Sean only had his Learner's Permit but he was happy to get behind the wheel.

Unfortunately, the rental car had a standard gearshift and Sean had never used a clutch. The trip back to the hotel consisted of jerks and stalls and sudden bursts of speed as Sean handled the steering and Bob, leaning over in the front seat, drunkenly handled the shifting of the gears.

If Bob enjoyed having a good time himself, he nonetheless expected the best behavior of his son. Tim had begun to follow his father's example and had turned his house in Grande Prairie into "party central." With four or five young males having a large house at their disposal, it was the ideal spot for keggers and all-night parties. Bob had received phone calls occasionally from neighbours complaining about the noise but he had blown the calls off and chalked it up to "kids being kids." He had mentioned it to Tim, though, and had told him that, as long as the boys kept the house in a clean condition, he was fine with everything.

When Bob and Ryan got back from Hawaii, they drove over to the house to give Tim some souvenirs. There were cars in the driveway, beer cans strewn on the lawn, and the front door was open. Bob walked in to the living room to find the place in total shambles. There were empty bottles all over, kids sleeping on the floor, pizza boxes and other garbage strewn around and the whole place smelled like a brewery. Tim was passed out in a drunken stupor.

Bob was furious. He hollered at everyone to get out and then he lit into Tim. Even badly hung over, Tim knew that his father was serious. They began yelling at each other and accusing each other of various examples of bad behavior and finally the quarrel erupted into a physical altercation. Ryan returned to his mother's house shaken and upset because he had never seen his father and brother actually fighting.

Bob was just as upset. He loved Tim and yet he had allowed himself to treat his son worse than he would treat anyone else. Although he was determined not to let it happen again, the promise he made to himself would sadly be broken.

By June, Tim was working for a paving crew and occasionally staying at the Beaverlodge Inn. He desperately wanted his father's approval and he had made a point of apologizing again for the scene that Bob walked into weeks before. Tim knew that he was fortunate to be living in a house while Bob was living in a single room.

One evening, Tim was finished his shift and some friends from the paving crew invited him to go for a beer. He had not been paid yet so he went to Bob's room to borrow twenty dollars. Bob had been having one of his power naps and Tim woke him up. Instead of being angry, Bob told Tim that he was welcome to take what he needed out of his wallet. Tim saw that a fifty-dollar bill was the only thing in the wallet and he did not want to take his father's last cent.

He looked around the sparse motel room and thought about his own furnished house and about the things he had been given over the years. He decided he did not need to go out with friends after all and told Bob that he would just stay in that night. Bob was having none of that. He got up and handed Tim the fifty, telling him that he was only young once and he did not need the money.

Tim did not hesitate with his response. He told Bob to come out for a beer with him; that they deserved a night together.

The gesture both surprised and touched Bob deeply and he still treasures the memory of that night. It brought the realization that his children were growing into adults and he had been missing precious time with them.

In June that summer, Kim was returning from visiting a friend in Heinsberg, just north of Lloydminster. In spite of the town being out of her way, she had promised her friend Twyla that she would be there for her graduation and Kim never broke promises.

She had decided to drive all the way home without stopping but, by the time she got to Edmonton, she wondered if she was getting too tired. Nonetheless, she pushed on, alone in the car. Just past Cherhill, she knew that she had made a mistake. It became harder and harder to shake off the drowsiness. Suddenly she was shocked awake when she felt her car careening off the highway. In her exhausted condition, she had fallen into an almost-hypnotic state and lost control of the vehicle.

Thankfully, she did not hit another car. She did survive the resulting accident but she was hurt. After being badly shaken up and injured, Kim had remained calm and had carefully assessed her situation and injuries. She knew she had to get away from the car in case it exploded but her sports training reminded her that she had to protect her spine.

Instead of trying to walk, Kim had the presence of mind to crawl slowly and purposefully away from the wreck, maintaining the integrity of her back as best she could. She managed to get to the side of the highway where she was seen and rescued.

Kim spent three weeks in the hospital in Edmonton. Her back had been broken in three places and doctors told the family that her core strength had kept the muscles together. Her years of playing basketball had kept her in excellent physical shape and her restraint in moving excessively at the crash scene had certainly been instrumental in preventing any paralysis.

After being transferred to Grande Prairie by air ambulance, Kim spent another month in hospital followed by an intensive regime of therapy.

Bob had only one daughter and she had grown up in the blink of an eye.

The shock of Kim's accident frightened him and, once more, he made a firm resolve to see more of all of his children.

That September, Kim enrolled in University in Brandon, Manitoba and Bob returned to his pursuit of success.

Eleven

"To lose a child is to lose a piece of yourself"
—DR.BURTON GREBIN, NY TIMES 30 OCT 1984

When Tim finished college the beginning of June 1990, he went back to building roads. This time he was working for Ledcor in Wonowon, BC. It was good money and Tim, just like his father, was never one to hide from hard work.

He put in long days and lived at the camp. On weekends he would stay in Fort St. John with Grandma Mandy and catch up with his old school pals. He had a girlfriend in Fort St. John, too, and that was even more incentive for going back. They were "steadies" but it couldn't be a serious relationship yet. She was only sixteen and Tim had plans for his future.

Tim and Bob had always been at odds with each other over Bob's affairs and, that July, when Bob told him that Janice McKinnon was pregnant, Tim reached the limit of his patience. He knew that Bob owned Janice's condo and he also knew that Janice had another man living there with her. Tim had no problem in speaking his mind and he pulled no punches.

JULY 14, 1990, SATURDAY
Knowing that Janice was at her condo, Tim confronted her about the pregnancy. He challenged Janice to prove that Bob was the father of the baby. He called her names and told her that he, along with everyone else in town, knew that she was involved with other men. When Janice told him to get out, he told her that he had every right to be there because he was Bob's son. The quarrelling escalated and got even meaner. Janice

told Tim she would call Bob to "do something about him"; that she was in Bob's life for the long term.

JULY 15, 1990, SUNDAY.

When Tim saw his father the next day in Beaverlodge, they quarreled about Janice. Although it didn't result in a knock-down, drag 'em out physical encounter, there was a lot of yelling and pushing. Tim called his father names and Bob told his son to get out of his sight. (Although Bob had serious doubts of his own about the baby's paternity, he was preferring to keep it quiet and he didn't want Tim to rock the boat.)

JULY 18, 1990, WEDNESDAY.

Kim asked her brother to come to Grande Prairie, pick her up and drive her to Dawson Creek. She had loaned her car to her boyfriend and wanted to pick it up. On the way to Dawson, Tim told his sister about the fight he had with Bob. He described how Janice had yelled at him, how he had told her that she was just a gold-digging tramp and how he had urged his father to leave her out of their lives. Tim also said that he told his father to get a paternity test done and then, if the baby was his child, to finally step up to the plate and act like a man, to try and be a real father to this kid; that he'd missed his chance with the others.

He also told Kim how angry Bob was at him and how they had pushed at each other and had parted on very angry terms. (Note: Bob prefers to remember that they parted on amicable terms; that he even gave his son a hug before Tim left.)

Tim hugged his sister, said goodbye and he headed back to work in Wonowon.

JULY 21, SATURDAY, 1990
2:00 AM, BEAVERLODGE

Bob was driving back to Beaverlodge from Grande Prairie. There was virtually no light on the long stretch of highway and he was speeding.

Bob suddenly lost control of his car and spun into a ditch. Shaken and bruised, he crawled out of the wreck, flagged down a passing motorist and got a ride to Wendy's house. Intending to call the tow truck in the morning, he wearily crawled into bed about four AM.

He got up and went to work a few hours later, around 7:30 AM.

He had just started his daily duties when he found two RCMP Officers grimly facing him. When he asked them if they had come about the accident, the officers seemed surprised and asked if he already knew about it.

Bob's retort: "Of course I know about it. I was in it. I'm fine. I'll take care of the car later."

The confusion on the officers' faces was clear and they continued by suggesting that perhaps they were speaking of two separate accidents. They were there about the accident on the highway north of Fort St. John. About six hours earlier. Around two AM.

It was at that moment that Bob realized the worst.

Tim Pomeroy had gone to Fort St. John to see his friends. There was a big house party on Friday night and Tim told his girlfriend that he would call her after he grabbed a bite to eat and then pick her up. When he got to town, Tim met a few of his pals and decided to have a beer with them. One beer turned into two and the guys ordered something to eat. With no cell phones handy in those days, Tim didn't manage to make the promised phone call. After the guys finished their beer and supper and caught up with the latest sports events, they headed over to the house party. Tim saw that his girlfriend had already arrived and she was steamed.

In spite of caring for Tim a great deal, she thought he needed a lesson in manners. She told her friends that she wouldn't forgive him until his next trip and she spent the next couple of hours avoiding his attempts to talk. The party wrapped up about one-thirty. Tim knew it was at least an hour's drive back to camp but he had a dependable car and only had finished a couple of beers all evening.

JULY 21, 1990, SATURDAY
2:00 AM, FORT ST.JOHN

About a half hour out of Fort St. John, Tim's car hit a large moose. A nurse living in a nearby farmhouse heard the crash and she rushed to the scene. Although she tried her best to save Tim's life, he did not survive.

The nurse stated the time of death to be approximately 2:00 AM, almost the precise time that Bob had lost control of his car on the other highway.

Twelve

"Most things break, including hearts. The lessons of life amount not to wisdom but to scar tissue and callus."
—*WALLACE STEGNER, "THE SPECTATOR BIRD" DOUBLEDAY 1976*

Marj, Grandma Mandy and Ryan had been travelling to Kelowna that weekend to stay with Judy. Ryan was registered for a two-week hockey school and, as Ryan's cousin was in the same school, they planned to make it into a holiday. They had picked up Grandma Mandy and left Fort St.John in late afternoon, stopping in Cache Creek for the night. Marj was tired from driving and fell asleep as soon as her head hit the pillow.

JULY 21, 1990, SATURDAY
2:00 AM, CACHE CREEK
Marj suddenly awoke and sat up in bed. She had not heard a sound but she had felt something, she did not know exactly what, but SOMETHING had jarred her awake. She lay down feeling unsettled but managed to fall asleep again.

Around seven AM, Marj woke up and called Judy from the hotel to tell her that they were going to have breakfast and then be on the road again. She expected to get to Kelowna right after lunch.

About the same time, Bob called his sister Joan in Grande Prairie. Her husband Brian headed out for Fort St.John immediately.

After speaking to Joan, Bob called Starr Martin about the accident. He told Starr he was on his way to the hospital; that he had to identify Tim's body to make it official. George had already gone to work at the "Cleanery" but Starr did not want Bob to be alone. She told him to wait for her and she would be right down. She called George and told him; then she woke their son Dan. Dan and Tim were the same age and, although they attended different schools, they had been pals so Starr wanted Dan to know right away. Leaving her son at home to notify friends, Starr rushed to the hospital and began looking for Bob. When she finally found the right elevator to take her to the morgue, the doors opened and there stood Bob with Joan's husband, Brian Scheck. Bob looked ashen and could only mutter two words, "It's Tim."

Starr hugged Bob and asked if Marj knew yet. Bob just shook his head and Starr said she would make the call. Joan had been totally blindsided by the accident. She did not know what to do or say and simply was in no state to call Marj with the news. Everyone all knew that the RCMP would be going to Judy's house in Kelowna but Starr wanted the information to come from a close friend, not the police. She told Bob not to worry, that she would break the news to the rest of his family. She also asked him to come back to her house when he was finished with what he had to do. Then Starr placed the dreaded call.

When Marj, Mandy and Ryan arrived in Kelowna, Judy seemed very somber. As her husband had passed away less than a year earlier, Judy's appearance was not really a surprise. She had been devastated by his death and was still finding it difficult to cope with being a widow. Judy told them not to bother unloading the car. She urged them to come into the living room; that she had to talk to them. Judy sat down and motioned for the others to sit as well. It was obvious that she was struggling with her emotions.

When Judy finally was able to convey the terrible news, Marj was very silent. In shock, she put her arm around Ryan and tried to process the information, tried to come to grips with the fact that her eldest son was dead. Although Ryan had heard his aunt Judy say something about a "Tim" being killed in an accident, the eleven year old figured that it must have been a friend or relative of the family. After all, the only "Tim" he knew was his brother and, of course, his brother was working in Wonowon. He would see him in a couple of weeks. When he looked at his mother's face and felt her tears, Ryan soon realized that the Tim they were talking about, his big brother, was dead.

A little while later, the RCMP arrived to confirm Tim's death. Bob had not been able to notify Kim as she had been visiting her boyfriend in Dawson Creek that weekend.

Thankfully, Marj had known Kim's plans and knew the young man and his phone number. She called her daughter and the rest of the extended family. Then everyone made plans to return to Fort St. John.

Meanwhile, at the Martin house, Dan had been making calls all morning. The radio station had been talking about the accident but the name of the deceased had not been released. Tim's friends felt the need to be together and they started to drop in to wait with Dan. When Starr got home, there were already over a dozen kids quietly waiting for news. Starr did not want to say anything until Bob got there so they all just sat quietly listening to the radio, some praying, most weeping. By noon when Bob and Brian arrived, there were almost twenty of Tim's friends gathered. Bob took one look and all the breath left his lungs. He looked at Dan and nodded and then he quietly told Starr that he had to leave, that he could not talk to anyone. Brian took him to get some of the arrangements started and Starr broke the news to the kids.

The next morning, Bob returned to the Martin home. Kim had already arrived and everyone was still silent in grief. Tim being dead was a hard concept for Ryan to understand. For young kids, death only affects old people. Brothers and sisters are immortal. Even when parents get divorced, your brother is still there for you. At least that is how it works in a perfect world.

When Bob and Marj were making the funeral arrangements, Ryan insisted on going to the funeral home with them. They tried to change his mind but he would not be deterred. Once they started their discussions with the funeral director, the reason became evident. When the man suggested one type of casket, Ryan interrupted and strongly demanded another type of wood. He made several surprising requests and finally the director asked how he knew so much. Ryan calmly explained that, during his last semester at school, the class had made a field trip to the Grande Prairie funeral home and they had learned about the choices available and the reasons behind each option. As usual, his inquisitive mind had retained all the information, not knowing that it would be needed so soon and under such sad circumstances.

JULY 25, 1990, WEDNESDAY

At the funeral, Ryan saw his brother's body and watched everyone in silence. Even at eleven, he was mature and thoughtful and the adults ignored him for the most part. Starr Martin noticed his demeanor after the reception though and she followed him outside to ask how he was doing. Ryan was not crying. He seemed more perplexed and she asked him if something was bothering him. Ryan told Starr that it seemed impossible for his brother to be dead. He had looked at Tim lying in the casket and he "wasn't messed up at all. He looked fine" so how could he be dead?

Starr put her arm around Ryan's shoulder and pointed to a parked TransAm. She showed him how low the car was and indicated how tall a fully-grown moose is. She explained that the car would have gone right between the legs and knocked the moose over onto the roof and windshield and that it was not like an accident where two cars end up all mangled. Ryan nodded his understanding, hugged her back and walked off to join the others, seemingly satisfied at the clarification.

Hundreds attended the funeral. Tim had been a very popular young man and, along with the many Pomeroy relatives, his former school friends, his coworkers at the hotel and the people from the construction site filled the chapel. Ledcor had taken an unprecedented move and had shut down the whole job for the day.

Bob's great friend Ray Yenkana gave one eulogy and Dawna Brown (the mother of Tim's girlfriend) gave the other. The reception at Dawna's house was packed.

When the funeral was over and all the goodbyes said, Judy and her children returned to Kelowna on the bus.

Bob headed back to Beaverlodge and threw himself into work, alone with his thoughts and his grief.

After a few days, Marj thought it best that Ryan return to some normalcy while the realization set in for the rest of them. She decided to return to Judy's home. Kim did not want her mother to drive alone so she persuaded her boyfriend to come along with her and drive Marj and Ryan back to Kelowna

Just a couple of hour's out of Fort St. John, they passed by a horrific car accident. Police cars and an ambulance had just arrived and there was a badly smashed car in the ditch. The sight of the accident upset Marj a great deal and they were glad to get past it and on to Kelowna. When they arrived at Judy's house, a message was waiting. The accident they had passed on the highway involved one of Tim's pallbearers. His cousin Sterling Pomeroy was dead as well.

Thirteen

"You can sort of be married, you can sort of be divorced, you can sort of be living together but you can't sort of have a baby":
—DAVID SHIRE, QUOTED IN TIME MAGAZINE 2 JAN 1984

That summer, 1990, Bob's personal circumstances continued to change. Janice McKinnon's pregnancy was progressing. She had been living with another man but was positive that Bob had fathered her child. If there was even the slightest chance of the baby being his, Bob wanted to be a participating father.

He began to support her financially but, realistically, he was still legally married to Marj and in no position to make any other long-term commitments. Janice was drinking heavily and Bob feared for the health of the baby. He had been furious at Janice during Tim's funeral. His last meeting with his son had been an angry one, the rancor caused by the pregnancy. In spite of Janice claiming to be carrying Bob's baby, the very week that Tim was buried, Janice was out of town camping with another man. It had not occurred to her to be available to give Bob any emotional support.

Tim's death had made all the family relationships even more strained.

Kim had heard from Tim that Janice was pregnant and she had mixed feelings. She wanted her father to be happy but she felt she had to be cautious—at least until they knew for certain of the paternity of the baby. Bob was an emotional wreck after Tim's death and he did not want any distance between himself and his other children. He wanted to spend time with them and he wanted them to try to accept this new forthcoming sibling.

He begged Kim to come out for dinner and meet Janice.

Before she could accept his invitation, Kim asked her mother how she felt about it. Marj was pragmatic about the situation and told Kim that she was an adult now, Janice was part of her father's life and she had no feelings either way. She had resigned herself to the fact that their marriage was over, once and for all, and nothing that Bob could do would change that. Still hurting from her parents' separation and her brother's death, Kim had some curiosity about the woman she had only heard about so she agreed to the meeting.

When Kim went to dinner, she was shocked.

Knowing her father's disdain for smokers at the best of times and seeing Janice's pregnant belly, she was appalled that Bob's companion was a chain smoker. She was further appalled when Janice consumed glass after glass of wine. Seeing Kim's reaction, Bob kept moving the wine glass away from Janice and waving the waiter away when he enquired about refills. As the meal progressed, Kim's comfort level was more diminished, and she felt it difficult to remain civil to the woman. Although she loved her father and could see his concern, she cut the dinner short and left as soon as she could. She was very happy to get back to her mother's house and she cried herself to sleep that night thinking about the mess that she felt her father had made of their lives.

Marj decided she needed to be closer to her family. She moved back to Fort St.John with Ryan and Kim enrolled in university in Brandon, Manitoba. Bob was still in Beaverlodge, throwing himself into his work and building the hotel and restaurant's reputation.

Dave Thompson was the chairman of the Board of Directors of the Dunvegan Inn in Fairview.

That business had been losing money and was now in the hands of the Alberta Receiver. Dave had the job of hiring a new manager and he had been hearing a lot about the incredible turn-around of the Beaverlodge Hotel. He drove out one Sunday to look at the celebrated Brunch and maybe meet the man who had made such an impact. He was very impressed, to say the least, and he asked Bob to drive out to Fairview and talk about a possible move.

Dave offered Bob the job almost immediately into the interview, and then they just started talking about the business. Prior to becoming a successful insurance agent, Dave had been an English teacher and he was a stickler for education.

When Bob happened to mention his own lack of schooling, Dave hesitated and said that he may have been too hasty, that he would never even consider hiring someone who could not read or write well. That did not faze Bob.

He confidently challenged Dave to ask him anything about running a hotel that he would not be able to answer. The position of manager remained in his hands.

Before he could start the new job, however, Janice went into early labor and Connor Pomeroy was born.

Janice had gone for her monthly checkup and the doctors in Grande Prairie noticed an irregularity in the baby's heartbeat. They admitted her to the hospital overnight for further tests and monitoring. When she wanted to check herself out for a few hours so she could go out for a drink, the doctors decided that she should be transferred to Edmonton's neonatal centre immediately. Connor was born there a short time later.

Because of the constant abuse of alcohol and tobacco, Connor was not only a small "preemie"; he was also born with a seriously damaged heart. Kim still remembers Bob's phone call telling her that she had a new brother but that the baby was critically ill.

Kim was not happy about Bob and Janice living together and she still hoped that her parents would somehow resolve their differences. In spite of these reservations, and in spite of her negative feelings about Janice, she could hear the distress in her father's voice and she rushed over to the hospital to be with him.

Whatever the circumstances were of this child's conception, they no longer mattered. Connor was here and he was her brother.

A few weeks later, Bob finally realized that his life had taken a path in a new direction and there seemed to be no turning back. He filed for the divorce that Marj had requested.

There was no hatred, no messy fights, and no rancorous end to their years together. They agreed to agree on the final arrangements. Marj got her house and a new car.

The "new car component" of the settlement was a compromise in sorts.

Marj had been driving a Mercedes. By selling that car, Bob could raise some much-needed cash. Bob got the Mercedes back and Marj got a new Chevrolet.

Even in their divorce, the two remained contractually bound. Bob did not have good credit so Marj had to arrange financing for her car through the bank where she worked. Bob made all the payments.

Looking back as an adult, Ryan realizes that there had to be loads of times in those years when there was virtually no money for the family. As a kid, however, he was never aware that there was any change in their financial situation. Bob always found some way to not only just provide necessities for them but also get them special gifts.

For his twelfth birthday, Ryan really wanted a dirt bike. He saw a used one for $200 but he did not have that much in his savings. When he asked his mother to buy him the bike, Marj said she could not manage the expense either. It was just a fact and Marj did not elaborate. Although Bob and Marj were divorced, Marj never once spoke badly of Bob to his children, nor did she bemoan the facts of living on a tighter budget.

When Ryan suggested going to his dad for the bike, Marj simply said that everyone was on a budget and he would have to wait a little longer or save for it himself.

Ryan was totally insulated from the cold, hard fact that Bob was not flush with money any more. He could not believe that his dad could not pull money out of a hat as needed so, when the $200 did not readily appear for the bike, he figured that his parents simply did not want him to have it.

When his mother said she was taking him to have lunch with Bob, he went along begrudgingly and he let his father know just how angry he was. For heavens sakes, all he wanted was a stupid two hundred dollar used bike! In other words, he behaved like a sullen, spoiled brat.

Marj and Bob said nothing. They simply enjoyed the lunch, shared a pleasant conversation and then got in Bob's car. Bob drove to the local bike dealership, they walked in and the dealer presented Ryan with a brand new dirt bike.

To this day, Ryan does not know how Bob managed to swing the deal. He does know that it was important to Bob that his son drove the best bike possible.

Fourteen

"The reward for work well done is the opportunity to do more."
—JONAS SALK

Bob started work in Fairview almost immediately. Connor was still in hospital in Edmonton and Janice stayed there to be with him. Bob was as proud of this little boy as he had been with his other children and he always brought out photos of Connor in the incubator to show people his newest addition. When Connor had his heart surgery, Bob carried new pictures of his son. True to form, Bob was not seeking sympathy for having a frail child; he was actually boasting about what a strong fighter Connor was and how his brave little guy was already proving to be a "real Pomeroy."

He and Janice became very active in the social life of Fairview. Managing the Dunvegan gave Bob the opportunity to use his marketing skills as well as his business acumen and he knew the importance of knowing everyone in the area.

When he took over the Dunvegan Motor Inn, Bob did an amazing job of turning around the financials. He spent weeks cleaning it from top to bottom. What may have appeared as acceptable to the former staff was unacceptable to Bob.

He did not just give orders; he rolled up his sleeves, scrubbed, polished, and painted like everyone else until the whole building was transformed into his standard of cleanliness.

To say that he is a "clean freak" when it comes to his property is a gross understatement. For anyone in the hospitality industry, this trait is a great asset.

At the Dunvegan, he thought outside the box when it came to increasing revenue and attracting repeat business. The lounge was a good source for profit, but only if all the chairs were filled. Bob worked with all the merchants in Fairview and supplied them with entry ballots for a "Win the Car" contest. Customers had to deposit the ballots personally at the lounge. At specified intervals, Bob drew twenty ballots. Each of the twenty finalists received a car key and, on the designated evening, each of the finalists had to be present at the hotel. Bob presented the car to the lucky person whose key opened the door. The contest was a great success and the lounge was always busy.

When Bob was not at the hotel or at home caring for Connor, he was visiting businesses in the entire area, getting to know people by their first name and inviting them to come down for a great night out.

During the major remodeling, Bob left the lounge for last. He wanted that spot to be perfect for the lucrative New Year's Eve party. He knew that more people than ever would turn up to be the first ones to celebrate in a brand-spanking new room but he also wanted the place to look good the next day. The year before, over fifty people had been involved in a brawl. The room had been left in shambles.

Bob knew he would have to resort to some innovation to prevent any trouble. His friend Willie was doing all the dry walling and Bob expressed the concerns he had about keeping the lounge in one piece during the current year's event. Willie offered to be on hand that night to act as security but he cautioned Bob that, although he was a big man, he was not a fighter. Bob told him not to worry.

A couple of weeks into December, Bob started a rumor in town that the Dunvegan was bringing in a "tough guy", a huge "bouncer" from a tough club in Edmonton and they weren't going to stand for any trouble. They would not be calling the police if there were a brawl. His "enforcer" would simply handle any troublemakers on the spot.

New Year's Eve, Willie turned up as promised and Bob handed him a t-shirt at least one size smaller than usual. The fabric was stretched taut across his broad chest and his biceps looked like they would rip through the sleeves if he simply breathed too hard. A gentle family man by nature, Willie nonetheless looked every inch a "thug" and no one tempted fate by causing trouble that night; except, perhaps, one middle-aged woman who could not handle her liquor. When she became very loud and then abusive to other partygoers, Willie sauntered over and quietly asked her to settle down. She continued her rampage.

Willie spoke to her a little more loudly the next time and told her to behave herself. Instead of settling down, the woman started swearing and loudly yelled, "You don't talk that way to a lady" to which Willie replied, "I wasn't." When her friends burst out laughing at this exchange, the woman calmed down in embarrassment and Willie walked away.

Darrell and Shelley Urban were local people who had invested in the hotel. The Urbans had a young family and they were close in age to Bob and Janice. The foursome became friends and spent a lot of time together. Bob even became Godfather to Stephanie Urban.

That first winter, Bob, Janice, and the Urbans entertained often. Everyone in their circle had babies or toddlers, so house parties were the most convenient way to get together. If a babysitter were not available, couples would simply bring the kids along and put them to sleep in any spare bed while the adults had fun.

It was the year that Murder Mystery parties became popular and Bob enjoyed playing characters.

When the foursome, along with a few others, tired of Murder Mysteries, they decided to have lip-synching contests in someone's home. In spite of Bob's outgoing personality and seemingly endless confidence, he was frozen with stage fright. Even among friends, he could not muster up the courage to sing one word. No problem. Bob was elected as the permanent judge, the Simon Cowell of the Saturday night party crowd.

When it was party night and everyone was in the same high spirits, many drinks were poured and everyone at one time or another drank more than their usual limit. Sundays were hangover days and then Monday the majority of people were back at work. What no one was noticing was that Janice's drinking continued over every day of the week. Even Bob did not see the extent of the problem until Connor's safety became an issue.

One day a cousin was driving through Fairview and decided to drop in for a visit. He knocked and knocked at the door but no one answered. He knew someone was at home, though, because he could hear Connor crying loudly. The door was locked so he could not go in to investigate. When the baby's crying became a choking scream and still no one came to the door, the cousin went to the hotel and found Bob. Sure enough,

Janice had passed out from drinking and Connor was very wet and very hungry.

From that day on, Bob juggled his work so he could disappear every couple of hours. He would rush home, change the baby and feed him, check on Janice, go back to work for a couple of hours, then repeat the process. When that system proved to be unworkable, Bob took his infant son to work with him in the baby carrier.

He bathed Connor at suppertime or before he went to work in the morning. No one except Shelley Urban knew that he was being mother and father to Connor. She often contributed babysitting duties so that Bob could get through meetings or evening functions. Bob kept Janice's secret but he continually implored her to get help. That, unfortunately, led only to constant quarrelling.

When Connor was about ten months old, Bob was going to a hotel convention and decided to take Janice along.

He thought she might feel better about herself if she got away from the house and baby. She had changed so much since they first met in Fort St. John. Always a stickler for style and personal appearance, Bob had been attracted to Janice initially because she always stood out from the other women at the hotel. Her hair was always perfect and she dressed fashionably. Little by little, she had been ignoring her grooming, never wearing makeup, and hardly combing her hair.

Although Bob bought her nice clothes, she left them hanging in the closet or still folded in bags, and just threw on tee shirts and old jeans. Anything else seemed to take too much effort.

Bob knew that Connor was always crying and neither of them seemed to be able to comfort him. He thought that maybe the premature delivery and weeks of worry in the hospital over the baby had created some depression for Janice. He knew she had been drinking heavily before the baby's birth but now acknowledged that it was constant. He thought that perhaps a weekend with new people and great entertainment would be a positive start.

Bob asked his sister Judy to come and stay with Connor for the weekend and Kim said she would drive out to Fairview as well. Connor started crying almost immediately after his parents left and Judy looked fruitlessly for some baby food. The only thing in the fridge was a supply of baby formula in bottles. No strained food, no cereal. Judy and Kim packed up the baby and headed for the store for some supplies appropriate for a ten-month old. After a couple of good feedings of Pablum, Connor slept soundly.

Bob and Janice returned Sunday afternoon and they seemed to be on good enough terms. Both were happy to see that Connor was napping peacefully and Bob asked Kim and Judy to stay for a while so he could catch up on family news.

When Judy mentioned having to buy cereal for Connor, that the baby was malnourished, Janice became quiet and stopped participating in the conversation. Kim still was not very enamored of the woman in her dad's life so she spoke directly to her father. Judy concentrated on Connor.

Bob felt the tense atmosphere and he kept trying to have "small talk" with his daughter, asking about university and about her classes. Finally, Kim told her father about the great guy she was dating, that it was getting serious. Bob turned to Janice to say, "Isn't that great". . . and, unfortunately, he called her "Marj." Janice erupted and stormed off to the kitchen. Bob followed, uttering apologies, but the damage was done. Kim and Judy put their coats on and hurriedly said their goodbyes over the noise of the escalating quarrel.

Once Connor became a toddler, Bob got a big dog to help watch him. Riley became Connor's shadow. The dog never left Connor's side, following the little boy around the house and barking like crazy if Janice fell asleep or if Connor wet his diaper. Riley even knew to pull on Connor's clothing if the toddler tried to climb up on something. Bob tried everything he could to keep his home life a secret even if it meant having a guard dog for his son and pulling away from his friends.

Bob had always taken an enormous amount of pride in his children. Marj had been a great mother. She always made certain that Kim and the boys were well dressed and well behaved in public. Their table manners were perfect at home as well as in public and they listened to direction from all adults. Bob and Marj took their children out to dinner from the time they were toddlers and they were always on their best behavior. When Bob saw other children running around the Dunvegan Inn lobby or throwing tantrums in a restaurant, he made no bones about telling everyone in earshot that his children would know better, that Bob Pomeroy's children would never cause a scene in public.

In just a year, his words would come back to haunt him.

Connor more than made up for any "spit and vinegar" that the other children lacked. To Bob's chagrin, his youngest son soon became known as the "unholy terror" of the Dunvegan Inn. As soon as he learned to walk, he learned to run. As soon as he learned to make little sounds, he learned to scream. By the time he was two, Connor Pomeroy ruled the roost.

There was not a shred of evidence that would indicate that he was anything but an extremely healthy, extremely rambunctious little boy.

Ryan spent his weekends and holidays with Bob and Janice and Connor. He and Robbie Urban were about 12 and Bob gave them both jobs as busboys in the restaurant. Robbie worked there regularly and both boys worked together when Ryan was in Fairview. In the late fall, Bob and Darrell Urban would take their sons hunting.

At the time, Bob was driving a little red Ford Tempo, hardly well equipped for backcountry roads. Late one day, the guys were heading back to Fairview after an unrewarding day in the countryside.

In a hurry as usual, Bob was driving too fast for the bumpy back road. Hitting a deep rut, the Tempo came to a sudden stop, the gas tank thrust up through the floor. Everyone climbed out to analyze the situation and the conclusion was that they were all in "deep do-do."

This was 1990 and only movie stars and big shots had car phones. It was getting dark, they were far from town and the young boys were getting scared and hungry. Bob knew that they needed to attract some help but he did not want the young boys to see his concern.

In his usual positive style, Bob announced that it was the perfect spot to break down. There was a clearing, lots of dry wood and they had plenty of food left. It was time for a wiener roast—a really BIG wiener roast. With the twelve year olds concentrating first on the excitement of building a huge bonfire and then on eating scorched hot dogs, the dads could concentrate in making sure that the fire was big enough to get the attention of nearby farms. Sure enough, within an hour or two, a farmer spotted the billowing smoke and came to investigate.

That particular trip did not end the hunting expeditions; it merely derailed the Tempo. Bob replaced the car with a sturdy van and, ignoring Janice's revulsion about hunting, the outings resumed. (It may or may not be true that the van's side doors provided a convenient, if not illegal, protection from rain while shooting coyotes.)

By this time, Kim was engaged to be married and Marj had met a man that she wanted to marry. The renewed fact that Bob and Marj were never going to reconcile gave Janice some optimism for her own future but she was still abusing alcohol and the quarreling between her and Bob continued. It was not a happy home and guests were less than welcomed.

Bob remained optimistic throughout the Fairview years. If things were tense at home, he simply changed his plans. And he really tried to put his children first.

When Janice was going through a bad patch and it coincided with time that Ryan was going to be with them for a few weeks, Bob took a holiday with his son. On one adventure, he took Ryan and a friend's son, Kevin Madden, to Las Vegas. Ryan was just 13 but Kevin was a few years older so if Bob was in a lounge or casino, the boys could be on their own for a few hours. Even in Las Vegas, Bob pointed out features of the hotels to Ryan, things that brought customers back repeatedly, features they could incorporate into the hotels they would build one day.

Whether Bob brought along a pal for Ryan on each trip because he remembered his fun with cousins Mike and Pat or because he wanted the freedom to be on his own during the evenings really does not matter. The fact is that Ryan always had a great time on the father-son vacations and still has good memories of each holiday. He also remembers each lesson his father taught about the hospitality business.

One trip had a greater impact than others did on Bob's plans for the future.

Janice had a sister getting married in Winnipeg that summer. Bob took a week off and headed out on the highway with her, Connor, Ryan and Robbie Urban. They did not book hotels in advance and when it was time to stop for a night, Bob let the boys choose a hotel. Their choice was always unanimous. If a hotel or motel had a waterslide, the boys were unrelenting. Bob had to stop there, no matter how early in the afternoon.

While the boys played in the water, Bob walked around the parking lot to count cars. He inspected the building structure and made notes on the size of the slides and the numbers of families eating at the restaurant. Once they got to Winnipeg and spent the weekend at the Country Inn & Suites, Bob started to formulate a plan. Somehow, he would buy a hotel and renovate it to include a waterslide. Then he would do the same with a second property.

Bob wanted to own a chain of Pomeroy Inn and Suites and offer extended stay rooms. He wanted hotels with the Pomeroy name on them and he wanted to operate the company with his sons. After the Winnipeg trip, Bob remained focused about their future together and he started Ryan's intensive training.

The following summer, 1993, Kim and Mike Gagnon were married.

Everyone knew about Janice's drinking by that time and Kim was terrified that Janice may make a scene at the reception. Bob promised his daughter that he would not let that happen. All through the day and evening, Bob stayed by Janice's side. He kept feeding her to keep her as sober as possible and the day went off without a hitch.

Bob had bought the couple a trip to Las Vegas as his wedding gift but as they both had so many sports commitments, Kim and Mike decided to postpone their honeymoon until the fall. Sadly, Mike was killed before the trip was taken.

After he had successfully turned around the Pioneer Inn, the Beaverlodge Hotel and the Dunvegan Inn, there was no doubt that Bob's future would be in the hospitality business. He loved it, for one thing, and he was good at it, for another. He had proven his ability to prevent losses and increase income and he saw hotels as a tangible way to leave his mark on the world.

Working for someone else would never give him what he needed. If a hotel bearing his name were the best, it would mean that he was the best.

Bob needed to get a hotel of his own.

With the Dunvegan Inn now operating profitably, Bob approached the Receiver about the possibility of buying it. He had become friends with Dave Thompson and the two of them thought they could do well as partners. They made an initial enquiry to the Receiver and talked about a price but they also said that they needed some time to apply to the Alberta Opportunity Company for funding. They were declined. As per required, the Receiver had notified the original owners that there was an offer to purchase on the table.

Bob had presented the investment proposition to his old friend Charlie Grubisich but, before they could come to an agreement or make a better offer, the Inn was sold to one of the original hotel investors. The new owner planned to manage the place herself so gave Bob notice.

He was out of work again.

The Second Half

"When it comes time to do your own life, you either perpetuate your childhood or you stand on it and finally kick it out from under"

—ROSELLEN BROWN, *CIVIL WARS*, KNOPF 1984

Fifteen

"Never fret for an only son. The idea of failure will never occur to him"
—GEORGE BERNARD SHAW

Bob still had financial commitments to Marj as well as a need to support himself, Janice and Connor. One of Charlie Grubisich's former accountants, Carrie Langstroth, shared office space with Dr. Smith and the dentist was one of her clients. She knew Bob from her work with Charlie and she recommended Bob as manager for the dental office. After Bob was on the job for a few months, Dr. Smith enrolled him in the Hollander Management courses. These courses specialize in medical, optical, dental practices so Dr. Smith felt it would be a good investment for his practice to have Bob better informed about the industry specifics. Bob flew to Portland a couple of times for the courses, accompanied by his girlfriend, Susan Jorgensen.

Working for Dr. Smith, he not only managed the Dental office, he handled the dentist's other businesses and properties as well; fixing the tenants' problems, collecting rents, making deposits, facilitating repairs. All the while, he looked for opportunities for himself.

The Igloo Inn had gone into Receivership and the same firm that had handled the Dunvegan Inn, Coopers-Lybrand, was acting as the Receivers for this property. Coopers-Lybrand had already hired Susan who was an experienced and capable accountant, as General Manager of the Inn.

Susan knew that Bob had turned the Dunvegan Inn around in a relatively short time and she urged Bob to contact the Receiver and see if he could take over the hotel operations. Coopers-Lybrand was extremely happy with the way that Bob had managed the Dunvegan and the company quickly made him an offer.

Bob jumped at the chance to be back in the hotel business and he assumed the overall supervision. He would be up at 5:30 AM, go over to the Igloo to check on the overnight business, have a quick breakfast, and then work for Dr. Smith from 8 AM until 5:30 PM.

After grabbing a quick bite of supper, he would work at the Igloo from 6 PM until midnight. (A lot of work hours, yes, but Bob happens to thrive on just five hours of sleep a night.)

Once he spent some time at the place, Bob realized that the Igloo just needed some work and some good marketing. Susan encouraged him to try and buy it as she knew all the costs as well as the potential for income. Bob knew he wanted to own it and he went to have another talk with Charlie Grubisich.

Charlie had no experience in the hotel business and was very dubious about any investment in the Igloo. Bob had to literally drag him over to see the property but, within minutes, Charlie was excited enough to take a chance. They shook hands on their agreement and then Charlie took Bob over to the Treasury Branch to see the manager. Any bid to the Receiver had to be backed by pre-arranged financing so they had to work fast. Bob, of course, had no cash but Charlie had dealt with the bank for many years and was a preferred client.

With a down payment of $145,000 from Charlie and $145,000 from his son Mark, they were able to get a preapproved loan. For his third share, Bob only had $35,000 from a second mortgage on his house. He still needed $110,000 cash to finish the deal. He did not have to look far.

Carrie Langstroth knew that, if Charlie Grubisich was backing a deal, she wanted a piece of the action. She had been watching Bob as he worked his way out of debt and she had a feeling that this new project of his would work. Before Bob started knocking on doors, she convinced her then-husband Al to offer Bob a personal loan of $50,000. Carrie arranged another loan of $60,000 from her parents. Both of those loans were signed under an agreement for Bob to pay them 10% interest monthly.

The sale of the Igloo had to go through the court system so Bob called his friend Ray Yenkana and asked him to act as his "buyer's agent." The deal was virtually completed when, at the last minute, a second offer came in. This second offer was made without an agent so all the monies would go to the Receivership account if accepted. Bob's offer took precedence because it had been filed first but, because the commission would be deducted from the proceeds, his offer would end up being a few thousand dollars lower. The bids were already in the hands of the Receiver but they called Bob and suggested that he have someone appear at the final decision. Bob called Ray and asked him if he would drop his commission. Ray agreed, and Bob sent a lawyer to the meeting. With Ray dropping his commission, the bids were equal. Luckily, Bob had given the lawyer the authority to raise their bid by $5,000. The other bidder had not sent anyone to the meeting so the offer was not countered. Bob and his partners got the Igloo.

When the deal was completed, Bob told Ray that he would never have to pay for a hotel room again.

The Igloo Inn was purchased as a partnership of Bob and G-Corp Investments Inc. (Charlie Grubisich and his family).

Bob took on the unpaid role of CEO of the Igloo. His future in hotels was at stake and he needed this to succeed. There were a number of newer, bigger hotels in Grande Prairie but Bob knew he could develop the Igloo into the best. He knew what to change and where to innovate. He had a good idea of what the traveling public wanted and how much they were willing to pay for it.

On top of his demanding work schedule for Dr. Smith, Bob worked tirelessly on the hotel project.

The first thing on his agenda was to clean the place up.

He repaired, replaced and renovated. Rooms were upgraded and amenities were added. Recalling the trip to Winnipeg with Ryan, Bob wanted to add a waterslide to the motel. Charlie was one of the owners of Amusements International, one of the companies that built waterslides, so he approved the additional cost of forty five thousand dollars to the budget. After all, that purchase would go right back to one of his own investments. What Bob neglected to mention to Charlie was that there would also be seventy-five thousand dollars in renovation costs to build the housing structure for the slide. Both Charlie and his sons were furious and they laid down the law—after the waterslide expense, there was absolutely no more cash. Bob would have to innovate if he wanted to upgrade.

Accepting the challenge, Bob went to see Joe Kalini of Towne Centre Furniture. He told Joe about the project; about how much he and Charlie had invested so far; and the fact that he had run out of money. He gave Joe a list of everything he needed—lighting, furniture, beds—and asked him to provide it all on credit. He promised to pay Towne Centre each and every month until it was paid off and Joe agreed to the terms. By the time the structural renovations were done, all the lights and new furniture arrived and Bob was back in business with an all-new Igloo Inn.

Within a month of the renovations being done, Bob knew he had a problem. The Igloo was not getting any new business and, if he asked people about the Igloo, no one seemed to know about its existence, even though it was right on the main road into the city. Not only that, but it was right across the road from the main shopping centre.

Bob wanted to see exactly how bad the situation was so he walked over to the Prairie Mall one weekend and spent a day pretending to be new in town. He would walk up to shoppers and ask them if they knew where the Igloo Inn was. Although the Igloo sign was clearly visible from the main doors of the Mall, nine out of ten shoppers could not help him with directions.

There were loads of outstanding invoices so it was time to start marketing.

Bob dropped in to see the Mall manager and asked him how often the owner came to Grande Prairie. Then he made them an offer: free accommodation in a suite at the Igloo whenever the owner was in Grande Prairie. In exchange, he asked the Prairie Mall to allow the Igloo to have a display table set up in the main concourse.

When the Management agreed, Bob made a video of the Igloo and sat at the Mall on weekends replaying it. He arranged with Towne Centre Furniture, Coca Cola and others to provide prizes for free draws. This brought people over to the table so he could talk to them about the Igloo and get them acquainted with the location, name and services.

Every Friday night that he sat at the Mall he booked ten to eighteen rooms.

The Igloo had the only waterslide in Grande Prairie so Bob's video really played up that feature. When he saw that kids got really excited about the waterslide, he started to offer the pool area for birthday parties. With the pool and slide virtually unused in the afternoons, there was loads of room for groups of happy children to enjoy the experience—especially in the winter months—and the birthday party schedule started to fill up quickly as word spread.

Seeing the reaction of kids to the Igloo, Bob also saw how their parents readily responded to the children's demand to stay at the Igloo. He made another unique addition to the lobby—a "kids only" check-in desk. Their counter was a mere two feet off the ground and the Igloo staff required that children check in first. Their parents had to wait until the kids were registered. This thrilled the kids and the attention to their importance and needs resulted in good behavior during their stay. After all, they were preferred guests.

The delight of the children also resulted in the Igloo being the only place they would allow their parents to reserve for future visits to Grande Prairie.

In addition to the waterslide, the Igloo was the first hotel in town to offer complimentary coffee, a free continental breakfast, ironing boards and irons in each room. In a very short time, all the airline crews and business travelers were loyal repeat customers.

Bob surmised that travelers always wanted four things from a hotel:

1. Quality, and that meant cleanliness, above all. Bob has made this a number one priority in every one of his properties. To this very day, he makes surprise inspections and his managers are trained to notice even the smallest detail. The Pomeroy properties even hire employees to keep the parking areas clear of cigarette butts and candy wrappers.
2. Comfort. When people get a good night's sleep, they remember. All Pomeroy properties are fitted with the best quality mattresses and pillows.
3. Value. Water slides, coffee, irons, ironing boards, full breakfast, top quality linens, flat screen television, business centers, spa quality toiletries, robes, exercise rooms—dependent on properties. Whatever a guest wants, the hotel will provide if possible.
4. Price. Bob's proven belief is that, if you consistently provide 1, 2, & 3, a traveler will not quibble about price.

He was, and still is, one hundred percent correct.

As the reputation of the Igloo grew, Bob increased the room rates. His guests kept returning and he kept giving them value for their dollars. The Igloo was always fully booked. In fact, it was more than fully booked. On one report, Charlie noticed that the Igloo had an occupancy rate of 105%. When he questioned Bob on the validity of the figures, Bob easily explained. Susan had told him that many travelers, especially truck drivers, or businessmen in town for an afternoon meeting, just needed a room for a few hours, a half day at most. The drivers needed a nap and a hot shower and they were on their way; a businessperson might need to freshen up, use the room to conduct an interview or two and then catch an evening flight.

Susan suggested that they had those rooms remade immediately for availability to rebook again that night. Bob agreed and that change alone made all the difference to the bottom line.

Initially upset by the huge expenditure, Charlie was more than satisfied by the rapid increase in revenue. Within six months, the Igloo had gone from twenty-five percent occupancy to an occupancy rate of more than ninety percent on a regular basis.

Charlie was also very satisfied with the partnership with Bob. A few months later, when the two men met for breakfast one morning, he was more than receptive to a second deal.

A fifteen-unit condominium project had come up for sale in Fort St. John and Bob assured Charlie that it was value-priced. He felt that, if they bought it and held on for a few years, they would do well. Once again, a partnership was formed between G-Corp Investments Inc. and Bob. Three years later, they sold the complex and shared in the profits.

Sixteen

"The pessimist sees difficulty in every opportunity. The optimist sees opportunity in every difficulty."
—WINSTON CHURCHILL

With the Igloo Inn thriving, and the Winter Games on the horizon, it seemed like a no-brainer to acquire a second property in Grande Prairie.

Bob was having lunch one day with Stewart Charchuk and mentioned his belief that it would be a good time to get another hotel. Stewart said that the Alpine Inn was for sale and that they should buy it together. Bob thought it was a great idea but added, "I have no money." After Stewart told him that he would put up any deposit needed, Bob agreed to do some investigating and get some figures put together.

When Bob called the owner in Fort Nelson, he found out that, in spite of offering rooms at only $19.95 a night, the Alpine was floundering at only twenty percent occupancy. He had heard that the man would accept $450,000 for the property if pressed. By this time Bob really wanted the deal so he agreed to the asking price of $500,000. To close the offer, Bob asked Stewart to send the deposit of $5,000. Then he went to talk to Charlie again.

Charlie still trusted Bob's instincts so he jumped in for a share. His son Garth became the second major investor and Bob's investment team was in for the last third. This team included Stewart and Bob's daughter Kim. Bob now had more than just his and Charlie's money at risk. He had invested his daughter's inheritance as well.

Kim's marriage in 1993 to Mike Gagnon had ended tragically. After just four months, her young husband died in a motor vehicle accident on his way back to Grande Prairie after coaching a badminton game in Red Deer. Mike was driving the college van and, approaching an intersection, he hit a patch of black ice, skidding into a large truck.

Although the students in the van with him survived with relatively minor injuries, Mike was killed instantly. The young couple had not even taken their honeymoon.

Because of Mike's death, Kim received a sizeable settlement from his life insurance and the Workers Compensation Fund. Her financial future was secure enough and she had an education but Bob thought she should consider getting into the family business.

Bob welcomed Kim as one of his new investment partners. Although he had always thought he would be passing on a business to a couple of sons, he was extremely proud to be working with his daughter.

Bob, Charlie and Stewart went to the bank and arranged a mortgage that included enough cash to cover the renovation budget that Bob had prepared.

The Alpine needed a lot of work to bring it up to the company's high standards and it had to be done quickly. The sooner the rooms could be rented, the sooner the loans could be paid. Bob set up a schedule that would be challenging and costly but he was convinced it was the right time to act.

The timetable was short and it was precise. Bob was on the site every day and he could account for every detail of every job. There was no "wiggle room" and he could not waste time waiting for subcontractors. He didn't have to worry about the Igloo because it was in Susan's capable hands.

At one point, the carpet layers arrived on site and worked so fast that they were finished before the last two rooms could be dry-walled. They told Bob that they were leaving and to call them back when the walls were dry. This was a busy time in the city and Bob knew that, once the installers started on another big job, it would be almost impossible to get them to come back to finish two small rooms. He told them to ignore the walls and install the carpet anyway.

Words were exchanged about "Standard Operating Procedures", a heated argument began and finally Bob told the men that he was paying the bills and they had to finish the work when he wanted them to finish. One of the exasperated tradesmen finally spouted off, "You're an asshole."

Years before, Bob would most likely have used his fists to make his position clearly felt. With his new confidence, the challenge was handled in a completely different manner.

The new Bob Pomeroy, the Bob Pomeroy with money, simply responded in a cool, firm manner. "Thank you. No one has called me an asshole for days. Now get the carpet laid."

Bob left and the carpet layers finished the last two rooms. The next day, working on plastic-covered carpeting, the dry-wall crew completed the walls.

Bob knows from experience that completing a project in the usual sequence does not always make sense. He knows that delays cost money and any added time affects his bottom line as well as the bottom lines of his investors. When he makes changes to a project or demands that jobs be done in a certain way, he does not do this without thought. Because he has done every job himself in the past, he knows what can be done.

The hotel needed more than simply a decorating job. Many of the problems were structural and needed some professional engineering and design.

Bob had initially contacted H.J. Scheunhage & Associates of Grande Prairie about the flooded basement but once Hank Scheunhage and Bob started inspecting the building, they realized that not only had the stairways been built far too narrow but they were open to the elements.

With the wind, rain and snowfall of northern Alberta being absolutes, it was obvious that the stairs had to be re-engineered as well. Bob wanted his new hotel to be top-notch and he was confident that Hank was the man to engineer a perfect refit.

Paint and carpets had been in the original estimate but Bob soon added more changes and upgrades. When Garth started getting phone calls from suppliers asking for deposits and verified purchase orders, he got a case of the jitters about the extra spending. This was not his usual environment and he needed a great deal of reassurance from both his father and Bob that they were not overdoing things. It seemed to Garth that Bob was ignoring the original budget altogether. By the time an order for first-class mattresses came from the supplier from Montreal, Bob was $350,000 over budget and Garth was livid. Charlie was a bit more pragmatic but even he was crossing his fingers.

Once again, time proved Bob right. He had read the needs of the city correctly and the Inn reopened to great success.

Marj and Herb had introduced Kim to a man they knew in the city and after about six months the man moved into her townhouse together. Kim had bought the home with her own savings but felt confident enough of the relationship to add his name to the title.

This new "paramour" was also the benefactor of the appointment as first manager of the "all new" Alpine, now renamed the Canadian Motor Inn.

Kim was going to rehab for a sports injury and she began working at the Canadian as her boyfriend's assistant manager. The arrangement was not a good one.

Bob originally liked Kim's new man. He seemed to have the same work ethic as Bob did and they both shared an appreciation for women. Bob did not spend much time at the hotel, though, and he did not see the truth in what was happening.

Although Kim was relegated to a tiny desk in a windowless office, she was gradually given more and more of the work to do. At the same time, her boss (her boyfriend) was managing to do less.

When accounts and reports fell behind, it was Kim who received the verbal abuse from Bob. He was frustrated by the way the office was being managed and he blamed Kim for bringing the slacker into the fold.

He also felt that a Pomeroy should be dedicated to the hotel business 24/7; that a college sports career was frivolous compared to the real world of hospitality and commerce. Like many "driven" parents, Bob expected more from his daughter than he would expect from an employee.

Many months passed before anyone in the family realized what a turmoil Kim was going through in her personal life. Not only had Kim been covering for the jerk's alleged mismanagement at work, she was also denying her own knowledge of the guy's numerous affairs.

Finally resigned to ending the dysfunctional relationship, Kim had a difficult time in purging the man from her life. The affection was definitely gone but the guy was not. He would not sign off from the title of Kim's home until she paid him off with a cash settlement. He would not quit his job. Kim's pleas did not budge him. When the guy demanded money from Kim, she became physically affected and the distress in her life showed on her face.

The accounting for the Canadian was handled through Charlie Grubisich's office and Kim would drop off the paperwork personally. Both Charlie and his son Garth noticed the change in Kim and they became very concerned. Finally, Charlie felt he had to step in. Bob was in Vancouver on business but Charlie called him there and suggested that he get back to Grande Prairie and talk to Kim. When Bob said he was busy, Charlie did not mince words. He told Bob that there would always be time for business but he only had one daughter and he should get home NOW.

Bob was home the next day and got to the bottom of things.

With a little subterfuge and a lot of assistance, he managed to get access to the man's new residence. Then, after hauling away every ounce of furniture and personal belongings, he sat back and waited.

When Kim's former partner got back from a short trip, he saw his empty place and immediately figured out what had happened.

Instead of calling Bob or Kim, he stupidly went to the police and reported that Bob Pomeroy had robbed his home. Then he called Kim and bragged about what he had done, thinking, in his arrogance, that this would bring both her and Bob to their knees.

He was wrong.

Bob called the RCMP and asked if they were looking for him. When the answering officer confirmed that there had been a complaint of theft filed, Bob calmly asked if there had been any mention made of Kim's missing $10,000 snowmobile—a new machine that was currently in the possession of the complainant. The snowmobile had not been mentioned. Realizing that there was a lot more to the matter, the officer knew at once that the whole business should have been handled as a civil dispute. He told Bob that he was closing his file.

Kim's "ex" was furious. He showed up at Kim's home armed with a hockey stick and threatened to break in. As he pounded on her door, Kim called 911 and her roommate called the family lawyer, Bob Lewis, to request a restraining order. The RCMP arrived just as the jerk had entered the house and was close to harming Kim with the hockey stick. The police put him on notice and sent him packing. By 8:15 the next morning, Lewis was at the Courthouse filing his own restraining order.

Bob negotiated the return of the personal property for a signature on the title release for Kim. It worked, and Kim got her life back. She paid for her poor choice of partner dearly. Her self-confidence had been shattered and her actual financial costs to extricate herself from the ordeal were over $50,000. She never did get the snowmobile back.

Bob may have been slow to recognize Kim's plight but, when he was called, he performed in spades. This was one of the few times that Bob really interacted with his daughter. He had grown up with sisters but had been raised with the rules of a man's world. He found it hard to communicate with her, rarely having conversations with her until she was well into her twenties.

Kim knows that her father has a difficult time talking about his feelings at the best of times. He does not open up until he has had a few glasses of wine or other alcohol.

"The long and short of it is that family is everything to my dad."

Bob taught Kim that, even though you may not like everything about a family member or everything he does, the fact remains that family will always be family and they are the only ones that you can count on forever.

Kim became the new manager of the Canadian Inn.

By 1995 both Canadian and foreign investors were showing interest in northern Alberta, specifically in Grande Prairie.

In spite of the regular patronage of the hotels, Garth was still feeling nervous about the partnership with Bob and about the hotel business in general. A realtor approached him with a purchase offer for the Igloo from a group of Koreans. The price represented a significant profit, so Garth persuaded Charlie to sell. They were the major shareholders, of course, and Bob had to agree to the transaction.

Charlie's daughter, Laura, had become a lawyer and she handled all the contracts.

At the last minute, the Korean group fell short of funds.

When they asked Charlie to approve interim financing through his bank, he almost called off the whole thing. As he puts it today, it was a hard decision, almost a coin toss, but he sided with his son and the deal went through. Although Bob hated losing the Igloo, he was very happy with his share of the profits. He knew that when he found his next project, he would have the cash to increase his share of the ownership.

Shortly after the Igloo was sold, a second group of Koreans purchased the Canadian Inn. Once again, Bob was financially rewarded. This time, he was able to see his daughter's investment grow as well. Bob knew in his heart that the Pomeroy family, HIS branch of the family, was on its road to a wealthy future.

Bob also knew that this major step towards achieving his dream was due in no small part to the faith and trust of Charlie Grubisich—the same man who Bob had trusted years before in Fort St. John.

Seventeen

"The price of success: dedication, hard work and an unrelenting devotion to the things you want to see happen"
—FRANK LLOYD WRIGHT

After the sale of the Igloo and the Canadian, Bob finally had some cash and he wanted to build a motel from the ground up.

Fred and Dave Tissington had been building hotels for Cam Christensen and Cam had introduced them to Marc Staniloff, the executive who held the Super 8 master franchise for Canada. Fred and Dave felt that Bob should consider building a Super 8 Motel in Grande Prairie.

Fred took Bob to Calgary where he made the introduction to Marc.

After Bob clearly defined the huge potential in the Grande Prairie area, Marc agreed that a Super 8 would do well in the northern city. He told Bob to go ahead and find a location.

Marc thought that Bob and Cam Christianson should also get acquainted. Cam was a reputable contractor, used only the best tradesmen and he was a good prospect as a future investor as well. Marc introduced the two men and the rest, as they say, is history. Cam became the contractor for the Super 8.

Bob knew just the spot in Grande Prairie for a new hotel but most people he talked to about it thought he was nuts.

Just around the corner from the Igloo was a large tract of swampy muskeg inhabited by mosquitoes and ducks. To the critters it may have been beautiful; to anyone else it was just plain ugly. Bob thought it was wonderful—wonderful enough to offer one million dollars for it, the highest price for any land sold in Grande Prairie that year.

Bob, Carrie Langstroth, Fred and Dave Tissington and Marc Staniloff became the partners for the land. Bob and Marc set out to secure financing for the building.

They arranged a two-level investment package: the "A" Group, which was comprised of Bob, Marc, Fred and Dave; and the "B" Group, which included associates of Marc and Carrie.

Later on, one of Marc's investors decided to pull out and Bob arranged for Kim to purchase the available shares by instalments.

Marc had strong connections with Barry Wershler at Central Credit Union in Calgary so the group got mortgage financing there, using both the purchased land and Marc's franchise fee as equity. Once the mortgaging was in place, the construction went up rapidly.

The Super 8 was almost completed when Bob got a phone call from Brian Walker, one of the owners of the Nomad Inn Fort McMurray.

"Hey, Bob, want to buy my hotel?" The immediate answer was "Yes."

Bob wanted to become a major player in the hotel business and he didn't want to pass up any opportunity to grow even bigger. Bob told Brian that he would be up to see the property as soon as he could.

Brian met Bob years earlier when Bob was managing the hotels in Beaverlodge. He knew about the sale of both the Igloo and the Canadian and he also knew about the development of the new Super 8. Brian was co-owner of the Nomad with Clint Cassin and they wanted to get rid of the place. The hotel had been poorly managed and they did not have any interest in trying to revive it.

Two years after the first inspection of the Igloo, Bob was back to see Hank Scheunhage; this time about the Nomad Inn. The men had become friends and Bob wanted Hank's honest opinion about the property he was considering in the boomtown. Bob and Hank headed for Fort McMurray.

First they stopped in Edmonton where they ran into two hotel partners—Ernie Wolver and Bill Ropchan.

In the early 80's, when Bob had asked them for a job in their hotel on Kingsway, they had turned him down. Bob always referred to the partners as "the two Ernies: Ernie #1 and Ernie #2". The men had been in partnership for fifty years and were as similar as brothers. (These longstanding partners even passed away in the same year, 2007, just a few months apart.)

As with any industry, the hotel business has its own rumour mills and people keep a sharp watch on what everyone else is doing.

The Edmonton hoteliers knew very well how successfully Bob had turned around business for other owners in both Beaverlodge and Fairview. They also knew that he had been making money for himself and his investors in Grande Prairie.

When Bob reminded them about their reluctance to hire him years before, Wolver's quick response was "Looking back, we both agree that we made a big mistake!"

After a good dinner and solid sleep, Hank and Bob headed for Fort McMurray. They inspected the Nomad from top to bottom and then sat down to discuss its possibilities.

Hank confirmed that the building had been soundly constructed with concrete and its structure still retained integrity. Bob had assessed two areas that he felt had been hurting the hotel's success.

First and foremost, the restaurant had been developed on the top floor. It was an elegant dining room with good food. The problem was that there was only one access elevator and it was small and slow. No one in Fort McMurray liked to wait for food – or look for it at a remote location.

The second flaw in the property was the absence of any amenities. There was no big drawing card to make travelers choose the Nomad over other hotels.

Hank agreed totally with Bob's ideas about the Nomad and he knew the changes were very possible—for a price.

Both the design and the construction would be expensive. Bob knew he could turn the hotel around but, after investing in the Super 8 project, he didn't have enough cash to move ahead on his own. It was time to build another investment team, and time to negotiate for services. Hank's fee was the first item to deal with.

With his usual candour, Bob told Hank that he had no cash available for engineering and design. He outlined his income projections for the hotel and proposed that Hank accept shares in the project instead of cash; illustrating his firm belief that Hank would do much better financially in the long run. Hank agreed and became one of the Nomad partners. With Hank's designs included in the proposal package, Bob figured out how he could buy the hotel using another two-level investment package.

His "A" Team, the group that put up twenty percent of the cash needed for the down payment and guaranteed the loans, consisted of himself, Fred and Dave Tissington and Brian Walker. (Brian had decided that he wanted to stay as an investor if Bob was managing the project.)

To get investors to make a commitment to participate on the "B" Team, (providing eighty percent of the cash but no loan guarantees) Bob flew all the interested parties to Fort McMurray.

He wined them and dined them, showed the town highlights and gave them a tour of the Tar Sands, all the while expounding on the huge potential for growth and prosperity.

They were convinced and the "B" team was finalized with a dozen investors including Ray Yenkana, Irene Hamm, Denis Rochette, Kevin Person and Kim.

Bob needed a total of $650,000 to close to mortgage and he had raised only $400,000.

He had already used up all his contacts so he knew he had to think outside the box. He walked through the hotel again, taking note of every asset and trying to think of a solution. One thing that kept flashing in his mind was the fact that the three hotel-owned liquor stores all had full shelves and full storerooms.

Bob looked over the agreement for sale again and thought that a solution might be right in front of him.

He faxed the inventory control records to Carrie and asked her to go over the numbers and confirm his own appraisal of the wholesale value. Carrie and her family had made money on their last deal with Bob and she had offered to help him whenever he wanted an opinion on any new acquisitions. She was also his accountant.

Carrie's response was just what he wanted to hear. Bob knew that he could raise the rest of the cash he needed if he could get Clint Cassin, the other owner, to agree to some unusual terms.

There was a long weekend coming up.

Bob met with Clint and asked him to structure the sale of the Nomad so that Bob would take possession on noon Friday with the four hundred thousand dollar deposit but not have to pay the balance of the

Scotty and Mandy Pomeroy with their children: Marie, Judy and Bob standing and Joan being held by her father.

Judy, Bob and Joan with their mother on Mandy's 86th birthday

Scotty and Mandy Pomeroy wedding photo.

Scotty and Mandy's anniversary. Marie, Bob, Judy and Joan standing.

Bob and Marjorie wedding.

One of Bob and Marjorie's first homes.

Bob in full western regalia.

Irwin Pomeroy and his adult family.

Bob training a horse.

Stars of "Dallas" with Bob: Steven Kanally, Bob, unidentified official, Patrick Duffy.

Buffalo Bob's mascot in costume, Marj, Bob, Kim and unidentified "buffalo hunter" in costume.

Bob modeling a parka at local fashion show.

His mentor and champion: uncle Ralph Pomeroy.

Bob in Fort St.John parade, full Arabian regalia.

Bob and Marj with Tim, Ryan and Kim.

Bob and Brian Surerus in Hawaii.

Bob Pomeroy

Land Purch.	$316,000.
B.C. Land Tax	4320.
Property Tax	2101.
	322,421

Interest for 64 days based
on 20% per annum — 11328
Engineering — 1000.
2 Plane Trips — 1350
My Mark-up — 10,000
Legal — 3350
Total — $349,449

This is price if closed on Oct 15/2000
If longer I must adjust.

Your lawyer handles both sides
no legal fees to me.

Hope this is what you need.

D. J. Will

Agreement between Dave Will and Bob – example of usual un-official documents.

Bob and Carrie – May 2002 – Scottsdale, Arizona.

Hank and Thelma Scheunhage, Bob and Carrie.

Ryan and Bob.

Ryan, Herb Millar, Bob.

Bob, Mayor Wayne Ayling, Joe Ferraro – opening of Holiday Inn.

Rick Vieira and Bob at construction site.

Willie Kempin and Bob, January 2006, Bob was awarded Grande Prairie Entrepreneur of the Year.

Pomeroy-sponsored Native National Fastball Men's "B" Champions – the Peavine Canadians (coach: Fred Cunningham).

Bob and his youngest son, Connor. (photo by Harj)

Willie Kempin and Bob — May 2009. (photo by Harj)

Brian Surerus and Bob — opening of Tony Roma's, Fort St.John 2008.

Ray Yenkana and Bob in Scottsdale 2002.

Kim.

Tim.

Ryan. (photo by Harj)

Connor. (photo by Harj)

Angel Marlo Cunningham, Zhivago, Bob — September 2009. (photo by Harj)

Ernie and Cathy Patterson in front of "Bob's wedding chapel" — 2007. (photo by Tanya Sedore)

Fort St. John — Scotty and Mandy's house where Bob grew up.

Rear and side views of Bob's new home in Grande Prairie — 2009 still under construction.

Exterior and interior views of the equestrian centre in Grande Prairie, just down the hill from Bob's new house

Home in Scottsdale, Arizona.

Barn in Scottsdale at rear of property.

New Pomeroy hotel sign, Fort St.John, BC. (photo by Harj)

Exterior new Pomeroy Hotel, Fort St.John, BC. (photo by Harj)

Original Pomeroy Hotel owned by Ralph Pomeroy.

Ryan and Allison's wedding, Scottsdale, Arizona, October 9, 2009. Rear, l to r: Connor, Allison, Ryan, Bob, Kim and Rod Gravengard. Front, l to r: Mallory, Hayley and Kaden Gravengard. (photo by Tanya Sedore)

final deposit until Tuesday morning. Further, Bob also wanted the agreement amended to leave the Nomad's Line of Credit for the liquor stores attached to the hotel for one full year.

Clint had heard that Bob was a blowhard and he really did not believe that he could come up with a quarter of a million dollars in a few days.

He accepted the terms in the confidence that he would not only have his hotel back by the following Tuesday, he would also have four hundred thousand dollars of free money from the forfeited deposit.

When the papers were completed, Clint met Bob in the bar.

He said he wanted to buy Bob a drink, as probably it was the last free night Bob would be spending in his hotel. He couldn't help but add that he thought Bob was a nice guy, ". . . just short on brains".

That Friday, as soon as he took possession, Bob told the staff of all three liquor stores to put up signs and spread the word that there was a "New Management Sale" at the Nomad Inn—that all the liquor prices were slashed.

The line-ups of eager buyers never stopped and the cash registers were humming all weekend. By the time Monday night rolled around, Bob had more than $300,000 in cash and he also had the Nomad's line of credit to replenish the shelves.

Tuesday morning, the balance of the deposit was paid and the deal closed.

Although he had assumed the original mortgage at the Treasury Branch, Bob still needed additional mortgaging and money for renovations.

He took his business plan and guarantor statements to the Royal Bank in Fort McMurray and received approval to buy out the original Treasury Branch mortgage and refinance a new mortgage for the hotel.

Part of his submission and application included financing needed for the addition of 40-plus rooms, turning the liquor store adjacent to the hotel into a banquet room and converting empty space into a new restaurant.

Receiving just verbal approval for the additional funds, Bob started renovations.

The restaurant was torn out of the top floor; replaced by ten large suites and a lounge.

A swimming pool was built adjacent to the lobby and all the rooms were redecorated and refurbished. Hank did all the designs based on

Bob's ideas and vision and the all-new Nomad started to take shape. The cost over-runs were beginning to take shape as well.

Bob had spent millions on both the hotel and the renovations—all based on the assumption that money would be forthcoming from the bank. Then the rug was pulled out from under him. The bank changed the decision and was no longer on board to fund the project.

Fred and Dave Tissington got skittish after the bank's decline and they wanted out as guarantors. They sold their "A" shares to Bob and, surprisingly perhaps, to Clint Cassin. Clint had come to know Bob better during the purchase process and thought it might be prudent to reinstate his involvement with the Nomad property.

A short time later, Brian decided that he wanted out. He didn't like the fact that there were so many investors. It seemed cumbersome to him that multiple discussions were always needed to make even the smallest decisions. He sold his "A" shares to Irene Hamm.

Although the shares were in Irene's name, the decision makers were now Bob, Clint and Henry Hamm and each of them had a reputation of making decisions fast.

Bob got together his financing proposal book and jumped on a plane. He spent the next week in Edmonton, visiting every head office of every bank in town. He got nowhere and the clock was ticking. The hotel was open for business but Bob had contractors and suppliers screaming for money and he was tapped out.

Checking in on the Super 8 progress, and needing to talk to a friendly voice, Bob called Marc Staniloff in Calgary. It was perfect timing. Marc told Bob that Merrill Lynch was having a special luncheon presentation the next day and the topic was hotel financing!

Bob hit the road again and headed for Calgary.

The next day he sat intently and listened to David N. Grieve describe how motivated his company was to help aggressive hoteliers get the financing they needed. As Bob was a late registrant to the meeting, he couldn't get an appointment with David before he left. He did, however, corner him right after the luncheon and asked for just one minute of the man's time. David said he was rushed, had no time to look over Bob's presentation book. He would take a second to listen if Bob just gave him the key points.

Bob had spent so many hours delivering his message to the bankers in

Edmonton, that he was more than prepared. He told David what he had, what he needed, what guarantees he had arranged and what he hoped to achieve.

David listened intently, paused to think a moment, then looked Bob in the eye, and said, "If what you've outlined is true, I think we can help you. Come see me in Toronto next week."

Bob was elated. There finally seemed to be a light at the end of the tunnel and he drove back to Grande Prairie to refine his presentation.

Back at home, the Super 8 was opening on an auspicious weekend. Ritchie Bros. Auction was having a huge event on the same date and the rooms were 100% booked.

The next day the investment partners all celebrated the obvious success of the new hotel. Bob refocused his thoughts on the property in Fort McMurray.

Clint Cassin, meanwhile, was doing some thinking of his own. His initial impression of Bob's abilities and intelligence had been proven very wrong and he astutely figured that the new Nomad was going to make a lot of money. He met with Henry Hamm and the two came up with a plan of their own. They called Bob for a meeting and said they wanted to streamline.

They proposed that the three of them apply a little pressure and buy out all the "B" investors, leaving just Bob and Clint and Henry's wife owning the whole property.

When Bob asked them how they planned to get rid of all the other investors, Clint's response was "Whatever it takes. If you don't want to do it with me, I'll do it myself"

Bob was furious. He told Clint that he asked his friends to invest with him based on good faith and he would force them out "over my dead body".

He knew that, with the other investors gone, Clint and Henry would have 51% of the "A" shares and 49% of the "B" shares; he also knew that he would probably be the next person to get stomped out of the deal. He left the meeting saying "Next time you hear from me, I'll be buying you out."

Bob contacted all his shareholders and told them what was happening. He told them not to sell their shares, to stick with him and he would not let them down. Denis Rochette is convinced that, if Bob had allowed the take over by Clint and Henry and then cashed out, Bob would have made more money personally. He is still grateful for the strong stand that Bob took. It resulted in nice windfalls for each and every minority investor when the hotels were eventually sold.

The next week, Bob was in Toronto meeting with the executives from Merrill Lynch. They were in full accord with his business plan and they were satisfied with the guarantees and equity presented. Bob not only got new mortgaging but he also got enough cash to cover all the renovations, including a shell for a new restaurant on the premises. (Bob still keeps David N. Grieve's business card in his desk.)

Merrill Lynch was using a New York underwriter and the guy had requested that all the liens and mortgages be filed immediately. When Bob suggested it might be hard to accomplish in just two days, the New York firm responded with:"If your local guy can't get it done by Monday, let us know and we'll hire someone who can."

Bob Lewis got it done. He burned the midnight oil and about ten packs of cigarettes but by Monday morning the papers were ready for signing.

Fort McMurray was growing at a frenetic pace and, with the top of the Nomad converted into suites, there was a shortage of finer dining spots. The city was ripe for a great new restaurant.

Bob had designated empty space in the Nomad for a steakhouse and the Nomad investors partnered with Kevin Person of Cool Line Refrigeration and a couple more businessmen to create a branch of the successful "Keg" franchise.

The building permits for the hotel had taken almost a year and a half to be processed and once the Merrill Lynch money was in place, Bob did not want to waste another month waiting for more approvals.

His original permit had allowed "space for a restaurant" so, using that as his "implied approval", Bob started renovating.

First, he went to one of the Keg's in Edmonton armed with a box of crayons, large sheets of paper and a measuring tape. Sitting in a booth, he drew a "footprint" of the restaurant and used the different colors of the crayons to indicate the placement of coloured lighting fixtures.

He measured the space between the booths and the tables, the distance between the seats in the booths and the centre of the tables and the length of the dining rooms and serving areas.

Back in Fort McMurray, he hired a friend to help him and, using a plumb bob and red masking tape, they laid out the whole floor plan. Once that was done, Bob started the installation.

Howard Butt was the electrician and he dug in his heels. He went to see Clint and complained that he was not about to start any wiring without proper drawings. Clint's response? He told Howard to go ahead with the work. He added that it would be cheaper in the long run to work with Bob's crayon artistry and then pay for any needed changes later, than to commission professional drawings.

Howard did the work using Bob's colourful plans. After the initial permanent fixtures were built and the wiring completed, Bob hired a professional to draw "as built" plans for the restaurant and, armed with those, he contacted the franchise office of The Keg.

They turned him down.

According to the Keg's guidelines for franchise areas, there was not enough population in Fort McMurray, therefore not enough business, to support one of their restaurants.

Bob hit the road again—this time to Vancouver to meet personally with Dave Aisenstat, the President and founder of The Keg.

He talked to Dave about the economy in Fort McMurray, the average income of the households and the lack of restaurants and he got the approval they needed.

Bob returned to Fort McMurray and finished the installation he had already nearly completed. It was amazingly concurrent with the Keg's spec book.

Once the money was in place, Bob called a shareholders' meeting and told them that he wanted to buy out Clint and Irene.

The investors were not completely in agreement with the idea of Bob owning all the "A" shares and having full control of the decision-making process so he agreed to have two new investors take over the ownership positions.

Joe Ferraro and Bill de Silva bought Clint and Irene's "A" shares as well as Henry's "B" shares.

By this time, Bob had found a house in Fort McMurray and Susan had moved there to be with him. Janice and Connor stayed in Grande Prairie. Having a clear definition between his two households helped Bob keep his eye on business. He had enough balls in the air trying to keep the group of investors happy without worrying about dealing with personal affairs.

In spite of the success of the hotel, the investment partnership of the "B" shareholders of the Nomad was full of tension.

Many of the smaller, less experienced investors expected to make profits right away and their whining and demands began almost immediately. There would not be dividends paid until after at least a year operating the expanded premises.

The cash flow of the hotel was as good as they had expected but Bob was never satisfied with any property until it was better than expected. He had continued renovating after the hotel reopened and he needed the early income to continue the improvements.

Ray Yenkana recalls many rancorous meetings. He had looked at the investment as being solid and he had gone in with the venture on a long term basis.

He had seen what Bob had done in Grande Prairie with the Igloo and the Canadian so he was prepared to wait and reap the benefits from a future turnover. Based on his experience in partnerships with Bob, Ray voted with him at all the meetings.

Denis Rochette, Kevin Person and Kim also stayed onside. This loyalty gave Bob the ability to continue his management processes. The loyalty was justified.

Times up north were not always full of stress and work.

Kevin Person and Jim Gretchen told Bob that they wanted to give him a surprise gift. They hired a helicopter and pilot to take Bob on a guided tour of the tar sands in Fort McMurray. The men had made some special arrangements with the pilot beforehand.

Not long into the flight, the helicopter started doing a lot of quick dips and dives and turns. Bob was getting slightly 'unsettled" but he didn't want to seem less than macho and so kept quiet. With a nod, Kevin let the pilot know that he needed to "up his game" and create even more turbulence. The helicopter took vertical plunges, careened around hills and became a wild rollercoaster ride. Finally, Bob yelled loudly "Stop. Right now". The tone of his voice meant business. The pilot was a professional and he knew when to be serious.

When he landed, Bob had mere seconds to jump out and puke his guts out.

Both Kevin and Jim kept their wits about them for quite a few months after that adventure, never knowing if Bob would find some nefarious scheme to pay them back.

Bob and his friends have always found ways to have a few laughs. More money has just meant more inventive, more expensive ways to act like kids. And most of his friends have made their money working with Bob.

When Hank Scheunhage was asked to trade his engineering services for shares in the Nomad, he was slightly hesitant about the deal but, nonetheless, agreed to become an investing partner.

As soon as the hotel paid off all the tradesmen and other immediate obligations, Bob was able to declare the initial dividend. He presented Hank and every other shareholder a framed copy of their first cheque. Each and every month the shareholders' dividends arrived on time and Hank's framed cheque still hangs in his office.

Scheunhage's company continued to provide engineering for the Pomeroy Group and Bob became a favourite client of the firm.

Hank's staff dealt with Bob on a very personal, direct level and they didn't need to go through Hank if they had a problem.

One December, Bob was very late in paying a large invoice and he got a call from Hank's bookkeeper. Annette was very tiny but she could be as aggressive as a Chihuahua when it came to collecting payments. When Bob proposed an even longer delay for covering the outstanding balance, Annette stood her ground.

She blithely informed Bob that he should be aware that not only wouldn't the small firm be able to cover the month end payroll but none of Hank's staff would be receiving Christmas bonuses that year thanks to him—and then she hung up.

Bob moved hell and high water to ensure that a cheque for $70,000 was ready before noon on December 24th. Hank's wife drove over to pick up Bob's cheque and the staff got their paycheques and bonuses. When Hank retired several years later, Annette was quickly hired by none other than Bob Pomeroy.

Eighteen

"The only way to find the limits of the possible is by going beyond them to the impossible."

—ARTHUR C. CLARKE

The late Ernie Wolver and his partner in Edmonton owned the Peter Pond hotel in Fort McMurray. The place had gained notoriety over the years and the dubious quality of both the clientele and the services offered made it less than attractive to guests who were simply seeking a clean room and a good night's sleep. The hotel was "party central" and housed Fort McMurray's most notorious strip club.

The Peter Pond was ripe for a takeover and, by buying it, Bob could not only get more rooms but he could also eliminate some competition. He called Hank, hoping once again to exchange shares for engineering services, but this time Hank wasn't interested. He didn't like the hotel, for one thing, as he wasn't certain that the past reputation for drugs and prostitution could be overcome. He also found structural problems that would be expensive to fix. Bob didn't agree with Hank about the hotel being stuck with a bad reputation but he appreciated his friend's concerns. He also knew that he needed Hank's skills to overcome the structural problems so Hank was hired as the design engineer, but this time as a paid supplier and not an investor.

Ernie Wolver had been dealing with the Royal Bank for years and had never missed a mortgage payment. In spite of that, perhaps due to the bank's reluctance to be connected to such a controversial property, they called his loan. Bob bought the hotel under an Agreement for Sale and, first, tried to assume the mortgage. The RBC declined the request. With Ernie still on the original mortgage, and the hotel being forced into Receivership by the bank, Bob started looking for investors and another source for mortgaging.

Traditional lenders were still a bit skittish in 1997 and 1998 so Bob ran into some roadblocks with the banks and mortgage brokers. Undeterred, he found a more positive response from men who had made their fortunes by investing not only in projects, but in the individuals behind them. After promising to manage the hotel personally during the initial months, Bob got investment commitments in writing from Doug Golosky, Bob Heinish, Paul Cronauer and Clint Cassin.

Then Bob started cleaning with a vengeance. He had huge dumpsters delivered to the hotel and his crew began tossing the old beds, draperies and furnishings into them—anything that was soiled, damaged or beyond repair. The piles of trash grew by the hour and the cleanup campaign probably looked like a total demolition was taking place. At least, that's what the management at the Royal Bank seemed to think.

The Peter Pond was situated right across the street from the Bank and, without walking over to ask what was being done, they took action. They called the Receiver and told them that Bob was destroying the property.

A few days later, Bob was on the site supervising the cleaning, when the representative from the Receiver turned up. The man said that he was there to inspect the damage and then begin action. Bob stood his ground. He sat down with the agent and told him exactly what had transpired over the past weeks. He told him about his plans for the hotel and his projections for profit.

Bob described all the effort he had exhausted to try to convince the Royal Bank to provide financing and he expressed his frustration at their reluctance to work with him. He showed the agent his "book" (full business plan) including the financial statements from all the investors, each investor solid and worthy of their guarantee. Finally, Bob told the agent that he felt that the bank was being uncooperative and that their tactics were both unreasonable and unfair. The Receiver's Agent agreed. He told Bob that he would help in getting the matter resolved.

Very shortly, Bob got a call from the Royal Bank's head office in Toronto.

There was an amicable conversation and a few days later a Royal Bank Special Loans Officer was in Fort McMurray meeting Bob for coffee in the old hotel restaurant. Once again, Bob presented his "book", outlined his business plan and described what he had done in the past years turning around other properties. The bank officer listened carefully and was impressed. Using nothing more than a restaurant paper napkin, he and Bob wrote down terms and conditions that both parties could live with.

That paper napkin was taken to Edmonton and was used as the basis of the new loan documents. The Royal Bank not only approved a new mortgage but they also provided funds for extensive renovations.

The Peter Pond was cleaned up and soon became a legitimate place to stay—and play—in Fort McMurray. The strip club was gone and Cowboys continued to attract the new clientele that the hotel wanted.

Paul Vickers and Brian Walker were the owners of Cowboys, but the management of the place was in the hands of Raphael Bohlmann. Raphael trained his staff well and didn't like to lose any of them. When he learned that Bob had lured away two of his most experienced wait staff for the Keg, he was furious. Not being one to shy away from confrontation, Raphael went right to Bob and told him just what he thought of his tactics. Bob, in turn, denied hiring the women. He told Raphael that one of his partners had been responsible, thinking that would get Raphael off his back.

That made no difference to Raphael. Whoever had done the actual hiring wasn't important. The fact was that Bob had poached his key employees.

When Raphael discussed the situation with Paul, his boss took a pragmatic stance. He said that all the yelling in the world would get him nowhere; that the only way to make a point with Bob was to hit him where it would hurt worst—in his wallet.

Prior to the pirating of Raphael's best female servers (and the best-looking!), Cowboys would book all the rooms they needed for visiting bands or entertainers at the Peter Pond. This was convenient for Cowboys and it was also steady income for the hotel.

Raphael knew just what Paul meant about hitting Bob in his pocket. Not another word was said about the employees but the next week, the band members playing at Cowboys were booked at a rival hotel. And the week after that.

By the third week Bob figured out the retaliation tactic. After nursing more than a few drinks, Bob called Raphael and told him to meet him in the laundry room at the back of the hotel. Bob asked "what the hell Raphael was doing" by booking the bands in another hotel. He said that he and the owners of Cowboys had a "gentleman's agreement" to support each other financially and that Raphael was threatening that agreement. Both men were angry and by this time Bob was poking Raphael in the chest yelling that he "worked too hard all his life to lose money"; that he "wouldn't stand for any of it."

Raphael thought that Bob was going to take a swing at any minute but he stood his ground. Normally the two men are about equal in size. This particular night, Raphael was wearing a big Stetson hat and heeled cowboy boots so he was towering at six foot eight. Moreover—Bob had been drinking enough so that he was not as steady on his feet as usual. Raphael let Bob rant; using every ounce of self-control he could muster to keep calm. Finally he turned and walked away from Bob saying firmly over his shoulder, "You've got my number."

The next morning, Raphael's phone rang very early. It was a sober, calm and businesslike Bob asking "How can we resolve this?" They discussed the sabotage on both sides and both apologized for resorting to such tactics. Cowboys resumed booking rooms at the hotel and Bob left their staff alone.

Months later, after Bob and Raphael had become better acquainted; Raphael asked Bob why he had not actually hit him. He said he knew Bob's reputation for using his fists and had really expected to be slugged. Bob just laughed and said he had held back because he had taken the time to look at Raphael's size and age and figured that this time he might have lost the fight.

Nineteen

> "Call me a braggart, call me arrogant, people have called me worse. But when you need a job done on deadline, you'll call me"
>
> —SAM DONALDSON, ABC NEWS

Grande Prairie was growing by leaps and bounds but the younger crowd really did not have anywhere to go and blow off steam. Bob knew that there was a real opportunity for a good nightclub in Grande Prairie and he knew just where to put it. Canadian Tire had erected a new building and their former property was on a prime location on the main road into the city.

The huge building was comprised of 27,000 sq.ft. of space and the whole thing sat far back of the lot leaving ample room for parking. The price was too good to pass up—only $44.00 a sq.ft. for the land and the building. It was perfect for a club.

When Bob and Clint Cassin approached Canadian Tire to buy the property, they hit a roadblock. There was a "List Penance" against the building (a list of liens or other legalities that must be cleared away before a property may be transferred to another owner) and, until that was settled, the building couldn't be sold.

Bob and Clint knew that a List Penance could take a half year or more to get resolved, and they also knew that renovations would take months. They didn't want to wait a year to open their club and so, once again, Bob thought "outside the box" and came up with an alternate purchasing plan.

The offer was for Bob and Clint to lease the building on a month-to-month basis while the List Penance was being resolved and then, as soon as the List Penance was removed from the property, they would enter into a Purchase Agreement.

That Agreement outlined terms wherein Canadian Tire would give them six months from the date of possession as owners to arrange a mortgage and pay the $1.2 Million purchase price. Canadian Tire agreed and the Lease to Purchase was signed.

Not having mortgage and financing cash, they needed a third investor so Bill de Silva joined the group. Renovations began the next day.

It should be noted that Grande Prairie was in a frenzied building era and tradesmen were in short supply. Schedules had to be monitored on an almost-hourly basis to get things completed on time. Bob spent his days driving from one project to another so he could personally keep on top of every aspect of construction or renovations for all the sites.

Three months after assuming the lease, the Corral finally opened.

The evening before the grand opening, there were no stalls or toilets in the washrooms and the main room looked like it was still under construction. Staff was dodging debris and ladders while they were stocking the bar and, one hour before opening, workers were still putting finishing touches in place. Bob had liked the layout of Cowboys back in Fort McMurray so much that he had copied it in every aspect, even to the operations. Bob had even swiped the club manager, Kevin Redman, from Cowboys.

The nightclub was so successful that it generated enough income to pay for the property in full before the List Penance was cleared and the purchase agreement activated.

With Ryan away at school and Connor living with his mother, Bob had only himself to think about—himself and making money. Everything seemed to be going well. The Nomad and Peter Pond were flourishing in Fort McMurray, the Super 8 and the Corral were both going gangbusters in Grande Prairie. He dabbled in a few smaller projects here and there but always kept his eyes open for new opportunity.

On one trip back to Grande Prairie, Bob stopped in Whitecourt to grab a burger. He was gazing out the restaurant window and noticed a large piece of land nearby. He also noticed that many travelers were being drawn to that location because of the popular burger franchise. He called the phone number listed on the realty sign, met with Leo Zelinski and made an offer on the spot.

It was the perfect location for another Super 8 so Bob called Marc Staniloff to get things going. Pomeroy Enterprises, Leo Zelinski, Can-Am Equipment (Clint Cassin), Stewart Charchuk, Marc Staniloff and Omni Construction (Ron Ghering), along with three or four others, raised $2.5 Million and the new Whitecourt Super 8 became a reality.

Bob had been in the right place at the right time and the move to build in Whitecourt was a good one. However, not everything that Bob touched turned to gold. The next venture in Whitecourt did not work out as well as he had hoped.

Bob had heard that the Whitecourt Travelodge Inn was for sale and he searched out the owner. The place was in rough shape but the price seemed right, the business was already operating and the location seemed to be good. With Bob's success in Grande Prairie, his frenzied activity in Fort McMurray, and the Whitecourt Super 8 exceeding expectations, investors were not hard to find. It took no time at all to put together a financing group for the second Whitecourt location. Clint Cassin was on board with Bob, joined this time by Doug Golosky, Stewart Charchuk and a couple others.

As usual, Bob was very upfront with having no operating cash, in fact he did not even a budget to pay salaries prior to re-opening. Tom Wright had been managing a rundown place in a small town so it was easy enough convince him to go to Whitecourt on speculation. Bob's excitement about the new property was contagious and Tom was eager to get on board.

The Whitecourt Travelodge Inn was renovated in a spectacular fashion. First class fittings, cherry-wood moldings and furniture, top of the line bedding—it was definitely an upscale move. The Inn became the second location for the Corral as well and, initially, the whole complex got a warm reception from the locals. The new Corral was a welcome addition to nightlife and many people booked rooms to see just how much the place had been upgraded.

Unfortunately, the travelers who passed through Whitecourt, the staple of the room bookings, were mainly truckers who wanted nothing more than a cheap night's sleep. Being a Travelodge franchise, the rooms and rates were expected to be on par with a "budget" motel. No one was prepared to pay more for luxury and the bookings began to dwindle. The Travelodge Whitecourt became an albatross—a beautiful albatross but a burden nonetheless. After a couple of years, Clint put the place into receivership.

Although they had become partners in several projects by now, Bob's working relationship with Clint Cassin was having its volatile moments.

The Whitecourt Inn deal had soured Clint for one thing and, in spite of the Peter Pond being a good investment, he had issues with Bob's company being paid management fees on a property where he personally had lost money.

Both men are "in your face" personalities with no patience for pussyfooting around an issue. At the same time, neither man confuses a single business disagreement with the overall working or personal relationship.

During one particular explosive argument between Clint and Bob, for example, Bob lost his patience and flattened Clint with one direct punch. Two days later the two were on a plane together. There had been a business problem. The problem had been resolved. There no longer was a problem. In Bob's thinking, holding grudges is a waste of time that could be better spent in making money.

In his mind, a man can be a complete asshole personally but still be respected for his business acumen. Bob may not want to consider him as a friend but he would not turn him away as an investment partner.

Twenty

"The right man is the one who seizes the moment."
—JOHANNE WOLFGANG VAN GOETHE

When the partners planned a second Corral for Whitecourt, Bob wanted to transfer Kevin Redman from Grande Prairie to that location. He knew, however, that he needed someone with nightclub experience to carry on in Grande Prairie to ensure the continued success there.

In 1998, Raphael Bohlmann had resigned from his management position at Cowboys to go backpacking in Asia and Australia. After his trip, he returned to Fort McMurray to visit his friend Nemr Najmedine and catch up on what was happening in the area. Some of the staff at the Peter Pond saw Raphael and mentioned it to Bob, who happened to be in Fort McMurray checking on the Nomad and Peter Pond operations. When Bob heard that Raphael was back in town, he did not want to take a chance that Cowboys would hire him back. He called him in the very next day.

Not only were past conflicts not mentioned at all, Bob was especially "palsy-walsy" when Raphael came into the office.

They talked about the backpacking adventures briefly but then Bob cut right to the chase—he wanted Raphael to move to Grande Prairie and take over the Corral. Raphael's initial response was "Run a club in Grande Prairie? I've never even been there before!"

Without saying another word or even taking the time to ask Raphael if he had plans for the day, Bob picked up the phone and called Clint in Edmonton. The call was brief.

"Warm up the plane"

Standing up and motioning Raphael to get up, Bob simply said "Come on" and headed to his car.

Four hours later, Bob and Raphael were at the Municipal Airport in Edmonton. Clint welcomed them on board his plane and the three of them flew to Grande Prairie. They arrived at ten PM, drove around the city and then stopped in to the Corral to socialize. The next morning, Bob and Clint drew up an offer for Raphael and headed back to Edmonton on the private plane. They sent Raphael back to Fort McMurray on a commercial flight and gave him a couple of days to consider his options.

As soon as he got to Fort McMurray, Raphael consulted his pal Nemr. Nemr's advice to him was clear. "Ask around town and then make your decision based on what you feel can work for you."

Raphael talked to anyone he could find who had worked for, or had invested with, Bob Pomeroy. Half the people he spoke to warned him not to take the job. They repeated old rumors of Bob's temper and broken promises.

The other half told Raphael that anyone who was given the opportunity to be involved in a Pomeroy project would be crazy to pass it up. Weighing rumors against his own experience, Raphael decided to take Bob's offer. It proved to be a smart decision.

When Raphael made the move to Grande Prairie, his training consisted of a half day with Bob. They did a walk-through of the Corral, Bob showed him the office and the books and they had a conversation about what was expected. Then Bob handed Raphael the keys and said "Gotta go". When questioned about his early departure, Bob simply said, "If you think you can't do the job, then I've hired the wrong guy." And he left.

Raphael began to manage the club just as he had done at Cowboys and, three months later, he felt it was time for a performance review.

Bob gave him a time to come in to the office but stressed that he only had a few minutes free. When Raphael arrived, Bob motioned for him to sit down and state his case. After hearing the request for a review of his new manager's work, Bob looked at Raphael for a couple of minutes and then calmly said "I haven't fired you so you must be doing something right. If you're here looking for a raise, that's up to you. Figure out a way that we can BOTH make money and get back to me. Okay?"

That was the entire meeting. Bob turned his attention back to the work on his desk and Raphael left the room. This management style was totally new to him. He was a bit shocked but the exchange made him think. He soon realized that his financial success was entirely in his own hands and that Bob had not given him just a job; he had given him an opportunity.

Bob and Raphael spent more and more time together.

Before Bob and Carrie were married, Raphael was a frequent guest at Bob's house in Sandy Ridge Estates. One afternoon the two men were sitting in the back yard talking about the great outdoors and their mutual love of camping. Suddenly Bob asked, "Hey, Do you know how to build the best bonfire?"

Raphael was not sure where Bob was going with the question but he "bit" and replied, "No, Bob, how DO you build the best bonfire?"

Bob jumped up and offered to show him.

He walked over to the site of a previous bonfire and built a modest pile of wood shavings and kindling chips. Then he created a teepee of some medium-size sticks of wood over those and very cautiously lit them. Once the whole thing was burning well, Bob walked over to a bundle of high-grade roofing cedar, opened it and proceeded to add some of the cedar to the flames.

"Isn't that lovely?"

Raphael laughed and, with some sarcasm, said, "Oh, so what you're telling me is in order to build the best bonfire, you have to burn only expensive wood!"

Bob seemed taken aback for a second but then said "Well, yeah, that and . . ."

He reached over and quickly picked up a canister of gasoline that had been hidden behind the wood,

". . . gasoline".

With that statement, he poured fuel on the fire. There was a giant "Whoosh" and the bonfire burst into mammoth proportions. Raphael was terrified but Bob stood his ground and laughed.

The ownership of the Corral locations changed over the next years. After the Whitecourt Inn demise, that location went into Receivership along with the hotel and was later sold. Clint Cassin sold his ownership in the Grande Prairie location to Joe Ferraro and Paul Cronauer. Then Paul sold his ownership and the club belonged to just Bob, Joe and Bill de Silva. In early 2005, during the Pomeroy restructuring process, Bob assumed full ownership.

Raphael Bohlmann began his career at the Grande Prairie Corral in 1999.

Against the advice of a handful of gossips in Fort McMurray, he had worked for Bob Pomeroy for eight years. He had become a friend of the family and a surrogate "uncle" to Bob's son, Connor. He had moved to Grande Prairie for just a job but Bob had given him an opportunity.

In August 2007, Raphael Bohlmann was in a strong enough financial position to become the owner of the Corral. He renamed it "Rock City".

Twenty One

"When friends stop being frank and useful to each other, the world loses some of its radiance"

—*ANATOLE BROYARD*, NY TIMES 1985

Although his long work hours and constant wheeling and dealing would seem to indicate that Bob is only after the almighty dollar, the fact is that Bob believes that he is working towards a happy, stable home where he can be surrounded by his kids, grandkids—and, of course, horses.

He is a businessman through and through but he is also a solid friend. He does not need to be with a person on a regular basis to stay close to them. Months may pass by but then, unexpectedly, the phone will ring late at night and it will be Bob calling just to keep in touch or reminisce about the old days.

Whenever a friendship is begun with Bob, it is based on trust.

His relationship with Ernie Patterson is an example of a friendship that began through a job contract. It is also a prime example of how long-standing business relationships work in the northern communities.

When a fast cash loan is needed, there is never any need for filling out loan applications and waiting for approval; there's no need for security deposits or legal documents. There is no mention of interest; there is no need for an invoice. Gentlemen of honour simply jot down a note in their folder. If the amount happens to be in the six-figure category and needed for longer than a few weeks, "maybe" a promissory note will be signed to protect the business in case of an accident.

If Bob is in a cash crunch, he can simply pick up the phone and tell Ernie he needs fifty thousand dollars "right now"—and he gets it as fast as Ernie can drive over with a cheque. If Ernie needs payment in advance on a contract to get him out of a pinch, there's no problem. Bob drives over to him with a cheque.

Sure beats dealing with a bank.

Other people may not understand the arrangement but they don't have to understand it. It works for this circle of pals. Their trust in each other is the foundation of real friendship. They work together, they play together, they invest together. Even if a deal goes sour, it does not change a thing.

When Charlie Grubisich forced the sale of two hotels, for example, it did not end the friendship. It was just business. If Bob needed anything—help, advice, cash—Charlie would never refuse him as their trust in each other is solid.

When Bob opened the Holiday Inn in Grande Prairie, the guest speakers were not all government officials or financiers; two of them were his friends, Charlie Grubisich and Ray Yenkana.

The truth is that Bob prefers being with people he knows and working with people he trusts. Even as a young man, when he went to Edmonton he chose to stay with his Aunt Helen and Uncle Les Collier.

Les feels that it was not a matter of saving money or being selfish. Bob just felt comfortable with family and he always reciprocated—not just with them but also with every one who has been good to him.

A few years ago, Les called Bob to catch up on how things were going. He had heard that Bob was doing well so he jokingly asked if Bob could loan him a million dollars. Without hesitation, Bob said "Probably. When do you need it?" Les was shocked because he had no idea just how successful Bob was becoming. He was very happy for his nephew because he knew just how hard Bob had worked and how he had remained optimistic even through the toughest times.

Every one of Bob's friends can recount times when Bob has done something special for them or has surprised them. Sometimes the surprises are not intentional and sometimes they backfire but Bob always more than makes up for them. All of his actions eventually result in laughter.

On one occasion, Bob decided to treat his friends Kevin and Maria

Person by taking them out for the evening. As a surprise, Bob and his girlfriend Susan turned up at the Person home in a limousine. Bob magnanimously welcomed the Persons into the vehicle hoping to impress them both. Before they even reached the Corral, though, the limo ran out of gas. Bob was embarrassed beyond belief.

A few summers ago, when the Persons were building their new home, Kevin ordered all his deluxe appliances through Bob's commercial account. He was especially happy to be able to purchase the unique double stacking wall oven that Maria had been admiring in a magazine. Kevin's order arrived and was put into storage along with appliances that Bob had ordered for his new kitchen in Scottsdale.

Months later, when Maria's dream kitchen was almost finished, Kevin went to pick up her appliances. The double ovens were missing. Kevin called Bob. Two days later, Bob called back to say that the ovens had been shipped to Scottsdale by accident. He thought it was hilarious—until Kevin told him that Bob was the one who had to call Maria.

Needless to say, Maria was not too happy with either of the men and she told Bob to get her ovens one way or another.

It would have taken ages to pack and ship the ovens from Scottsdale, clearing customs and handling paperwork, so Bob simply called the wholesalers and ordered a second set. He paid a premium to have them express-shipped to Grande Prairie so Maria's kitchen could be completed on time.

The irony is that the double ovens could not be used in Scottsdale. Bob and Carrie had ordered their own preferred appliances for that house so the ovens sat in their garage for months. Eventually they made their way back to Canada and were installed in the kitchen of the equestrian centre.

When the Person house was completed, Kevin called Bob to invite him to a housewarming party. Carrie answered the phone and said that, unfortunately, they could not attend because they were in Scottsdale. Then she handed the phone to Bob.

After Kevin expressed his disappointment that Bob was out of the country, Bob told him that, whatever it would take, even if it meant getting a private flight, he would show up.

That weekend in Grande Prairie, when the Person party was in full swing, the doorbell rang. It was Bob and Carrie.

In the summer of 2007, Kevin and Maria, Bob and Carrie decided to attend the "Bud country concert" with a group of other friends. As this was a weekend event, they all planned to set up their recreational vehicles on the grounds. Bob cleared three days from his calendar, asked one of his employees to get his RV all gassed up, and then he pulled up at the gate Wednesday night, ready to enjoy some good country music.

Unfortunately, Bob forgot to bring his tickets to the event and he was directed to pull out of the line at the entrance. Unhooking his trailer, Bob drove back home and found his VIP tickets. Finally, after the gate staff was shown that the Pomeroys did have VIP tickets, Bob was allowed to move his vehicles to their over-size RV parking spot and Bob proceeded to set up his "camp" for the weekend.

The next day, Kevin walked over to Bob's encampment to touch bases. Bob's truck was parked alongside his RV and in the back were twenty huge 18-litre bottles of purified glacier water.

When Kevin asked Bob if he had acquired a terrible thirst, Bob's response was "Nope. When I asked my guy to get gas, I forgot about asking him to fill the water tank. We were bone dry and this was the best solution I had without disconnecting and moving the whole unit out of the park." It was the first time that Kevin had ever seen anyone use bottled glacier water to flush toilets.

In 1982, Brian Surerus stopped in to the Pioneer Inn for nothing more than a quick drink in the lounge. Bob was the manager at that time; the two "hit it off" immediately. Brian became one of Bob's closest friends.

Bob does not need a large circle of friends. He prefers to surround himself with solid people that know him well; people he trusts; people he loves like brothers. Ray Yenkana would share the list with Brian.

Another longstanding friend is Willie Kempin. Each of these men knows Bob's strengths and faults and accepts him without compromise or censure.

A friend who has remained close since school is Viggo Pedersen and, over the past fifteen or twenty years, Charlie Grubisich, Gerry Tucker, Hank Scheunhage, Kevin Person and Ernie Patterson have become close and important to Bob. He has a lot more acquaintances, people he does business with or sees socially, but he is cautious who he actually calls a friend with a capitol F, because, once Bob considers you to be his friend, he can be trusted with your money and your life.

Willie and Bob had met in 1980 when Willie was selling hotel cleaning supplies to the Pioneer Inn. He had been a drywaller but the crash in the economy had left him without work and without a cent. Their friendship eventually resulted in operating Northern Linen together for a short time in Grande Prairie.

Willie and his wife Marla welcomed Ryan into their home one spring when Bob and Marj went on a holiday and the couple has remained close to Bob through the years. When Willie moved to Kelowna for a time, his daughter wanted to stay in Grande Prairie and Bob did not hesitate to hire her. For that reason, and many more, Willie feels that he can always depend on his friend. He is the first person that Willie would call in an emergency, whether it is business or personal.

Willie has been an unwavering supporter of Bob through the years. In 2006, when Bob accepted the award for "Businessman of the Year" at the Chamber of Commerce event, Bob omitted mention of his office manager and his wife but he remembered to acknowledge his friend Willie Kempin.

What Bob lacks in education, he more than makes up for in empathy and understanding.

He listens to people and he cares about them. Willie has said that Bob has not changed one bit since they first met. He is the same man whether he is flat broke or worth a fortune. Money does not seem to affect him one way or another; his generosity is based on where he sees a need.

When all has been said and done, the fact remains that Bob Pomeroy is an average guy with an above average will to succeed. He has faults; he has weaknesses; he has more "gonads" than a ring full of bulls.

Every person he meets has a "Bob story" to tell when he leaves his or her company. Sometimes, even the most average of days can end up being a "Bob story".

One night Bob was having a late dinner with Ryan, Susie, Kevin Szakacs and Vern Boyd. Vern offered to give Ryan and Bob a ride home and, halfway there, Bob nodded off in one of his power naps.

When they dropped Ryan off, Bob woke up and invited Vern in for a nightcap. The two men sat on the deck spinning tales and talking about their future.

Bob asked Vern a question and then, while Vern was giving a detailed answer, Bob fell asleep again. When Vern realized that he was alone in the conversation, he got up and got Connor out of bed. He showed the boy where Bob was sitting and told him to stand guard; to be sure his dad did not stay out there all night. Then he left.

On the way home, Vern recalls thinking,"Man, how does that man deal with all his stress! What he's got now, starting with no money and no investors, is amazing. He built an empire with just "balls to the wall"!"

Bob is certainly a unique individual. He makes everyone he meets feel special and he tries to share his good fortune wherever he can.

Sometimes it's in a big way. In 2008, the Grand Opening for the new Pomeroy Arabians International Equestrian Centre was held at Bob's new estate. Bob used the event to raise over $100,000 for the Peace Area Riding for the Disabled Society (PARDS). It was the largest single donation the society ever had received.

When Julius' wife Kathy asked to hop on board Bob's plane to be able to make a connecting flight in Edmonton, Bob insisted that his pilot fly her all the way to Calgary so she would not be tired for her meeting.

Ernie Patterson credits Bob as being the catalyst for the way he met his wife Cathy.

Ernie was the drywaller for the Holiday Inn in Grande Prairie and Cathy was working on the same site doing taping for his crew. They became friends but just on a casual basis. Some months later, Cathy got a position at Langstroth & Company, doing bookkeeping.

Ernie often dropped by the office about his accounting issues or contracts but his visits started to become more frequent when Cathy started working there. Bob noticed the mutual attraction and started ribbing his friend about all the accounting problems that seemed to be popping up. When Ernie admitted that he was smitten, Bob encouraged him all the way.

Once the romance blossomed and became public knowledge, Bob played a part in Ernie's marriage proposal.

Shortly after the big hotel transaction, Ernie told Cathy that they were invited to fly to Edmonton with Bob, Carrie, Willie and Marla to celebrate the deal. Even Ernie's mother Laura (a fun-loving woman that Bob calls "mom") was invited.

They all boarded Bob's private plane and the champagne was uncorked; but when Cathy congratulated Bob on his big deal, Bob acted surprised. He said, "This trip isn't about me, Cathy, it's all about you."

Before she could figure out what was happening, Ernie pulled out an engagement ring, got on his knees and proposed to her at 20,000 feet. She accepted and the champagne toasts began in earnest.

When they were planning their big day, Ernie and Cathy knew that they wanted a rustic, intimate wedding and Bob offered the use of his property in Sandy Ridge, which they were happy to accept.

The couple had seen a false-front chapel at a photographer's salon and they planned to replicate it for the ceremony. Ernie told Bob about his plans to build a simple garden shed, adding a taller façade in front that could be removed later. He ordered materials for a basic 12 x 24 work shed, set it up in Bob's back yard and then he and his crew erected the roof trusses.

One evening, when Bob saw Ernie and Cathy looking over the progress, he joined them and expressed his dissatisfaction. "This still looks just like a work shed. It's nowhere near looking like a church". Bob's eye for perfection and his attention to detail had been activated.

The next day, he had the trusses removed and threw a "truss-burning barbecue" for emphasis. Then he ordered materials for a proper sloping roof, a small bell tower and stained glass windows in the appropriate arched shape.

Once the new exterior was finished, Ernie dry walled and wired the interior, added a pretty front porch and, finally, a bell in the tower.

What had begun as a simple garden shed that would serve as a makeshift backdrop for a wedding had ended up being an exquisite miniature chapel, the materials alone costing over twenty three thousand dollars.

The wedding was beautiful. (see photo)

Ernie says that he has never had a friend as good as Bob—in or out of business.

When he is feeling stressed over a project, he can call Bob and within a few minutes of conversation, he feels better, more confident. Bob always makes time for his friends, no matter how busy he is himself.

The wedding chapel is just one example of Bob's preference for doing thing first-class. He operates his hotels that way and he expects the same quality when he travels. He knows that, with more effort, the other hotels could provide better service. He rightfully considers that giving first-class service is the best way to show respect for the money that guests spend. It is the best way to ensure that they return.

Bob treats his friends, his family and the women he has known with the same attention to detail.

When he takes a woman to dinner or on a trip, he makes every effort to treat her like a queen and that is why women like to be with him. He is attentive, he is generous and he sees to every little detail to make it a perfect evening.

Janice still recalls going to Hawaii with Bob and going for dinner at an elegant restaurant. The décor was romantic and beautiful; the meal was perfect but Bob wanted to be certain that nothing was left out of the experience.

He spoke to the manager and shortly after, the couple was escorted to the restaurant's legendary wine cellar for a private tour and wine tasting.

Janice still talks about that "perfect" evening.

When asked to summarize Bob's traits, Ray Yenkana offered the following observations:

"As a business partner: Bob is motivated, hard-working and honest. He has the uncanny skill of finding innovative ways to put projects together; as a friend: Bob is loyal, direct and honest; as a man: Bob is caring, generous and, above all, genuine. Bob has amazing people skills. He can build a rapport quickly and he sees every person as an equal. He will clean toilets alongside a housekeeper and he will share a meal with a waste remover."

Bob has always worked harder and longer than anyone he employs. He loves work; he thrives on it. So much so that he finds it hard to understand why not everyone else is ready and willing to work as much.

He knows a great deal but he is smart enough to recognize where and when he needs skilled help; and then he knows when to back off and allow them to do their jobs. Bob seems to have a gruff, tough exterior, but people close to him know Bob as a man who is very sensitive to people and to their families.

He does many good things quietly and without fanfare. His own extended family has always been treated well and they continue to enjoy the fruits of his hard work.

Children, siblings, nephews or nieces of friends and relatives are given employment just for the asking; family members are included in holiday and vacations. Whatever Bob has, he shares.

One family member pragmatically observed, "Because of his basic good nature and generosity, everyone takes from Bob. As a result, no one makes him accountable for any of his shortcomings. Perhaps, in that respect, a cynic could say that Bob is manipulative. He knows that as long as he keeps giving, no one will criticize him or refuse him any request." (sic)

While that may be true to some extent, everyone who knows Bob also knows that he will never refuse a requested favour from anyone—whether it be an acquaintance, a family member or a friend.

The list of Bob's friends has to include his cousin Mike.

They went through thick and thin together as boys and Mike was a reluctant witness to Bob's abuse. Mike feels that people would be surprised to know just how rational and mature Bob has been all his life. He acquired somewhat of a "wild man" reputation because of his womanizing and his tendency to use his fists to settle disputes but when it came to his body and his business, Bob has always exercised amazing self-discipline. He had a need to succeed so he chose not to smoke in order to be the best swimmer.

Bob's dedication to swimming skills has served him well. In 2006, Bob's entire family was enjoying a houseboat vacation in the Okanagan. His sister Judy, a swimmer herself, was enjoying the cool lake waters alongside the boat when suddenly she got too close to the undertow of the engine and began to be pulled downward into possible danger.

Connor noticed her first and, after alerting his father, he swam towards his aunt and tried to provide assistance. Bob dove in and pulled his sister to safety.

Bob does not know how to just participate in a hobby or sport just for the enjoyment.

When Fred Tissington invited Bob to join him in some early morning bike rides for exercise, every ride became a race. Even with two bad knees. Bob was fast and he continually impressed the young college kids who rode alongside them.

Fast wasn't good enough, though, and when Fred beat him one morning, Bob turned up the next day with the best racing bike he could find in the city, just to have a better "edge".

Tissington speculates that a diploma from a graduate school might have held Bob back. He feels that, if Bob had ever stopped to read pages of regulations and requirements, he may never have taken the first step on some projects. By forging full speed ahead, unhampered by the warnings of "possible downsides", Bob allowed his instincts to take control and his energy to carry the workload.

In April 1969, the Texas billionaire, H.L.Hunt, was being interviewed on CBS' "Sixty Minutes" and, when asked about his early business moves, he said that he "…didn't go to high school and I didn't go to grade school either. Education, I think, is for refinement and is probably a liability" That could probably apply to Bob Pomeroy as well. Although he has little formal education, his entrepreneurial "sixth sense" has hardly ever let him down.

Regarding the refinement aspects of education, Bob has learned through osmosis and observation. He has made some mistakes along the way. He can still be politically incorrect in the workplace. And, yes, his salty language occasionally makes ears burn.

While these traits do not reflect the refinement generally associated with today's business executives or the genteel "horsey set" of Scottsdale, the truth is that Bob effuses charm and that charm gets him a long way with people.

His manners are impeccable. His appreciation for elegance and beauty is well documented.

His new appreciation for wines has been helped along by his business relationships and travel. (Joe Fodor, for example, introduced him to the wonders of Italian Amaronne.)

His kind heart and generous, forgiving nature are solid truths. For those reasons alone, Bob should be known as a gentleman and that, folks, is about as refined as he needs to be.

Twenty-Two

"What separates the winners from the losers is how a person reacts to each new twist of fate."

—*DONALD TRUMP*

In Fort McMurray, Bob had opened a Keg restaurant with the Nomad Hotel group, Kevin Person and a couple of other minor investors. Kevin's main focus was still Cool Line Refrigeration and his company was busy doing all or most of the work on properties developed by Bob.

Kevin had become a friend of Bob's over the years and often did personal favors. When Bob and Marj had finally divorced, for example, Kevin got involved in the settlement.

As part of the financial arrangements, Bob had to buy a new car for his former wife. He found the make of the car she had requested but the Grande Prairie dealer only had a basic model on hand. Marj had been agreeable to the car but Bob wanted her to have more options. He called Kevin and asked him to install air conditioning prior to delivery.

Kevin picked up the car, installed the air conditioning and then got one more request.

Bob asked him to put a dozen long-stemmed roses on the front seat when he delivered the car to Marj—Bob's last grand gesture!

In the fall of 1997, Ryan began college in Grande Prairie and he moved in with Janice and Connor. Janice was functioning relatively well that year; she kept the house clean, fed the boys and managed to provide a stable home—from Monday to Friday. By the weekend, she started to wobble but, for the most part that school year, she was a responsible parent. By the end of the school year, though, her problems with alcohol worsened. Bob could not see the point of increasing child support payments if the money would not be spent on Connor's wellbeing. He applied for full custody.

Although Susan and Bob had a house together in Fort McMurray, Bob knew that he would need a stable home in Grande Prairie for the court to approve his petition. After buying a new house in Crystal Estates, Bob got full custody and moved both of his boys into his house in late August.

His intentions were good but, realistically, Bob was an absentee father. He was always on the road or in Fort McMurray with Susan.

Ryan was stretched thin between college courses, volleyball and practices. He was still just a kid and it was a big enough job to care for himself, nonetheless ensure that his seven year old brother was fed, clothed and ready for school. Frustrated and exhausted, Ryan called on the one person he knew was dependable—his sister Kim. She had remarried and now had a baby girl to care for. In spite of her own workload, Kim opened her arms and her home to her youngest brother. Ryan concentrated on his education and his passion—volleyball.

The two Corrals, both the Best Western Nomad Inn and the Travelodge Peter Pond were all in good hands, the Whitecourt Super 8 was functioning well, and Kim was caring for Connor. Bob was able to focus on new business and his new relationship—with Carrie.

He was still involved with Susan; in fact they were engaged and she was sporting a magnificent diamond ring. But she was in Fort McMurray and Carrie was in Grande Prairie. Plus—the relationship with Susan was having some bumpy spots and Carrie didn't bring any baggage to the mix. She didn't have any problems with alcohol, she was financially independent and she didn't have any children.

Bob managed to handle the balancing act very well.

He even found time to participate in a couple of projects with Grande Prairie College—perhaps to the dismay of Ryan.

Part of the curriculum was to participate in a case competition and be judged by businessmen in the "real world." The faculty rightfully believed that comments from the corporate world would have far greater impact than more "edu-babble" from teachers.

During one session, Bob chaired the panel of judges and worked well with the other participants, including Henry Hamm, arguably the most successful real estate developer in the area.

Both Bob Pomeroy and Henry Hamm were business icons, their status in Grande Prairie equivalent to that of Donald Trump's in New York.

Bob's cousin Terry Collier was an instructor at the college. Ryan was a bright student but Terry felt that he only exerted academic abilities when absolutely required. The perception was that Ryan was far more dedicated to his pursuit of sports than to his academic experience. Up to that day, Bob was not aware of his son's laissez-faire attitude toward his studies.

Several groups made their presentations ahead of Ryan's group. The early presenters had each spent many hours preparing their cases and they turned up in business suits or, at the very least, carefully chosen "school dress."

When it was time for Ryan's group to present their analysis, it became painfully obvious that they were ill-prepared. Ryan walked into the lecture hall wearing a track suit and carrying a large soda. Although his statements showed remarkable insight and business acumen beyond his years, it was very clear that he was "winging it." His overall presentation was in sharp contrast to the ones of the other students, and not in a good way. Bob was mortified but he hid his emotions well.

After all the students had finished, Terry asked the judging panel to step outside for a briefing. At that time, he also told Bob that he would not be able to comment on Ryan's team due to their relationship. Bob gave Terry a cool stare and calmly stated "You don't have to worry about me being biased towards my son. Just the opposite is true. My son should be worried that I may end his life tonight and he will be moving from his cozy bedroom into my freezer in the basement."

The day was not in vain. One of the students had given an exceptional presentation. Bob was so impressed by Trevor Boychuk that he gave the young man a position in his company. As for Ryan, that night Bob gave him a lesson in compliance.

After dinner, Bob told Ryan to sit at his computer and be ready to work. He stood behind his son and carefully dictated ten rules for giving a successful presentation, taking time after each rule to clarify the point and be certain that his son understood the validity of each one.

By the fall of 1999, Connor was still in Kim's care and Bob was still being Bob. He was commuting between Grande Prairie and Fort McMurray and bouncing from Susan to Carrie. He wanted to start acquiring horses again so he bought an acreage in Sandy Ridge and started living like a "country gentleman." Ryan was either in Manitoba at University or half way around the world playing volleyball.

Connor was in Bob's full custody but he needed a stable home. Kim's family was growing and she insisted that Bob care for his son; that he had to stop depending solely on her; that it was time he ensured that Connor had a proper schedule, regular meals and someone to see that his medical and educational needs were met. Kim meant that someone should be Bob. Bob thought otherwise. He got a housekeeper for himself. Kim kept her younger brother for another year and a half.

The Grande Prairie Corral was still doing well but, after Raphael Bohlmann had assumed management, he noticed that there was a large amount of space not being used to any advantage. In the original planning, Bob had intended to have a cigar room but this had never really taken off. The main area of the Corral was busy but the unused area was just an expense to be heated.

Raphael questioned Clint and Bob about the rationale for keeping such a large empty space. When Clint suggested a pub, Raphael asked "What kind?"

Clint challenged Raphael right back with "You're the hot-shot. You figure out something."

Raphael returned in a few days and told them that Grande Prairie could use a really friendly theme pub and the area next to the Corral was just the right size.

Bob and Clint agreed and sent Raphael and another staff member on a "snoop and report" pilgrimage all over Alberta. They told them to take notes on successful pubs and to really analyze the ones that were floundering.

One of the most successful Irish pubs in the province was Ceili's in Calgary. Coincidentally, this pub was owned by none other than Paul Vickers, the man whose Cowboys nightclub in Fort McMurray had been virtually cloned by Bob for the Corrals in Whitecourt and Grande Prairie.

Raphael was impressed by Ceili's and told Bob and Clint to fly down to Calgary and meet him there for lunch. When the three men got settled into their chairs, they noticed that Paul was at the pub.

There were still undercurrents of bad feelings over Bob's unabashed copying of Cowboys but, instead of "leaving well enough alone", Bob decided that this was a perfect opportunity to pull another of his notorious pranks.

Once he was certain that Paul was watching them, Bob leaned over to Raphael and Clint and whispered "Watch this."

Taking a pen and notebook from his shirt pocket, Bob purposefully strode over to one side of the room and, with Paul glaring at his direction, he began pacing off the measurements and making notes in his book. He made certain to pace off the area directly in front of Paul before he sat down to jot more notes in his book.

Seeing Bob adding more notes, Paul finally lost his cool and stormed over to the table. "Hey, Pomeroy! What the hell are you doing now? You gonna rip off this concept the same as you did with Cowboys?!"

Bob remained calm, the coolly responded with "Well, Jeez, Paul, you did such a nice job of doing up this pub, why on earth would I consider copying anyone else?"

Raphael didn't say a word. Clint was chuckling under his breath. Bob just shut up and kept grinning innocently at Paul.

After a few tense seconds, Paul turned and walked away. He was very angry and it was obvious that he wanted nothing more than to throw all three of them out the door. Being an intelligent businessman however, he knew that the best thing to do was to do nothing. He avoided a public scene and didn't give Bob the pleasure of seeing him lose his control.

After Paul walked away, Bob opened his notebook to show the pages to Clint and Raphael. He had been scribbling nonsense on the pages. His only goal was to get Paul choked up.

When Egan's was completed, Bob's floor plans were not similar in any way to Ceili's. In fact, preliminary stages had begun prior to the visit to Calgary.

The new pub was built without blueprints. After Raphael had left on his fact-finding tour, Bob had gone down to the building, paced out the area and sketched out a floor plan on a napkin. Then he used photos of other pubs with ideas he had come up with himself, adding freehand drawings to his file.

As the interior began to take shape, Bob, Egan Ungurian (the project manager) and Carrie used duct tape to lay out the floor plan for the carpenters and installers to follow. (Wayne Korol of Heartland Cabinets confirms that his company has produced many projects using only "Bob's blueprints" on restaurant napkins, scraps of paper or, at best, lined notepaper.)

Eventually a sign had to be ordered for the new pub. In his haste to get the place built, Bob hadn't stopped to consider a name. On the phone with the sign-maker, Bob stopped suddenly and looked Egan. "Hey! Isn't Egan an Irish name?"

The project manager laughed and said that he was actually Ukrainian but, yes, Egan definitely was an Irish name that had been passed down from his mother's family.

Bob was elated. He had a name for his pub. "Close enough! We have an authentic Irish name. The pub is now officially Egan's."

To be certain about his choice of names, Bob contacted the head of the marketing class at Grande Prairie College. He gave them a student project: to do an actual market survey. He provided them with a list of ten Irish names and asked them to see which name would be most readily acceptable to a cross-section of the population.

It was another win-win situation. The college students got a legitimate professional survey to conduct and Bob didn't have to pay any research fees. As it would happen, Egan's was the was the right name after all. The student panel embellished it a bit but the end result was "Egan McSwiggin's Irish Ale House and Pub."

Although the Corral was a successful nightclub, Egan's needed to be managed differently. Bob built the pub on a shoestring as usual so cash flow had to begin as soon as construction was complete. He didn't have six months to have untrained staff floundering around learning the ropes.

During the final stages of construction, Bob sent Raphael, his kitchen manager and a shift manager to Fort McMurray and surreptitiously had them hired as new management trainees for The Keg. He didn't mention to the supervisor of The Keg that the new employees were going to jump ship as soon as they completed their education in food service.

Three weeks later, Raphael and the two managers resigned from the Keg and returned to Grande Prairie. Coincidentally, a couple of the Keg's best "front of house" people decided to take their two weeks' vacation time on the same date. Bob had persuaded them to trade two weeks' of their holidays in exchange for air fare, meals, free accommodation and doubled wages if they would go to Grande Prairie and train the new staff at Egan's.

It didn't take long for the owner of the Grande Prairie Keg to find out that another Keg franchisee was pirating staff in direct competition. He reported Bob to the Keg's franchise head office but any ramifications proved to be of no consequence. By the time any paperwork had been filed, the staff members had returned to Fort McMurray from their "holidays" and Bob had already divested himself of any Keg ownership.

Kevin Person had discovered that he preferred being a "restaurant man" more than being a "hotel man." He was happy with the income that the Fort McMurray Keg could generate with efficient management. He asked Bob to do a share swap. Bob bought Kevin's ownership portion of the Nomad and Kevin bought the Nomad's shares of The Keg. This deal happened before the sale of the Nomad so Kevin didn't participate in the profits of that property. However, the Fort McMurray Keg has performed so well that he never once regretted his decision.

Although he originally had no intentions of being so actively involved in the hospitality business, Kevin Person eventually built two more lounge/restaurants—this time in Grande Prairie—Jake's and The Lions Den—and he continues his ownership of the Fort McMurray Keg.

He credits Bob with setting an example for him of always being prepared for opportunity.

Back in Grande Prairie, the company was beginning to get complaints from guests at the Super 8. There was no restaurant in the hotel and none close by. The Super 8 partnership, along with Bob and Carrie, owned the land adjacent to the Super 8 as well as a building so they began looking for a franchised restaurant.

Bob knew Roy Hildebrandt, the man who owned the Ricky's Restaurant franchise rights for Alberta; in fact, the two men were buddies.

It was a relatively easy step for Bob to get a Ricky's franchise. Because of his relationship with Hildebrandt, the usual personal guarantee was waived and Bob negotiated a discounted franchise fee as well. Bob, Carrie and a group of investors were now proud owners of a slick new Ricky's Restaurant. Bob was especially happy to be operating a Canadian-owned franchise.

Ricky's was the perfect compliment to the Super 8—a bright, clean restaurant offering a wide menu, generous portions and reasonable prices. Guests at the hotel appreciated the next-door convenience and the place soon became a favorite spot for regulars. Ricky's was arguably the #1 breakfast spot in the city. Each morning the booths were filled with members of the RCMP and guys from Eagle Built Homes along with Fred and Dave Tissington, Kevin Szakacs (Hi-Tech Business Systems Inc) and Bob.

Kevin even installed the wireless access at Ricky's in exchange for space to have all his meetings there!

Every morning, Bob would have breakfast with Connor at Ricky's. Anyone looking to have a few words with him could simply stop by the restaurant between 7 and 7:30 AM and find father and son starting their day together.

(The franchise was successful as long as there was a good manager in place. Profits ebbed and flowed according to the labor market in Grande Prairie. For the most part, Ricky's was the perfect franchise for the location but eventually the restaurant was sold and became a sushi place.)

During this period, Bob had noticed a need for a good car wash on the north end. There was still a huge space at the end of the Corral and Egan`s and during the daytime, the lot was virtually empty.

Bob leans towards opening businesses that he has liked personally in other cities and he had been impressed with the Bubbles Car Wash outlet in Edmonton. He told Clint about the franchise and they went to look it over.

A car wash was whole new territory for Bob but, as he's always up for a challenge, they went ahead with the deal. Even though Bob and Clint already owned the land, it still took over $3 Million for the Bubbles franchise and massive installation.

Although a car wash seems like a relatively simple operation, the equipment, mechanical requirements and refit of space is a complex project and there was a great deal of relief when it was finally complete.

Ryan had a few free months from university that summer but he wasn't ready to get involved with Bob on a full-time basis. Coincidentally, Terry Collier had moved to Fort Worth, Texas to open a business and he invited Ryan to spend the time there and help him get things going.

Bob and Terry both felt that it would be a good idea for Ryan to work in another industry and Terry was happy to have someone working with him who had both business education and practical experience. As it was a small project, Ryan's business knowledge wasn't fully utilized.

Terry soon found himself in the position of having to assign heavy manual chores to Ryan. In spite of his duties being changed, Ryan never complained. Terry was impressed by both his work ethic and his acceptance of the jobs he was asked to perform. Terry was also impressed by Ryan's commitment to his training over the summer. It was clear that Ryan had focused on his dream of playing professional volleyball and he had inherited his father's understanding that it took constant hard work to achieve any goal.

That fall, Ryan entered the University of Manitoba in Winnipeg and quickly became one of the stars of their Volleyball team.

Bob forged on with his development in Grande Prairie.

Twenty-Three

"Perpetual devotion to what a man calls his business is only to be sustained by perpetual neglect of other things."
—ROBERT LOUIS STEVENSON

The next addition to the Pomeroy portfolio was a Best Western in Grande Prairie.

Peter Biegel from Top Realty approached Bob and told him about the available piece of land that was a short distance west of the Super 8. Biegel said it was the perfect spot for another hotel. With the Whitecourt Travelodge losses being too fresh in his mind, Bob's immediate reaction was to say ``No." He and his investors had all lost money on the Whitecourt deal and he was feeling the pinch.

Peter was insistent. When Bob told him that he had no money for the land, Peter simply said ``Come with me. I want you to meet the guy who owns the land".

They went to see Mike Didyk, the Grande Prairie magnate who was behind the Royal Oaks subdivision. After Mike and Bob had a chance to talk about the land and the prospects for the city, Mike said, "Why don't we do a hotel together? ``

Being in partnership with one of the most respected developers in Northern Alberta sounded like a good deal to Bob. Mike had the land and Bob had the hotel experience so they shook hands on their proposed deal.

Bob immediately set out to acquire a franchise and he began construction planning. He had completed that stage of the project when he was stopped in his tracks.

Mike had begun to think about his stage in life and decided that he really did not need to start any new ventures. He certainly did not need to make any more money. He changed his mind about becoming an investment partner and told Bob that he preferred to just sell his land and see the area developed.

Although he was out of the package as an investor, Mike was astute enough to recognize that a good hotel would be the best "anchor" possible for the location. He offered Bob an incredibly generous purchase deal—an offer that was too good to pass up.

Not only would he finance the purchase, he would defer the four equal payments for as long as necessary.

Using the land as equity for the entire project, Bob's investor group applied to the Toronto Dominion Bank for mortgaging through a broker.

They received their approval quickly and the construction of the Best Western began in earnest. By the time the group needed a large draw on the financing to pay contractors, the building was already built up to the roofline. That's when Bob got a kick to the groin.

All the fees to the broker had been paid as soon as the approval was received and everything seemed to be in order.

However, when Bob went to draw on the mortgage, the TD Bank informed him that, in fact, the mortgage was not going ahead. The manager who had signed the agreement with the broker did not have the authority to approve a mortgage of that amount. The TD Bank, in its infinite wisdom, cancelled everything.

Carrie had often voiced her concerns over the way Bob approached his projects. In the past, he would get an idea, raise some seed capital and start building. His concept was always to wait to get the final financing until the project was completed. That way, income would be generated as soon as interest started accruing. With the Best Western, Bob had taken Carrie's advice and had gone the traditional route. He had worked through a broker and had arranged for the TD Bank's approval for financing before he started building. Half way through the project, of course, the financing was pulled and Bob had to scramble to find money.

His reaction? "Why bother doing things the RIGHT way? I get further ahead doing things MY way."

And that's what he returned to doing.

The contractors needed to be paid for the work already done and the roof had to be installed immediately. For a brief moment, Bob panicked. Then he got on a plane, headed for Edmonton and made a beeline for the Royal Bank. The bank officer there put everything together and, in no time, Bob got all the mortgaging he needed to finish the project.

Bob took the hard lessons learned in Whitecourt and he built the new hotel just one level upwards in ambience and quality. The Best Western was close enough to the Super 8 that the company got business from both levels of a discerning traveler's wallet.

Mike Didyk never waivered in his support of the development.

The final payment for the land was not due until 2005. (It was actually paid after Bob received investment funding from Manulife for the company restructuring.)

All the while the new hotel was being built, people talked about the stupidity of building another hotel so close to the Super 8. They also talked about Bob's dual lives; one in Grande Prairie and the other in Fort McMurray.

The city's rumor mills, however, did not always revolve solely around Bob Pomeroy. Long winters and the boredom of cable television can bring speculative talk about just about anyone. Sometimes the gossip was about both Bob and another wealthy developer.

Dave Will was the owner of the Casino in Grande Prairie as well as many hotels across the province and Bob considered Dave to be a friendly rival in the hospitality business. No one would fault him if he envied the man's list of properties.

There was restaurant space available close to Dave's casino and it was anyone's guess what would be developed in that space. The most popular guess was that it might be a Tony Roma's.

Then people started hoping that it would be a Tony Roma's.

Knowing of Bob's competitive nature, one of the hopeful rib-lovers put a bug in Bob's ear.

He told him that "word around the city" was that Dave Will was thinking of buying a Tony Roma's franchise.

Ricky's was next to the Super 8 and catered to the early morning guests as well as the dining traveler with a modest wallet, but Bob and his investors had already been considering a more substantial restaurant on the same lot as the Best Western.

Bob had always liked Tony Roma's and he was determined not to be one-upped by Dave Will. If there was going to be one of the popular rib houses in Grande Prairie, it was going to belong to Bob Pomeroy!

Thinking that he would have to act fast, Bob called the Head Office of Tony Roma's in Texas and asked to speak directly to the President of the company.

In a stroke of luck, it happened that the man was flying to Red Deer, Alberta the next weekend to attend the opening of a franchise there. Without mentioning the small detail of the six-hour drive between Red Deer and Grande Prairie, Bob offered to pick the executive up and take him on a little tour of the northern city.

The offer was accepted. After the Red Deer opening, Bob and Carrie were waiting. They all headed off for "parts unknown"—at least that is what it must have seemed to the unsuspecting Texan.

Luckily, they had a friendly drive and some lively conversation. By the time the six-hour trip and subsequent tour of Grande Prairie were finished, Bob had the approval for the Tony Roma's franchise rights.

An investment group, one that included both Bob and Carrie, was created for the franchise cost and the renovations. This partnership was separate from the land ownership.

Tony Roma's was a step up from Ricky's and filled the need for a "dining" place as opposed to just a good "eating" place. It remains a popular spot for locals.

It was years later when Dave Will informed him that he had never held even the remotest interest in the rib franchise.

Bob has always operated on the concept of "find a need and fill it."

Grande Prairie needed moderately priced accommodation so he built the Super 8. When he noticed a lack of accommodation that was one step higher, he built a Best Western. When a restaurant was needed in the Best Western, Bob chose to go another step up.

He loved Sorrentino's Italian Bistro in Edmonton and felt that an upscale "date night place", a more high-end dining room, would fit right in with his other properties. Bob and Carrie committed to the project and created another investment group to seal the deal.

Bob asked Raphael Bohlmann to go to suppliers and purchase all the kitchen equipment for the new restaurant. Raphael was a nightclub manager, not a chef or kitchen designer so his first reaction was to beg off the job.

Bob was not interested in negotiations. He simply said "Learn." Raphael headed to Edmonton.

After three days of gathering prices and quotes and specifications, Raphael called the office and said he would fax the information for Bob's decision. Instead of the expected response, Raphael got a tongue-lashing.

Bob let Raphael know in no uncertain terms that he had assigned the job to him because he was busy.

"If I have to make all the little decisions, I might as well have gone myself. Don't come back without buying what we need."

Bob hung up. Raphael did the deals.

To anyone who does not know Bob, this might seem like a frivolous command: assigning the allocation of hundreds of thousands of dollars to a relatively new employee. To anyone who has worked for Bob for a long time, this is a normal procedure.

He makes his initial selections of his managers based on a combination of experience, qualifications and references, just as any other employer.

When it comes down to his final choice, he looks for people who are confident, people who can think for themselves. He doesn't have time to nurture or coddle and he expects his employees to hit the ground running.

As Raphael looks back on the experience, he continues to be impressed by Bob's willingness to give his managers both the freedom to think and the responsibility to see things through to completion.

Bob's own viewpoint is that, if he is going to use his energies in developing properties, he needs people around him that can work without supervision.

Sometimes, his own need for pushing through projects has brought him some unwelcome attention from the municipal authorities.

When he was building his Chelsea Villas project, a city inspector showed up one morning asking to see permits or approvals. The Phase One basement foundations were already completed and the footings were being installed for Phase Two but Bob had no paperwork to present to the inspector.

"You don't have ANYTHING?!"

Bob, with his usual candor, raised his eyebrows in puzzlement, waved his arm toward the project and simply said, "I sure do. I have two basements right over there."

After some discussion, the inspector left, Bob filed the appropriate paperwork and the project was completed without delay.

Twenty-Four

"Ambition is so powerful a passion in the human breast, that however high we reach we are never satisfied."

—*NICCOLO MACHIAVELLI*

The next year was the beginning of an intense building period. Ryan had moved to Germany to play professional volleyball for a season and then in January of 2002 had moved on to do the same in Indonesia.

Carrie had been Bob's business partner for a few years and, in May of 2002; she became his marriage partner as well. Bob's life, and his relationship in Fort McMurray, was left behind.

Together Bob and Carrie were a formidable team. Bob created projects and made deals. Carrie kept the cash flow moving in the right directions. He moved the big wheels and she found the oil to keep them moving.

Although she often became very frustrated at Bob's quick decisions, they worked towards one goal: the company's expansion.

In the fall of 2002, Ryan returned to Grande Prairie to work with Bob for a few months. He was not surprised to see how much the company had grown as Ryan knew his father's need to be recognized as a person of worth.

Although he knew that Bob would have loved to have him stay at home, Ryan also knew that he still needed time for himself. He had his own passion and his own career just as Bob did. He realized that eventually, perhaps sooner than he might have wanted, he would be expected to take on a major part of the family business so he returned to his sports career while he still had the opportunity. He left his father to build the hospitality business on his own for another year.

And build he did.

Marc Staniloff not only had the franchise master license for Super 8 Motels, he also had the franchise rights for Ameri-Host, the American mid-range, family-oriented chain of hotels. He convinced Bob that this would be another recognizable name to add to the company portfolio.

Marc, Carrie, Bob and a handful of other investors purchased a large piece of land in Grande Prairie half way between the Best Western and the Super 8 and they contracted Omni Construction as the building contractor. Bob did not know that the builder was already in a precarious position and by the time the Ameri-Host was 90% finished, their finances collapsed. The investment partnership, under Bob's direction, took the project to completion.

In September 2003, the Ameri-Host opened and it did not take very long to realize that the franchise brand meant absolutely nothing to the travelling public in Canada. After a couple of year-end reports, it was obvious that the franchise relationship was a waste of money. The fees that had been paid to Ameri-Host had resulted in only two referral bookings in almost two years.

It was time to cut the losses and cancel the franchise.

Bob had fitted the hotel with bedding and linens that far exceeded the standards of Ameri-Host. He had built the interiors and bought furnishings that reflected his own requirement for quality. The truth was that the Ameri-Host Inn was really a Pomeroy Inn in every concept but the sign.

With a quick redesign of the basic neon sign on the corner of the lot and new stationary, in January of 2006 the old Ameri-Host officially became the first Pomeroy Inn & Suites.

Bob finally had his name, his "brand", on a long-stay hotel. It was the culmination of the dream he had shared with Ryan on their trip to Winnipeg many years before.

While the Ameri-Host was under construction, Bob had been eyeing more locations for hotels.

He convinced Dave Will to go and look at land in Fort Nelson and Fort St.John.

Dave never closed a door on any possible opportunity to expand his holdings, so the two of them flew to Fort Nelson.

Most people would describe Bob as being a "colorful character", or a straight shooter; always a man to be counted on to say exactly what is on his mind. Dave Will outshines Bob in that department.

Bob had agreed to drive a National rental car back to Grande Prairie, so, after stopping by the pick-up location and getting the car, Dave and Bob had a vehicle to get around town. They explored the entire area for a while and, as they passed through the residential parts, Dave commented on the kaleidoscope of colors that dotted the landscape. There was no neutral anywhere. Dave could not get over the mish-mash of cheaply painted houses.

Stopping to visit an old friend of Bob's, Dave could not help but comment about the overall appearance of the city. "Don't you have a store that sells good paint here?" When the man responded in the affirmative, Dave shook his head in amazement saying, "Sure doesn't look like it."

Dave was not interested in seeing any more of Fort Nelson. There were not many good locations for hotels and, even after he saw the land that Bob wanted to buy, he gave the city a pass. In Dave's estimation, Fort Nelson was too far north for him to invest any money or time. Cross Fort Nelson off the list.

The two men headed south to Fort St. John that same night.

Unfortunately, the proposed partnership deal for Fort St. John did not fare any better.

Bob wanted to buy a 6-acre parcel along the Alaska Highway, at the corner of Airport Road. When the two men stopped to look at it, the parcel was not much more than a marsh. In fact, Dave pointed out a family of ducks enjoying the pools of water that covered the area. In spite of the rough condition of the acreage, both men saw the potential for development. They stayed overnight to make an offer to purchase the next day.

Bob was feeling a squeeze for cash that year and he had hoped that Dave would buy the land as his part of the investment, enabling the partnership to use the equity of the down payment as leverage for full financing. Unfortunately, Dave was already committed to many large projects of his own. Further, he had made a promise to himself that he would never participate in anything where he did not have full control. He learned many years before that, if he were going to have longtime value in his portfolio, he had to own the majority ownership.

When Bob stated his need for Dave to invest the initial money for the land, Dave offered an alternative. He wanted out of any partnership, but he would put the cash down for the land to enable Bob to secure the purchase.

Bob set about raising the cash he needed and subsequently he was able to buy the parcel outright. (Although it took a few years, eventually the 6-acre parcel was the home of the Super 8 Motel, the Pomeroy Inn & Suites, East Side Mario's and Egan's Irish Restaurant and Pub.)

Before Bob could even start the transfer of shares and payment, Dave sent him a handwritten, one page deal memo outlining everything he wanted reimbursed, including payment for the land. Bob still has the invoice. (See photo pages)

Dave's invoice is a striking example of how business continues to be done in many areas of western and northern Canada between men whose handshake or word is considered as bond.

There is no need for lawyers to complicate simple deals between men who have worked hard for every penny they have earned. They prefer to stick to the facts and keep it simple. "Here's what you owe me." Period. The lawyers can handle the papers at the end.

Bob bought the land in Fort Nelson as well as another parcel in High Level with Marc Staniloff and Cam Christianson.

Cam had taken over the construction projects from Omni and the first property that the new partnership built was the Super 8 in High Level. Finances were tight and they were short $300,000 for completion. Needing an immediate addition of cash, Bob called Lyman Brewster. Lyman still remembers the call because it was the dead of winter and in the middle of the night. Bob sounded almost desperate and Lyman admits that he may have taken advantage of the situation.

Knowing that Bob had his back against the wall, Lyman agreed to loan the project the $300,000 but he asked for ten percent interest. Bob agreed and the High Level Super 8 got finished on time.

It should be noted that the loan was not paid in cash. Lyman ended up swapping the debt for "B" shares in the Clairmont Ramada Inn project a few years later instead. He remains part of that investment group.

In Fort St.John, the land sat empty for about a year. The Super 8 was going up in High Level and the Ameri-Host was being completed in Grande Prairie. Bob still needed to raise the investment capital for the Super 8 in Fort Nelson but the marshy land did not look much like hotel property.

He made a deal with his friend Brian Surerus to clear off four acres of the Fort St.John land on credit. At least this way the land would look more presentable to investors and it would be ready for construction work as soon as funds became available. Brian removed all the trees, leveled and graveled the property. Then he waited for payment.

Months passed by and finally Brian's bank forced him to put a lien on the property to protect their interests.

Bob had been busy getting his investment packages together. He had already secured the franchise for the Super 8, and so he was able to convince the bank that it would be a better deal in the long run for them to release the lien and allow Brian to take shares in the Super 8. The bank agreed and Brian added hotels to his own growing empire. Eventually, Brian became a shareholder in four Pomeroy properties.

This was just after 9-11 and everything was falling apart in the financial communities. Mortgage funding that was near to signing suddenly was cancelled. Investors with deep pockets were nowhere to be found. Caution and Deferral were the keywords of the day.

The Fort Nelson Super 8 had financing delays, as did many of the company's projects, and some of the contractors began to stop work or start collection procedures. It was happening to developers all over North America.

One plumber registered a lien against the Super 8 and, unfortunately for all the other contractors, the lien was preventing Bob from getting any completion financing.

Bob and Cam flew to Fort Nelson along with Bob's drywaller, Ernie Patterson. Ernie had been doing drywalling for Omni Construction as well as for Cam's hotels for years and now he was both a contractor and investor in Bob's projects. Ernie had become a friend as well and he was more than happy to go along with Bob and Cam to speak to the plumber.

The man had never worked for Bob before and, when the financing was delayed, he started to worry. He made the unfortunate mistake of talking to some of Bob's detractors from years long past in Fort St.John. He heard some of the rumors and started to panic. He did not believe he would be paid.

Bob has never felt the value in wasting time on trying to convince others of the unreliability of gossip. He spoke to the plumber about the matter at hand—that the lien was the problem and that everyone would suffer if it were not released.

Ernie talked to the plumber as well and told him of his own positive experience with both Bob and Cam over the years.

With the other tradesmen urging him to concede, the plumber started to waiver but each hour that the work was shut down cost the project money.

Time was of the essence for everyone. There was no more room for negotiation.

Bob and Cam put personal cash in a trust fund as assurance, the lien was released and the hotel was finished on time. All the contractors, including the much-chastened plumber, received their full payments.

Twenty-Five

"The right moment for starting on your next job is not tomorrow or next week, it is right now"
—*ARNOLD TOYNBEE,* EXPERIENCES, OXFORD 1969

The first project that Rick Vieira managed for Bob was East Side Mario's in Grande Prairie.

Bob wanted the restaurant to open quickly. He insisted that Rick's crew finish the job in three months. He told Rick that the crews in Ontario worked within that period for all the East Side Mario's built in that province and he expected the same results. Rick doubled his crew and employed two shifts a day to meet the deadline.

When Mario's opened, Bob admitted that he had fibbed about the construction schedule in Ontario: the other restaurants had actually taken four months to build. From that day forward, Rick had a better understanding of Bob's sense of urgency—and his tactics when it came to dealing with his managers.

Bob's communication with employees is always interesting, to say the least.

He dropped in on one building site after there had been a few difficulties. The site manager was on his first project with Bob and, although he was very experienced, he was nonetheless a bit nervous having the boss come for an inspection. Through his efforts, the job was now going well but he did not know if the boss was satisfied.

Bob walked around the whole area, saying very little. Then he stopped suddenly and looked the man straight in the eye. There were a few seconds of silence and then Bob said, in an utmost tone of sincerity, "You know, this is coming along just fine. I've changed my mind. We're not going to cut your wages after all."

And he walked away. The confused manager was speechless until he heard both Bob and Rick chuckle loudly.

Occasionally, the tables are turned and even an office employee can make Bob the target of a practical joke.

Ashar Minhas has known Bob for at least fifteen years. She worked for Carrie when Langstroth and Company was just starting and she moved over to the Pomeroy Group with them, eventually becoming a Pomeroy employee. Bob considers Ashar to be a friend and confidante and one evening, when they were discussing personal likes and dislikes, Bob mentioned that he absolutely hates elephants. He hates all types of elephants, not just the huge real animals but even ornamental elephants. Ashar stored that bit of information and, when one of Bob's regional managers at the time, Mohan Bilgi, went to India for a holiday, Ashar suggested that he bring back a gift. She told him that Bob adored elephants and Mohan could really impress Bob if he brought back a large porcelain elephant.

Mohan was so appreciative of this bit of "inside information" that he went a bit overboard with his shopping.

On his return, he presented Bob with a large collection of elephants of every size, color and material.

In spite of his aversion to the pachyderms, Bob, in his usual politeness, thanked Mohan profusely—perhaps too profusely, because from then on, whenever Mohan travelled anywhere, he brought Bob another elephant.

Ashar has not refrained from doing her own part to add to the collection. In fact, in 2002, for Bob and Carrie's wedding in Scottsdale, she had no problem with selecting a gift for the man who has everything. She presented the couple with a large elephant statue.

In the early years of the company, Bob made a point of appearing at every site on a regular basis, almost daily in fact. He always wanted to see exactly what was happening and where he could cut time or cost.

Once projects began to take place simultaneously in different cities, his personal inspections became less frequent.

At the same time that East Side Mario's was being built in Grande Prairie, for example, both a Holiday Inn and a Tony Roma's Restaurant were being built in Fort McMurray. Bob often had to make quick trips back and forth to keep better control of things. One night, he was heading back to Fort McMurray with Rick and the woman who was his second-in-command, Joanne Butt. Rick was in the back seat, not paying too much attention for most of the trip as he had work to review. Overhearing a bit of phone conversation, he glanced up to see that Bob was talking on the cell phone. That, in itself, was not unusual. What WAS unusual was that the phone was tucked under Bob's ear and, in Bob's left hand was a pen and a half-eaten banana. In his right hand was his open notebook. He was writing notes. He was taking bites of the banana. He was carrying on the phone conversation. Rick jolted ahead and looked at the speedometer. Bob was driving 140 kilometers per hour and steering with his knees.

Joanne seemed oblivious. Rick was horrified and made his feelings known. The note taking stopped but just before they arrived at Fort McMurray, Rick felt uneasy about the fluctuating speed of the car. He looked over the back of the seat again and saw that Bob kept dozing off and then snapping awake. Everyone knew about Bob's frequent catnaps but Rick was not about to meet his end due to one. He yelled at Bob to wake up, that he would drive the rest of the way. Bob shook his head and seemed to get a second wind, just long enough to get to their destination!

The frequent high-speed commutes had long since become a requirement for the company. It was a rare few who would drive with Bob. The corporate plane quickly became a necessity to protect life and limb.

The Holiday Inn project in Fort McMurray was actually put together by Bill de Silva and Joe Ferraro. They purchased the land and were already building a hotel when Bob got involved. After meeting the district representative for the Holiday Inn Corporation, Bob, along with Carrie, Joanne Butt and a few others, had purchased the popular franchise for Fort McMurray. That franchise, along with Bob's skills at hotel management, would bring added value to the de Silva/Ferraro project if they joined forces. The two men gave Bob and his investment partners shares in their project to come on board.

Bob and his partners also acquired a Tony Roma's franchise for Fort McMurray so that was the logical choice of restaurant to open along with the hotel. The principals of Tony Roma's master franchise for Alberta, including Henry Cinnamon, invested their franchise fee to become part of the Fort McMurray restaurant team.

Tony Roma's opened six months after the Holiday Inn and both were successful additions to the city's social scene.

Within a year after opening, Bill and Joe bought out everyone's shares of the hotel and continued to operate it on their own. With the Tony Roma's business, they just bought out Bob, Carrie and Joanne. (Eventually, that restaurant became "Spaghetti Joe's")

Bob and his investment partners took their profits and channeled them into new projects.

Bob needed to implement an extensive IT network for the company to keep up with the technology that came along with such a large portfolio. Along with the installation for East Side Mario's came the contracted IT specialist for the franchise chain, Susie Goodwin. Her work was impressive and Bob contracted more work with her. Susie's experience and capability happened to come packaged in a trim body and Bob did not always see beyond the blonde hair and blue eyes.

During one meeting with Bob and Raphael at the restaurant, the conversation became very technical and Bob was getting more and more agitated, complaining "all this techno-talk is over my head."

He began to talk directly to Raphael and, as an aside, asked Susie to get him a cup of coffee. Totally nonplussed, Susie responded sweetly with "I can certainly find someone from the wait staff to bring you a cup of coffee" and she called a server over to their table. Bob was mildly shocked but did not respond. Susie had not felt insulted. She understood that Bob was a maverick employer who had not been accustomed to the political correctness of the new workplace.

She had already heard about some of his sexist comments at the office and she had made up her mind to accept Bob's quirks as a challenge rather than a stumbling block. She soon had another opportunity to stand her ground.

Bob was trying to micro-manage every aspect of every project and his manner often became brusque. He made decisions by the minute and his office became a small-scale conference room. There was rarely time to discuss options. Time was money and Bob just forged ahead. He did not want to hear opposing viewpoints.

During yet one more meeting, Bob seemed to be more stubborn and uncompromising than usual.

Susie became exasperated when he seemed to be telling her how to do her highly technical job. Finally, when she felt she was getting nowhere at all and was ready to throw in the towel, she blurted out "Oh fuck off!"

There were a few seconds of dead silence and then Bob let out a loud roar of laughter. The discussion became more cooperative and Susie received far more respect in future.

The incident speaks as much about Bob's general character as it does about his outdated views on women.

As one of his business associates has learned, "Bob is the type of person who pushes and pushes, even to the point of being a bully, until you stand up to him. That is the only way to get his respect—to prove that you know and believe you are his equal." (Sic)

Twenty-Six

"The conventional definition of management is getting work done through people but real management is developing people through work."
—*AGHA HASAN ABEDI*, LEADERS, JULY 1984

In January of 2003, Ryan returned to Indonesia. That summer he played for Canada's National team one last season and then signed a contract with a professional volleyball club in Azores, Portugal.

Back at home, Bob was busy with more expansion plans.

Bob and his investors had acquired the franchise for the Holiday Inn brand in Grande Prairie in 2002 as well as for Fort McMurray.

About six months before his wedding in 2002, Bob took a couple of his managers to Phoenix to attend a Best Western meeting. After the day was over, they dropped by Barcelona for a late dinner. About ten o'clock each night, the restaurant turns into more of a nightclub and gets quite lively—a real hot spot for singles.

While it has been acknowledged that Bob's former hobby was chasing skirts, the fact is that he did not always chase them for himself. This may lend credence to the theory that it is the chase he really loves—not necessarily the catch.

Bob will demonstrate his flirting techniques at the drop of a hat. He considers his way with women as much of a skill as being a great hunter or great orator.

After they had finished their meal, the three men were nursing a drink and discussing the day's events when Bob spotted a table of beautiful young women nearby. He got up, walked across the room, introduced himself and chatted for a while as the others watched in amusement. Within minutes, Bob and all the girls walked back to Bob's table. Bob gallantly introduced them all. Then he bid them goodnight and went to bed.

This trip to Scottsdale was also another of Bob's "fact-finding" jaunts.

Barcelona was his favorite restaurant in the Arizona city and he knew he wanted a similar look in the hotel he was building in Grande Prairie.

Carrie had selected Barcelona as the site for their wedding reception and she continually told Bob how much she enjoyed the ambience of the elegant restaurant. Bob was eager to please his new wife so, when she mentioned once more how much she loved Barcelona, he said he would build her one of her own in Grande Prairie.

The next day, while the men waited for their lunch at the restaurant, Bob started taking snapshots of the well-appointed dining room. It did not take long for the manager to rush over and demand that he stop. Bob started to compliment the fellow on the elegant décor and excellent service and eventually discovered that the manager was a fellow Canadian. The conversation quickly turned around and Bob's "newest pal" not only allowed him to keep the pictures he had already taken, he encouraged him to take about a hundred more.

Some time later, Bob made another trip to the property, this time with Larry Ungurian and an associate from Russell Food Equipment.

The cooperative manager allowed them to take extensive measurements and even more notes. On their return to Grande Prairie, Bob started to design his own Barcelona.

Bob wanted the hotel's restaurant to be better than any other restaurant in the city. He also wanted the most beautiful spa.

The Grande Prairie Holiday Inn partnership was comprised of Bill de Silva, Joe Ferraro, Cam Christianson and Bob along with a few others. The plans were for the Holiday Inn to open in August of 2003.

By early spring of 2003, with no permits and no drawings yet filed, Bob started excavating. The city officials called on him and, once again, Bob managed to avoid any major problems. When they asked what he was doing, he simply said, "Building a hotel that the city will be proud of." The inspectors obviously agreed.

Even when some problems arose with compliance, the city officials told Bob to keep building.

They knew from experience working with Bob that he would make any changes required and that everything would be done to regulations if not exceed them.

The Holiday Inn project was begun in Fort McMurray after the Grande Prairie property was already under construction. (The Fort McMurray property opened before Grande Prairie.)

Barcelona Restaurant was originally a separate investment package between Bob, Cam, Bill and Joe. When all the original investment money was gone into completing the basement and concrete pad, it made more sense economically to roll the restaurant into the hotel partnership. As well, the restaurant was attached to the Holiday Inn and the catering was built in to the hotel's amenities package.

With the final drawings on file with the city, Bob decided to change his building plans.

The walls were up and floors were being built when he told Rick that he needed the banquet room changed. He insisted on having huge exterior doors added so that cars could be driven inside for special events. Rick knew that major changes could not be made over the parkade and he had serious concerns with this last-minute structural edit. Nonetheless, he and his engineer found a way to make the change and the doors were added.

Adjustments and inspections aside, Bob's team pushed on and the paperwork was handled in due course. The occupancy permit was issued on opening day.

When it came to the Spa area, Bob wanted to be certain that Rick knew just how beautifully the spot should be built. Once again, he did not have any professional drawings, just memories of elegant spas that he and Carrie had visited. He tried to describe Spa Utopia in Vancouver but was not convinced that Rick understood the level of opulence that he wanted in the Holiday Inn spa. This was a joint project of Bob and Carrie's and they both wanted it to be perfect.

Finally, Bob said, "You should just go and see them for yourself. I mean it, Rick. You should go to Vancouver right now. Take your wife. Then you should go to Phoenix."

With that, Bob called Carrie and asked her to book flights and hotels in both Vancouver and Phoenix. Rick still had not spoken to his wife. When he could finally get a word in edgewise, he called home and told Cathy to get a sitter for a few days because they were going on a trip together. When she asked what day they were leaving, Rick laughed and said "Tomorrow morning."

Rick and Cathy visited Spa Utopia as well as several spas in Phoenix and they took a good look at the Barcelona Restaurants in Scottsdale and Chandler. When Rick returned to Grande Prairie, he not only had a folder full of photos to use for reference, he had a much clearer understanding of exactly what Bob wanted to create.

Carrie meanwhile was busy on the internet. She sourced spas all over North America and she and Lisa Desgagne flew to Connecticut to take a course in spa management.

Lisa had esthetician experience and was well versed in the top spa products; Carrie and Bob had the financial means to secure the distribution rights for the product lines. Carrie did all the negotiating of contracts.

Paul and Lisa Desgagne became Bob and Carrie's equal partners in the new Mirage Spa at the Grande Prairie Holiday Inn.

By the time the plans for the Spa were implemented, the Holiday inn was virtually completed. Extra ventilation, an item not included in the original plans, was necessary. Once again, Rick was faced with a small fortune in cost over-runs due to structural changes at such a late date.

He told Bob that he wished he had known a lot sooner about the spa and the pool area. He felt that the extra expense would be massive and Bob might think he had mishandled the construction costs. When he approached Bob about it, Bob's response was, "Oh, don't worry. I knew. I just forgot to tell you."

At the grand opening of the Holiday Inn, a beautiful new Mustang sat front and centre of the ballroom. Every person who toured the new hotel received a key to try in the lock and one lucky visitor won the car.

The Mirage Spa was completed exactly as Bob and Carrie had envisioned. Not only was the Mirage the first in Grande Prairie, it was arguably the most beautiful spa in Alberta. Lisa worked tirelessly to build a solid team of experienced estheticians and masseuse professionals and open times for appointments quickly became a rare commodity.

When the Mirage opened, Carrie and Lisa estimated that they would sell $200,000 in gift certificates the first season. Both Bob and Paul called them crazy optimists. The women met their goal.

The agreement was for Lisa to be the salaried manager of the Mirage and, initially, that arrangement worked. Things began to fall apart when Lisa hired a close relative to share the management responsibilities. According to Carrie, Lisa changed the agreed-upon employment situation. Under Lisa's new plan, the two women would be sharing the work and yet both would receive full salaries.

Although she loved the Mirage, Carrie was not as enamored of the new arrangements. In spite of the workload being far heavier than first expected and the increased income justifying an additional manager, she was not happy about the expense of two management salaries cutting into profits. She convinced Bob to sell their ownership position to Paul and Lisa before any friendship between her and Lisa was irrevocably damaged. The transfer of ownership shares was completed and Lisa assumed full control.

The Desgagnes continue to operate the wonderfully successful Spa Mirage.

As for Rick, and others on Bob's team, they soon learned to take the time to ask Bob if he "happens to have any ideas percolating that he wishes to share." They have come to appreciate that Bob's projects are always "in flux" and, more importantly, they are usually in his mind and rarely on paper.

Bob does not expect employees to do any more than he would do himself. He is definitely "old school" when it comes to management and he is not afraid to roll up his sleeves and work in any position in any of his properties. He still does surprise "walk-throughs" of his hotels and restaurants.

It is not unusual to see him pull out a flashlight to check corners or a blue-light to check bathrooms for urine stains. He is not being critical of his managers or spying on staff. He is simply ensuring quality accommodation and service for his guests and setting an example for his managers.

Bob is very protective of the Pomeroy name on anything he owns or manages and he is constantly on alert for shortcomings or problems. He will notice a dusty ledge, a crooked picture, a small crack in a window before anyone else does and he will point out the matter, not as criticism, but as a matter-of-fact statement of something to change.

When Allison was managing the Holiday Inn, for example, Bob stopped by one day, did a walk-through and then asked Allison if she had done the same. When she responded in the affirmative, Bob asked her to go down the front hallway with him. Stopping by an office window, he pointed out an old piece of scotch tape still hanging where a notice had been removed. A small thing? Yes. Inconsequential? For most people, yes. Important for Bob? Yes. In his eyes, if one small item is overlooked, the negligence is multiplied and soon the entire property looks shabby.

At Ricky's restaurant one night, the hot water tank gave out during the last shift and the next day there were no clean dishes for the lunch hour. In the morning, the kitchen manager called Raphael in a panic.

When Raphael told him to boil water on the stove, the manager said that his staff members were not hired to wash dishes by hand in boiling hot water.

Raphael knew that Bob would be furious if the restaurant closed over the lucrative lunch hour. He ordered the manager to put the "blankety-blank" water on the stove and he would wash the dishes himself. Then he stopped by Bob's office to tell him where he was going.

Without a moment's hesitation, Bob jumped to his feet and said, "Let's go."

Bob and Raphael spent the next three hours decked out in aprons and rubber gloves washing dishes by hand to ensure that the lunch trade was saved. None of the customers in the front of the place knew that the owner was sweating it out in the kitchen to protect his investment and the investment of his partners.

Bob will do almost anything to keep his customers happy.

In his early years at the Pioneer Inn, he even considered skirting the law to ensure that he could offer full service. During the beer strike in BC, the hotel bar ran dry and Bob needed supplies fast.

His best friend, Brian Surerus, traveled between Fort St.John and Grande Prairie almost daily and, as he was desperate, Bob gave him a large amount of cash and asked him to bring back a load of beer on his next trip. Not wanting a quarrel, and hoping for a strike settlement any day, Brian took the cash and agreed to the assignment.

He did not buy any beer.

Very late that night, Brian called Bob and told him that the RCMP had stopped him on the way back from Grande Prairie and had confiscated both the beer and his truck. He also said that he had caved in under pressure. Worrying about losing his truck, he told the cops who had actually bought the beer.

Bob could not sleep a wink. First thing in the morning, he called the owner in Vancouver to tell him about the loss of cash and the potential problem for the hotel.

A short while later, Brian stopped by to confess and to return the money.

He was doubled over in laughter knowing that Bob had lost sleep and had even contacted his employer. Bob was not amused. In fact, he was totally pissed off at his pal and told him to get the hell out of his sight and out of his hotel.

They did not talk for days but when they did, Bob told Brian that he respected him for not agreeing to bend the law. Then they both laughed about the entire incident and the friendship resumed.

There is no doubt that Bob has great "people skills" and, in spite of expecting a lot from his employees, he gives a lot in quiet ways. His generosity comes without conditions.

When Tom Wright moved to Grande Prairie, he was suffering from dental problems. One day, Bob commented on the sorry state of Tom's teeth and Tom told him he could not afford the work that the dentist had quoted.

Bob said nothing but the next morning, Tom got a phone call from Bob's dentist confirming an appointment.

Tom was puzzled but went to the office as requested. When he asked the dentist who made the appointment, he was told that he had nothing to be concerned about. Bob had arranged for all Tom's dental work to be completed.

For many years, Bob employed a developmentally challenged man called Alan Dietzen. Alan was relatively high functioning but he had no education and no skills and Bob always watched over him.

He employed the man to keep the parking lots clear of cigarette butts and do simple maintenance chores around the motels. Alan had a wife but, when the woman walked out, he began to drink heavily and wander around until he passed out. Bob instructed his front desk people to let him sleep it off in one of the empty rooms and he asked one of his closest employees, Ashar Minhas, to check on him occasionally. When temperatures dipped, he had Ashar buy Alan warm clothing, gloves and winter boots. Unfortunately, one morning, the housekeeping staff found Alan dead in his room. Bob took care of everything, even the funeral, and was thoroughly disgusted when members of Alan's family showed up just to enquire if there was anything of value left behind.

In 2005, Darlene Black's daughter was grievously injured in a motor cycle accident in Grande Prairie.

As the family wished for her organs to be donated, she was kept alive until she could be flown to Edmonton for the medical procedure to be performed immediately after death. Without being asked, Bob and Carrie took action. They provided a limo for the family the day of the funeral and paid for the luncheon at the Best Western Inn.

Darlene had already been on a two-month stress leave when the accident happened and was in a state of shock.

Carrie suggested that she return to work at head office so that she could be around people who cared about her and could keep busy as she coped with her loss. This proved to be the right move and Darlene was able to return to her usual effectiveness. Four months later, still fragile from her family tragedy, Darlene fell ill with pneumonia and was off work for two full months. Bob and Carrie kept her on full salary.

In 2006, one of Steve Good's family members lost a child. When Steve asked Bob for a few days off to drive to Calgary for the funeral, Bob told him not to waste time on the road. He told him to go home, pack and head for the airport.

Within hours, Steve, his wife Katy and their two children were flying to Calgary for the entire weekend in Bob's plane. Bob never mentioned the cost and he has never told anyone about his gesture.

The things that Bob does for others are not limited to his own friends. Nor are they limited to his current employees.

When Ethel Mohr's partner, Bill Hynne, passed away, it had been more than twenty years since she had worked for Bob at the restaurant. Nonetheless, when Bob learned of Bill's death, he and Carrie flew to Fort St.John to attend his funeral and show Ethel that she still could count on his support.

In the winter of 2007–2008, Charlie Grubisich was in Phoenix golfing with his friend Rick Hart. Rick got a message at the course saying that his wife had taken ill at her hairdresser's and had been taken to the hospital.

A couple of days later, Charlie happened to mention casually the incident to Bob and they talked about the high cost of medical care in the U.S. as well as the emotional comfort of being home during an illness. Then the matter was dropped. Less than forty-eight hours later, when Charlie was visiting LouAnn and Rick at the hospital, his cell phone rang. It was Bob enquiring about LouAnn's situation and offering the use of his plane to fly them back to Canada in comfort and at their convenience.

Not all of Bob's kindnesses are large or costly; some are as small as employing the daughter of a friend or offering a place in his home to a young teenager whose parents abandoned him. If Bob knows about a need or a problem, he steps in immediately. He never asks for thanks, compensation, or repayment.

He is not always appreciated.

One young painter he employed had a list of personal problems. Bob helped him in many ways and, when he continually screwed up, Bob gave him chance after chance. Was he grateful? Hardly.

A few months after his last reprieve, when Bob's back was to the wall with labor shortages, the kid quit for an offer of a couple of bucks more. Bob would never mention it.

He is not a whiner. He does not hold grudges. He just lets things go and moves ahead.

One clear example of Bob's reluctance to hold on to past hurts occurred in the lobby of the Super 8 Motel just a few years ago.

Bob and Carrie had stopped by to talk to the manager when Bob spotted a very old woman walking towards the elevator. He nudged Carrie and said, "Look. There's the teacher who said I was too stupid to be in a classroom." Carrie asked if he was certain and when he said, "Absolutely", she suggested that he introduce himself and let the woman know that she was checking in to one of his hotels. Bob shrugged and said, "What's the point of that? It wouldn't make any difference."

Albert Einstein said that "Anger dwells only in the bosom of fools" and Bob Pomeroy is no fool. He fully understands that holding on to anger from the past does nothing but slow a person down from making progress in the future.

Twenty-Seven

"Business, more than any other occupation, is a continual dealing with the future; it is a continual calculation, an instinctive exercise in foresight."
—HENRY R. LUCE, WORLD OF QUOTES

Clairmont was, and still is, considered to be a bedroom support area for Grande Prairie as well as a stopping/refueling spot for trucks headed up the northern highway. Athabasca was uncharted territory and also a key spot for truckers doing long hauls.

Bob set his sights on both towns. Clairmont got a Ramada Inn & Suites, along with a Husky House Restaurant, a convenience Store and Gas Bar. Athabasca got a Best Western.

A couple of days before Bob and Carrie's wedding, May 2002, Bob received a phone call telling him that a couple of guys were going to Clairmont to buy land for a hotel and truck stop. The caller knew that Bob had been thinking about the same thing. He warned that Bob had better hurry if he didn't want to lose the opportunity.

Bob called Darcy Hare and was adamant, "Do not sell to those guys. I will buy it. Guaranteed. I just need a couple of days to get married."

Darcy agreed to wait—but not more than a week or so.

Two days after his wedding, Bob was at his home in Scottsdale. He was placing calls, making promises and hoping for a miracle. Carrie, meanwhile, was sitting by their pool. She was not happy about spending her honeymoon alone.

Finally she picked up the house phone and started to repeatedly dial Bob's cell.

Eventually, she got through. Bob had just started to dial out on another call when he heard Carrie's voice telling him to stop what he was doing.

She told him to look outside; that she was sitting all alone by the pool waiting for him. When he groaned in protest about not having any time; that he had to find a way to buy some land, she added, "And I didn't bother to put on my bikini."

Bob put down his phone.

A half hour later he was back at work.

The deadline was approaching and he still didn't know where he would find the money he needed. He just knew that he wanted the land in Clairmont and he had promised Darcy that he'd buy it.

Returning to Grande Prairie a few days later, Bob's first action was to get the offer for the land in writing. He got some unexpected good news. Darcy agreed to carry the financing if Bob paid a quarter million dollars as the down payment. Bob gave Darcy the impression that the down payment would be no problem but inwardly he knew that the pressure was on!

When he returned to beating the bushes, a friend suggested that Bob talk to Bill Jenkins in High Level. Bob had never met Bill so he didn't want to take a chance on making a "cold call" on the phone. He was running out of options fast. He got on his plane and headed up to High Level to meet Jenkins personally.

Just before landing, he called Bill and said he would be in High Level in a few minutes and needed to speak to him about a possible investment.

He almost missed his window of opportunity.

Bill was just preparing to leave town himself. He agreed to meet Bob but made no promises. The two men sat down together at the airport and Bob told him about the project. Forty-five minutes later, Bill called his wife and told her he had just invested a quarter million dollars with a complete stranger.

The Clairmont land was safe.

The land deal proved to be an interesting experience for Bob in another way as well.

When he was putting together the large land purchase, Bob wasn't dealing solely with Darcy Hare. He was actually negotiating with Darcy and a partner as both men owned the tract at the intersection. Bob wanted all twenty acres but he only wanted to pay for nineteen. The deal was, for all intents and purposes, in place but the parties were still negotiating over a difference of $100,000 in the purchase price.

Bob and the younger partner had arranged a meeting in Bob Lewis' law offices to sign the final papers but neither side would budge on the price. It was a deadlock. Time was passing and the lawyer was getting tired of the back and forth haggling. Out of sheer frustration, Bob finally suggested, "Why don't we just arm wrestle and be done with it?!"

Confident in his own physical prowess compared to the old guy with a limp (Bob), the young man felt he had it "made in the shade." In fact, he felt a match might be a little unfair and told Bob so. Bob feigned disgust and sarcastically commented that he wasn't afraid of any young guy. He taunted him even more by saying he could "even beat you left-handed." The match was on.

After assuring Lewis that they would both abide by the outcome, the men sat across from each other and Bob offered his left arm.

When the younger man hesitated and offered Bob one more chance to reconsider, he just scoffed and renewed the left-handed challenge. A short two seconds later, the young man had his arm pinned to the table. There was no contest. Bob won handily. He was happy. The lawyer was happy. The young man was not.

He had not only misjudged Bob's strength, he had not stopped to consider that Bob was left-handed. What's more, he had not asked Darcy for permission to arm wrestle for $100,000 of their company's money.

The papers were signed at the reduced price but the next day Darcy called Bob to express his dismay. The original prospective buyers had been offering the full price. Darcy felt that by waiting for Bob, he was "out" $100,000. Being a gentleman, and acknowledging that the deal was made in front of a mutually-selected lawyer, he honored the price.

A week later, the partners realized that they needed one acre of the land for one of their own projects and they had to buy it back from Bob. Bob negotiated their buy-back price to reflect the $100,000 he had gained on the earlier deal. He was satisfied enough to have the bragging rights to winning that much cash in an arm wrestling match when he was pushing fifty-six!

Eventually the Ramada Clairmont partnership involved Bob, Cam Christianson and Bill Jenkins as the "A" shareholders. The "B" shareholders included Lyman Brewster, who had swapped his $300,000 loan from High Level for shares in the Ramada project.

The Ramada Clairmont brought a new investment partner to the Pomeroy Group.

The Peavine Metis Settlement just outside of High Prairie had been looking for opportunities to maximize their oil lease payouts from the Federal government. Their Council recognized the potential in Clairmont and was happy to invest in the new hotel complex. The Peavine group became 29% owners of the "B" shares of the Ramada. That first investment began a strong relationship between the Peavine Group and Bob.

The deals were complete and the drawings were submitted. Weeks began to pass by, though, and nothing was being built on the site. Finally Lyman Brewster called Bob and asked him what was going on.

There was no getting around the issue. Bob told Lyman that they couldn't proceed because they were still short one million dollars.

Lyman couldn't see the point in any more delays and he believed that it was the right project for the right place at the right time. He also believed that Bob would get the job done as promised. He loaned the partnership the million dollars. He also made certain that Bob showed his appreciation for the bailout in the best manner possible—money. Once again, Lyman charged ten percent on his loan.

As the building progressed and expenses soared, Bill Jenkins got a little case of buyer's remorse. He liked the idea of the investment but he didn't like the idea of being one of the guarantors. As an "A" shareholder, his name was part of the security on all the contracts and that made him uncomfortable. He wanted out.

Lyman wrote another cheque. The Ramada "A" shares were now held by Cam, Lyman and Bob.

Once the Watershed deal was concluded a few years later, Cam was bought out and his shares were transferred to Bob. The "A" shares are still held by Bob and Lyman. The "B" shares are held by Lyman's company and the Peavine Settlement.

Bob's intention was to incorporate a Subway restaurant into the Ramada, complete with a drive-through window. He just happened to have the ideal window in storage so it was a logical decision. He gave the window to his crew and told them to build a drive-through alongside the hotel. Unfortunately, securing the Subway franchise didn't happen. More unfortunately, the window had to be un-installed and the entire exterior wall had to be refinished. It was just another "blip" on Bob's planning table.

Meanwhile, the Pomeroy Group opened both a second Egan's and a second East Side Mario's in Fort St. John. Egan's was attached to the new Super 8 and East Side Mario's was on the other side of the company's land across the parking lot. Bob planned on building another Pomeroy Inn & Suites on the same tract of land but, at that point, he had not put together an investment group for the hotel.

In July that same year, a tornado ripped through parts of Edmonton and Northern Alberta.

It had been seventeen years since another horrific tornado took lives in the area but memories of that event were still sharp in peoples' minds. Word spread fast about the impending storm.

Susie Goodwin had left the office to see how things were going at the new Ramada Inn. She was half way to her destination when her cell phone rang. Trevor was calling to tell her that a tornado had already touched down in Clairmont and she was in very real danger. Making a quick U-turn on the highway, Susie headed back to Grande Prairie. She switched on her car radio just in time to hear that the tornado had suddenly switched direction and was swirling towards the city. At that precise moment, a severe gust shook her car and she saw the huge KFC sign blow off the restaurant building as if it were a piece of tissue.

Susie called Bob to tell him where she was and told him to warn the staff to take cover.

Without missing a beat, Bob said, "Get back to the office as fast as you can! You need to protect your leader. Hurry."

It had turned very dark by now and the high winds made it difficult to control her car but Bob's humor helped Susie remain calm in spite of her fear.

When she got back to the office, the other employees were gathered together to decide what steps they should take in case the tornado hit their building. Bob walked into the room and, very seriously, asked for their attention. The room became silent as he proceeded.

"Listen. We are going to incorporate a new Emergency Measures Plan for the office—starting right now."

Pause for effect.

"If the tornado hits—in fact, any time there is a similar event—the closest female staff member will immediately lie on top of the company leader—that being me—to save him from danger. Oh, and I'm going back to my office to write up a schedule for some practice drills."

With that, he turned on his heel and walked back to his office amid shrieks of laughter.

In another office, with another executive, this statement may have prompted a call to the Labor Board and a complaint of sexual harassment in the workplace. With Bob, it is impossible for his staff to be insulted. He often comes up with things that may be construed by an outsider as being politically incorrect. His employees know that he is without discrimination or malice and he uses "old school" humor to diffuse tense situations. Simply put, he has a charismatic personality and they love him, warts and all.

Susie had originally been hired for one contract for East Side Mario's. The company's growth had resulted in more work and there seemed to be no end in sight. Her position had become full-time, she had moved to Grande Prairie and she already had a few memorable exchanges with Bob. He passed her in the hallway frequently but was usually deep in thought. One day, as they crossed paths, he suddenly stopped in recognition. "Are you working for us again?"

Susie smiled a bit as she responded, "Actually I've never left."

"For how long?"

Susie burst out laughing as she told an incredulous Bob, "Uhhh, eight months."

He didn't forget her after that. Moreover, he became intrigued by a young woman who had no qualms about risking her job by standing her ground and speaking up for herself.

Ryan had been signed to play volleyball in Dunkurque, France. The European Volleyball League is the goal of most young players and very few Canadian players reach this level of success. The scope of this accomplishment was not lost on the twenty-five year old from Fort St.John, BC.

On a professional level, going to France was a great move. On a personal level, however, it was demoralizing. Ryan was younger than most of his team-mates and he didn't speak French.

As well, he had nurtured his sports ability around a life of exercise and clean living. This was contradictory to the lifestyle of most of the European ballplayers who felt that womanizing and hard-drinking was almost their contractual obligation to their fans. After a couple of weeks of feeling absolutely alone in a strange land, Ryan was miserable. He called his father and told him he was going to quit the team and come home. He wanted Bob to say "Come home, son. Here's your ticket."

Bob wasn't buying it. He listened while his son pleaded his case.

Ryan clearly remembers Bob's words," You made a commitment. Be a man. You don't get anything from quitting. I'll visit. I'll send you money or whatever you need but DO NOT QUIT."

The response wasn't the one that Ryan wanted to hear. He wanted his father to feel sorry for him, to support his decision, but Bob saw the situation in a different light. He knew that his son had signed a contract and had a responsibility to his team; that he had been given the choice of working with him or playing professional ball.

Bob told Ryan that he loved him but he would be prouder of him if he acted like the man he knew he was.

If Ryan had been miserable before the call, he was even more miserable after Bob hung up the phone. He knew his father was right but that didn't help his homesickness.

Bob may have seemed stern on the phone but, as usual, his heart turned to mush when he thought of his son sitting alone on his days off.

Within a week, Bob dispatched Marj, her husband Herb and Ryan's fourteen year old brother Connor to France for a visit. Ryan's mood lifted considerably.

Bob's insistence for Ryan to stick with his decision proved to be wise counsel. The experience not only strengthened Ryan's belief in morals, values and commitment but it also resulted in his obtaining a Professional Volleyball championship.

"Through struggle comes strength." Bob taught Ryan that edict and he has come to live by it.

After one last summer with the Canadian National Team in Winnipeg, Ryan returned to Grande Prairie to live with Bob, Carrie and Connor and to run volleyball camps for a few months. He also became totally smitten with a young teacher from Prince George named Allison Lloyd; so smitten that, when he landed in Argentina that fall, he came to one strong realization: if he wanted the girl, this would have to be his last volleyball tour.

By November Ryan was working alongside his father in Grande Prairie.

He was welcomed with open arms. Bob not only wanted to have his son at home, he needed him. The surge in building and expansion was spreading the employee pool very thin.

Staff members were working long hours and it was a horrendous time for managers. The employee shortage in the area created a situation where people jumped jobs at the first offer of a pay increase and staff loyalty was rare.

The Pomeroy Group was no exception to the fragile staffing situation and the lack of experienced food and beverage managers.

Bob was very happy when Julius Van Wyk showed up at his office.

Julius had been working in London when he met a young woman from Grande Prairie and immediately fell in love. He wasn't keen on England and, with a poor economic situation back in his home of South Africa, he found it very easy to pull up roots and follow Kathy to Canada. The trip had originally been intended to be a visit but Kathy's father had other ideas.

After he learned about Julius' extensive food and beverage career, he called his friend Bob Pomeroy. He knew Bob needed experienced managers and he insisted that Bob meet his future son-in-law.

Bob always tries to accommodate friends so he agreed. He told Julius to meet him for breakfast at Ricky's at 6:15 AM. He would give him a half hour. That was his only free moment—and Julius' introduction to Bob's work ethic.

The two men had breakfast and just talked about life in general. The short meeting turned into two hours and then they headed to the Pomeroy building. After Julius was introduced to Raphael, Bob disappeared into his own office. They had just touched on Julius' restaurant and beverage experience, when Bob returned to interrupt. He told Raphael that he wanted Julius to start as soon as possible.

Bob's reputation as a hotel owner can not be questioned. Today, in both Fort St. John and Grande Prairie, there are many large companies that direct their employees to reserve rooms only at hotels managed by the Pomeroy Group. Finning Tractor, for example, is a loyal customer because that company has come to know for certain that the rooms, beds and service will exceed expectations.

Many years earlier, when Bob was first assigned to the Fort St. John hotel, the owners sent him to a Holiday Inn in Vancouver to take one of their ten-day crash courses in hotel management. Bob became a hotel man with a capital "H." He loved it. He knew he had found his calling and his future. He instantly understood the difference between operating a good hotel and operating a very good hotel. He kept his eyes and ears open and quickly learned how to detect and prevent employee theft, one of the industry's biggest problems.

Millions of dollars are lost annually in hotel kitchens simply by staff setting bottles of wine or frozen meat just outside the back door or in a dumpster for retrieval after a shift. Millions in revenues are lost when rooms have to be "comp'd" (provided free of charge) due to guests complaining about dirty bathrooms, lumpy beds or broken amenities.

Bob not only managed the business aspect of the Pioneer Inn, he talked to guests and he asked questions. He soon grasped the fact that people will pay a premium rate to be guaranteed quality and guests will return time after time if service was consistent. Instead of continuing the former trend of hotels in the area (running the most basic of operations and undercutting each other's rates), Bob upgraded the Pioneer Inn and added first class amenities.

Then he raised the prices to reflect the superior accommodation. This move set a precedent for upgraded hospitality services in northern BC and Alberta.

Bob learned the importance of doing regular walk-throughs (inspections) and he conducts them at his own properties as well as at properties he is considering buying. He trains his managers to check around back doors, to watch employees leaving, to run fingers along ledges; to use a flashlight to look under beds and behind toilet bowls—even to check the dumpsters.

His attention to detail and cleanliness has made him the ultimate hotelier. He notices every one and every thing entering and leaving his hotels and he expects the same diligence from his managers. A guest at a Pomeroy property should never have to call down to the front desk to report a dirty bathtub or broken television. A guest at a Pomeroy hotel should never see stained carpeting, dusty plants or burnt out light bulbs. That's the way Bob wants it and he knows that his guests want the very same. He has never changed his policy of putting the guests first.

Everything gets set aside when it comes to business.

When his friend (and cousin's husband) Ron Barker drove his motorcycle into the lounge of the Pioneer Inn and caused a near-riot during an important function, the lounge manager, Janice McKinnon, was more than furious. When Ron returned to the hotel, she told him to get out and stay out. Bob had executed some revenge on Ron so had put the incident behind him. Not Janice. Ron remained barred from her lounge area and he complained to Bob. This time, Bob backed his staff. Ron's prank had frightened paying patrons, messed up the carpets and ended a lucrative night's income for the lounge. Ron was "persona non grata" for the next week. It clearly showed Bob's intolerance for anything that might compromise his business reputation—and it gave Janice a few extra days to cool off.

Bob always tried to teach his children the business from the ground up. He taught them that the best hotel manager is one who treats a hotel as if he is the owner, that the hotel represents the manager personally.

No one taught Bob how to succeed in business. He just figured things out for himself. He knew that, if he liked the best, surely other people liked the best as well. He learned quickly that, if he could be the best, people would like to be with him. He had been low man on the totem pole during his growing years and he was determined that his children would never feel that pain. He started teaching them how to be independent from an early age; how to get respect by doing things right. He didn't simply tell them what to do, he showed them through example.

Whether it was running his property, managing the clothing store or building a hotel, Bob always put the time and effort required to get it done. He learned how to do everything himself so he wouldn't have to depend on anyone but himself if required. He wanted his children to take pride in whatever job they did and to always do their best. It was never a point of "Do what I say" when it came to work of any kind. It was always "Do what I do" and all of Bob's children say they learned more from watching their father than anywhere else.

When Bob is raising money or getting a project completed, he literally does not rest. Weeks may pass with him going to bed at three AM and then rising again at five AM to be at his desk before seven. He survives on sheer energy and an occasional cat nap. Even now that he's past sixty, he drives himself on the same routine. For most people, it would be a risk to health. There are a few who can manage well on the napping principle.

Bob Hope lived to be almost one hundred and he followed the same regime. He would do a show, tour the troops, fly all night and start all over the first thing in the morning. The reporters on his USO tours couldn't keep up with him. Hope swore by his frequent cat naps throughout the day and he remained alert and energetic right to his last days.

Sometimes, near exhaustion combined with a heavy meal and ample amounts of wine can bring on a nap when least expected. One day, after hours of tedious financial discussions without one minute of break, Bob and a group of investors headed to the Barcelona for dinner. Bob knew he was tired as he had just a few hours sleep the night before and he knew he would have to minimize his wine intake to stay awake.

Before the group sat down, Bob noticed Susie was working in the office. He told her that he was totally "beat" and he asked her switch his wineglass for a smaller one so he could just sip a bit to be polite. Susie found a smaller glass for Bob and then returned to work. She was busy making adjustments to the IT equipment between the office and the kitchen so it was some time before she found a moment to peek into the dining room.

It was a very quiet scene. Bob was fast asleep sitting up in his chair and the investors were murmuring quietly to each other. Susie called the General Manager over and said that they should do something.

Without any hesitation, the manager walked into the noisy kitchen, tapped for attention and coolly announced:" Please keep it down in here. We have dinner guests trying to have a nap."

Nothing more was said. Eventually Bob and another guest who had also nodded off snapped awake and the evening concluded.

The little nap restored Bob's energy and he was back to his congenial personality.

Bob has the ability to transfer his uncanny energy to others. The project sites generally move along at a respectable pace but, if Bob happens to drop by to do a walk-through, there is an immediate buzz and the tempo is quickened. He doesn't arrive with fanfare. He simply appears and takes an interest. He asks questions, makes comments, hands out compliments and then leaves. Long after he has gone, the job site has a different energy because Bob seems to instill a sense of pride of workmanship in his crew. He doesn't coddle people. He treats everyone as a capable, equal adult and so he inspires an adult work ethic.

Once you've worked for Bob for any length of time, he becomes your friend. You can go to him and discuss not only work issues but also personal matters and he listens without discrimination or criticism.

He has the ability to conceptualize. He isn't afraid of hard work and he puts in grueling long hours to get things done. He has the ability to find enough investors to provide the needed money to get a project underway and, in the past, he never turned away a potential investor, no matter how small the amount the person had to invest.

When he was beginning his career, he was able to work with large numbers of very small investors under the old "close friends and associates" clause. Unfortunately, the changes to the Securities Exchange Commission prevent any small investors from participating in large projects now.

Bob keeps himself so busy that he not only gives his managers the authority to make decisions and solve problems, he expects them to do it. He allows anyone to make mistakes as long as they admit them, learn from them and then move on. His managers don't always agree with things that Bob has requested of them but they absolutely respect him.

As Raphael stated, "It's impossible not to respect a man who has accomplished so much. Bob has the energy of three men; he has the foresight and natural instincts that are necessary to seize opportunity; he's never afraid to go ahead with an idea. Bob not only meets challenges, he invites them."

Although Bob understands and accepts most aspects of business requirements, he hates life insurance. He hates the concept and he hates the pages of fine print and clauses. He hates the very idea of paying great sums of money to a company that will only give out a return if he dies.

In 1989 Bob was carrying a half million dollar personal policy. When he started working in Fairview, his policy got transferred from Grande

Prairie to the local office to the desk of Dave Thompson. Dave was the same man who had hired him to manage the Dunvegan Motor Inn.

When Dave called him in to review this policy, Bob was very cranky and almost belligerent. In spite of his dislike of the concept, however, he recognized that the policy gave some protection for his children and he never missed a premium.

After Bob bought the Igloo and the Canadian, his investment partners demanded adequate partnership insurance. Although Bob still hated insurance, he liked Dave so he called him. For Bob, this also saved time with casual conversation and limitless personal questions. It was a matter of dealing with "the devil you know." Dave placed the partnership coverage policies.

A few years later, on a Saturday night around ten PM., Dave Thompson's phone rang at home. It was Bob enquiring "What's up? Got anything going on right now?"

When Dave assured him that he wasn't busy with anything at the moment, Bob told him that he was calling from a shareholders' meeting in Fort McMurray. There were four partners who needed a two million dollar policy each and they needed them placed immediately.

Dave got off the phone and called his friend, Dr. Cooper. The Doctor owned a twin engine plane and liked to make use of it, especially if the costs were covered by business. By eight AM, Dave and the doctor arrived in Fort McMurray. Doctor Cooper completed four medicals and picked up his cheque for his services. Dave wrote up four $2,000,000 insurance policies. Needless to say, Bob's partners were impressed with his connections as well as Dave's service.

As Bob's deals increased, so did his need for even more coverage.

Most of the wheeling and dealing was done at the last minute and often there was no time for the usual paperwork involved with placing large insurance policies through a company headquartered in Eastern Canada.

After a lot of wrangling and personal assurances, Dave managed to convince the insurance carrier to issue a large group of generic policies that could be transferred from one deal to the next so long as the principal partners remained the same. This was not a normal procedure for an insurer. It was a special arrangement made to accommodate the Pomeroy Group and his agent. If one particular project lasted only a few months, for example, and then replaced by a new project, Dave could, by the stroke of a pen, transfer the insurance to the new project. Ten of these large policies on Bob's life were placed in one day! Needless to say, with the new restrictions placed on all insurers, such a thing would be impossible to accomplish today.

Who would have thought that Bob Pomeroy would, within ten years, go from being Dave's salaried hotel manager to become his most important client?

Bob's partners and his friends soon became Dave's clients as well. The Pomeroy Group kept getting bigger.

Usually when Bob called, Dave came running but Dave's company was growing just as quickly thanks to the association with Bob.

Dave wanted to be certain that the Pomeroy Group always had excellent service so he assigned an agent to be dedicated exclusively to Bob's needs. He thought he was doing Bob a favor.

When the new agent dropped by the office, Bob said he was too busy to see him. When the agent called for an appointment, Bob wouldn't speak to him. When the company needed a half million dollar policy placed, Bob called Dave personally. He was very explicit and he was not very happy with Dave turning him over to a "lackey" from the office. Bob told Dave in no uncertain terms that he was too busy to break in a new agent and that he fully expected Dave to handle his business personally. Bob knew that he had earned personal attention from Dave and Dave recognized his mistake. He reassigned the new agent, placed the policy that day personally and returned to handling the Pomeroy account.

In 2005, Bob needed to add a $10 Million policy to his insurance coverage. Dave arranged an appointment for Bob with a Doctor in Fairview. To get everything done in one day, the tests and x-rays started early in the morning so Bob stayed overnight with Dave and his wife. First stop was the ECG at the hospital.

A little more than half way through the procedure, the technician stopped and told Bob not to move, that he was in the middle of a heart attack.

Bob told the technician that he was NOT having a heart attack; that he was perfectly fine and he was leaving. Dave was summoned into the room to lend assistance and, only after both Bob and Dave swore to go directly to the Doctor's office on the grounds of the hospital, the technician let them leave.

When they got to the office, the Doctor was standing by the door. He read the ECG and said that he had to admit Bob to hospital; that he was, indeed, having a heart attack according to the report. Bob pushed his way inside and refused to leave.

He was adamant about being in perfect condition and informed the Doctor that he had just recently undergone a complete physical at the prestigious Mayo clinic in Scottsdale and had received full clearance.

"In fact", Bob said, "I brought the medical reports with me in case Dave needed them for the insurance. They're at his office."

Hedging his bet somewhat, the Doctor insisted that Bob stay in his care until Dave could fetch the medical reports. When he read the reports, he was astonished. Apparently, Bob was more fit than most active sixty-one year olds. The Mayo Clinic's investigations found that Bob has an unusual blockage on one side of his heart. It is not life-threatening but its presence sends of warning signals in regular ECGs.

The doctor let Bob leave and the new policy was issued.

Twenty-Eight

"Business is a game, the greatest game in the world if you know how to play it"

—THOMAS WATSON

In the spring of 2004, Carrie, Bob and the Pomeroy Group owned about twenty-eight percent of the properties in their portfolio. One hundred and twenty investors owned the other seventy-two percent. According to Carrie, two of the major investors became "demanding and aggressive." She admits that they had a right to be expect more control over their investment as they both were enormously successful and had seemingly unlimited finances. They had provided much needed capital when Bob needed it very quickly and they had provided that capital without audited statements.

Both of these businessmen recognized the potential in northern Alberta and BC and they knew that Bob had started a real "growth" product. They also knew that their financial capabilities, education and contacts were far broader than those possessed by either Carrie or Bob. When the company began to acquire properties even faster than expected, they started pushing for more reporting and more meetings.

Bob and Carrie had been married less than two years, they had Connor living with them full time and they started to feel as if they were being pushed from all sides.

It was not unusual to get a call from one of the investors demanding a meeting the next afternoon—even if it was a Sunday and plans had already been made.

It became more difficult to balance personal family commitments with the demands of business partners, this being made even more awkward by the fact that the two major partners were not local.

The spontaneous meetings were one or two day marathons. Working with local investors, Carrie and Bob were more accustomed to lunch or dinner updates on a flexible weekly or monthly basis.

Bob wanted to expand again. He had locations in mind but no cash of his own. He knew he could not go back to the same pair of investors without giving up even more control of his company as well as the decision-making power.

The only solution was to buy out the investor interest in the hotels. In order to avoid any accusation of preferential treatment, they would need to arrange sufficient financing to be able to buy out all one hundred and twenty investors in nine hotel partnerships.

If they wanted to develop more properties and keep control of the company, they would also need to refinance all the projects based on current values. That move would provide the cash resources they would require to operate independently.

Initially, Bob was reluctant to start the ball rolling. He appreciated the financial commitments of all the smaller investors. Many were family members and most were friends who had reinvested over the years.

He certainly did not want to "rock the boat" with the two major investors either. Their recent participation had been instrumental to his success and he did not want to do anything to endanger the relationship.

Carrie, however, was insistent that they pursue other options. She convinced Bob that there would be no harm in at least making some enquiries.

Mike Didyk's son, Mel, was an entrepreneurial freelancer who often referred associates to Watershed Capital in Vancouver. When Bob discussed his situation with Mike, he suggested that Mel get involved; that he may be able to help. After reviewing the key points of the Pomeroy proposal, Mel introduced Bob and Carrie to the principal partner of Watershed Capital, Richard Whittall. Whittall saw potential in the proposal and began his due diligence.

The first thing he needed was facts and figures.

Every property in the Pomeroy Group operated as a separate company and every company had a different year-end. Many of the properties were newly started or just completed. In most cases, there were no financial statements available or audited year-ends. It took almost a month for Carrie to provide suitable documentation to meet the demands of Watershed.

By the beginning of May, Whittall had reviewed enough material to at least know that the deal was going to be much bigger than he had expected.

The "little company from Grande Prairie" had been flying under the radar in the investment community and Watershed wanted to become part of its growth. He called in for reinforcements, and investment banker, Joseph Fodor, was added to the team. Joe had his own successful firm but, for the Pomeroy deal, he became an integral part of the Watershed team. Joe's role would be not only to find the money but also to help structure the deal to ensure that it was completed.

Bob and Carrie flew to Vancouver to meet with Richard, Mel and Joe and they worked together to complete the proposal using just spreadsheets, bank statements and monthly operating reports.

Over the next fourteen months, Joe Fodor would fly to Grande Prairie almost every week. Richard Whittall and Joe worked as a team and Richard made almost as many trips to Grande Prairie as he was heavily involved with Joe in the structuring and negotiations with the various existing partners.

Joe became, "de facto", the Head of Finance for the Pomeroy Company and prepared the paperwork necessary to satisfy not only the major financial institutions they would be approaching but also each and every one of the one hundred and twenty investors.

A lawyer himself, Joe knew that Bob needed some powerful corporate tax advice and extensive legal work for all the contracts. He knew the then head tax attorney for Borden Ladner Gervais (BLG) in Vancouver, Robert Kopstien, and after Robert was familiarized with the finer points of the legal requirements, he referred the project to BLG's Calgary office. From that point on, a BLG Calgary team led by attorney Marilyn Paterson handled the Pomeroy tax portfolio.

With the numbers crunched and a sense of equity established, Watershed concluded that an MBO (Management buyout) was the best way to go. In that scenario, they would bring in one major investment partner, pay out the partners and have the Pomeroys own much more of their company.

Watershed felt that the equity in just five of the hotel properties was enough to provide cash to pay out the partners for all nine properties and so they began pursuing financing sources.

Although comfortable with the working relationship, Bob and Carrie returned to Grande Prairie without signing any final commitment with Watershed.

Richard Whittall and Joe made a list of potential partners: the two top contenders being Manulife and the Stern Group. Joe had introduced the Stern Group to Watershed and had worked with them in the past; he also had close ties with top executives with Manulife. He knew that either company could handle the deal.

GE Capital was already involved with the Pomeroy Group on some of their mortgages. Watershed worked closely with Edward Khediguian (GE's then Vice President in charge of hotel real estate finance for Canada) in particular, to increase their participation in the overall financing plan.

The paperwork that Watershed provided fulfilled the due diligence requirement for GE Capital to increase their mortgages substantially and become the senior debt provider. Over the next years, GE Capital would continue to be a mortgage lender for the Pomeroy Group and the account manager for GE Capital in Vancouver, Salim Gulamani, would become a valued connection for the Pomeroy Group.

For the large investment financing, there remained two options. Bob flew Richard Whittall from Watershed, as well as both the Stern people and the Manulife team, to Grande Prairie for meetings and then he took them all to view each property listed in the proposal.

Joe Fodor did not want Manulife to underestimate the opportunity simply because Grande Prairie was so far from their head offices in Toronto. He took things one step further. He called one of his former partners, Warren Thomson, and told him about the Pomeroy deal. Warren in turn referred the proposal directly to Bill Eeuwes of Manulife. In January of 2005, Joe spoke to Bill and told him that he absolutely had to fly to Grande Prairie to meet with Bob Pomeroy and see the operations in person.

He also told Bill that he would have to get on a plane the very next day. As an afterthought, Joe added that perhaps Bill should take a warm coat because it was currently minus 35 degrees Celsius.

When Bill choked slightly, Joe assured him that it would be worth the trip; that he believed the deal would be good for both parties. Bill got on the plane. (An interesting note to add is that Joe's friend, Warren Thomson, is now the Chief Investment Officer for Manulife)

After the weekend of discussions and property inspections, the principals from both the Stern Group and Manulife expressed their interest in proceeding.

Stern's people did their own extensive due diligence. Kevin Budd was a recent addition to the Stern team and, after the initial trip north, he flew back to Grande Prairie to get more comprehensive details and to see just how the operations were managed.

Tom Vukota from Manulife also returned along with a Senior Manager, Kent Kirkpatrick.

Ron Stern and Bob could relate well to each other personally but Bob and Carrie both felt that Ron's partner would insist on micro managing the company if they became involved. Their suspicions were validated when the draft proposal was presented. The Stern proposal had included clauses for explicit authority to take immediate possession of any property at any time they felt it was warranted. They would also want fifty per cent ownership of the company. The comfort level changed. This proposal sounded like things would not be changed much from having the two original controlling investors.

Tom Vukota had been impressed with the Pomeroy Group and with the potential of northern Alberta and BC. He returned to Grande Prairie a third time with a Senior Financial Analyst to review the company's bank statements and accounting records. He felt certain that the analyst would confirm his own positive opinion of the business operations.

The immediate reaction was not good. The Analyst was especially concerned about the absence of audited statements—a usual prerequisite for any investment of such scope. He would not give his stamp of approval.

Fortunately, Tom believed in the strength of the Pomeroy Group and in Bob's personal commitment for the success of the company. He left with the promise to try to persuade his head office to move forward.

Feeling uncertain about the final decision, Bob and Carrie did not want to depend solely on Manulife. They did not want to have to start all over again if Manulife backed out of the financing. Because they had to keep their restructuring plans confidential, there was a certain sense of urgency. They continued their discussions with Ron Stern and Kevin Budd in Vancouver.

Both companies were solid financially and both companies were prepared to consider the total amount of financing needed.

Bob and Carrie liked the personal, down-to-earth manner of the Stern team but they still were not comfortable with the amount of control the company wanted in their proposal.

Manulife, on the other hand, was interested solely in being an investor. That company's mandate was not to manage hotels; the mandate was, and still is, to invest in companies that already had good management.

In the early negotiations, Bob played his role like a fox. He kept up the façade of "no formal education", "hick from the farm" and kept his eyes and ears open. As time passed, the scope of Bob's intelligence became obvious. He absorbed information like a sponge.

Manulife was the preferred option.

On one evening in late August in Vancouver, a dinner was arranged with Ron, Kevin and two others sitting along one side of the table and Bob, Carrie, Richard Whittall and Joe Fodor along the other.

It was meant to be a congenial evening of business and pleasure but the seating plan was a good indication of the actual atmosphere.

The Stern group tried their best to pressure Bob into making at least a verbal commitment to them and Watershed. They mentioned the fact that their office on the West Coast was so much closer than Toronto. Bob finally pushed back his chair and commented that: "In my experience, where there's water, there's bound to be some sharks."

The comment was followed by nervous laughter on both sides but it was obvious that Bob was leaning towards Manulife. Their terms were far less onerous and, best of all, Joe had negotiated a twenty-five per cent ownership of the company if Manulife were to become the investment partner—half of the position that the Stern Group was demanding.

Stern did not give up easily. Knowing that Manulife was moving forward slowly, they hired Stewart Prescott to crunch the figures again and do a forward analysis.

Both Kevin Budd and Stewart "got" the Pomeroy Group and they wanted the deal. They flew up to Grande Prairie again to try personally to convince Bob to change his mind.

They all thought that Bob was a great "hotel guy" but they believed that he needed more professional help with investment financing and financial reporting. They felt they would be protecting both their equity and Bob's by demanding an active management role.

It was too late. All bets were off. Manulife's head office team had taken the advice of Vukota. They were prepared to move forward.

The Pomeroy Group turned total focus on the deal with Manulife for the development financing.

By the time that aspect of the restructuring was proceeding, the company had received the proceeds from the Watershed/GE mortgage loan and the Pomeroy Group had bought out most of the smaller investors. The Pomeroy Group, Joe Ferraro, Bill De Silva and Cam Christianson now owned the lions' share of the nine hotels.

When Manulife began working with the Pomeroy Group, Tom Vukota spent a lot of time in Grande Prairie. His initial impression of Bob was that he was a charismatic host, a very focused and determined businessperson. As time went on, he saw Bob in his role as an employer and noticed that he was very approachable. "If an employee or associate disagrees with him, he asks them to validate their point. If he's wrong, he will change."

In October 2004, Manulife presented their "Term sheet" for review and discussion. A second "Term sheet" was drawn up in December of 2004. There was also an extensive Inter-Party agreement to be drawn up between GE Capital and Manulife with the equity security positions being carefully protected and clearly defined for all the subordinated debts, the mezzanine loan and the mortgages. Borden Ladner Gervais had their work cut out for them.

Bob and Carrie were spending that Christmas and New Year's in Hawaii.

They were using this time to plan the best way to go ahead on their own, how to remove even the larger investors and how to approach them all without alienating them. On December 23, when they felt secure with their decision, they contacted Manulife and verbally agreed to a tentative deal.

On December 30, Manulife responded and an agreement was struck.

Surprisingly, on New Year's Eve, Bill de Silva phoned them in Hawaii with notice that he and Joe Ferraro wanted to reduce their ownership. They wanted to know exactly what Bob could afford to take over. Bob told Bill that he would call them back in a week, after he got home.

The same day, the Controller of the company faxed them his immediate resignation.

Bob and Carrie spent the next few days discussing just how much they were prepared to commit to the buyouts.

Bill and Joe, meanwhile, unaware of any restructuring or refinancing plans, informed Cam Christianson that they had asked Bob to buy them out of their investment in the hotels. This would, of course, place undue financial hardship on the company. Cam did not make his position known right away. Before Cam made a decision, he wanted as much information as possible to be certain that this was the best move for his own interests. Once he knew the amount of ownership that Bill and Joe were forcing, he joined forces with them, possibly feeling that such financial pressure could leave the company in a fragile state and thus affect his own shares.

With the knowledge at hand, the investors decided to divest themselves of as much of the hotel ownership as possible and they asked Bob to buy out the maximum the company could afford.

They were surprised when he said, "We'll buy all of it."

They had been unaware that he had been raising money from outside sources and their reaction reflected their shock. They changed their demand and now insisted that Bob buy them out of everything they had invested in—not just hotels, but land and restaurants as well.

Bob's quick response and the resulting increased demands caused more than a few anxious moments and a lot more compromise.

The Term Sheet from Manulife had covered the cost of buying the partners out of the nine hotels only. It was also supposed to provide Bob with four million dollars for his own investment and Carrie with two million dollars personally.

To meet the new demands of his partners, Bob would need all the proceeds of the Term sheet, including both his and Carrie's portion of the proceeds. That still was not enough.

He would need, above that, another two million dollars to buy them out fully.

To add insult to injury, property taxes were coming due in the spring.

Joe Fodor had run into many challenges when he was putting together the exact figures needed to buy out each partner. If Bob gave him a list for Bill de Silva's shares in a few properties, for example, Joe would begin to negotiate for those properties but then Bill would add, "Well, sure, but what about this other property?"

This domino effect turned up repeatedly and the actual buy-out figure snowballed. At the end of the day, to get all the investment partners to agree, Bob was forced to pay much more than he had initially estimated. The original investment proposal to Manulife had been $25 Million. It ended being $50 Million.

In June 2005, thirteen months from the beginning of the deal, the financing closed and the last of the partners were gone.

To conclude the negotiations, Bob, Carrie and Ryan flew to Toronto. The offices were a distinct contrast to their own corporate headquarters in Grande Prairie. Marble floors, cathedral ceilings and mahogany desks were accented with original works of art. Wide hallways were dotted with sculpture and fresh floral displays.

When they entered the corporate dining room for lunch, they were met with elegant tables set with exquisite custom-designed porcelain and crystal. The chef offered a menu to rival any four star restaurant. In Carrie's words, they felt like "the Beverly Hillbillies."

None of them fully realized that it was growth businesses like their own that helped Manulife grow to its successful position; that they, in fact, were the valued guests at the table.

When the undertaking had started, the Pomeroy family owned just twenty-eight percent of their company and they had one hundred and twenty partners. Their equity position was worth $18 Million.

After the Manulife deal was concluded, they owned seventy-five percent of their company, had just one partner and their equity position was $85 Million.

That was the good news. The not-so-good news was that the company had no cash to fund future projects; there was still no Senior Financial Officer; and Bob and Carrie were losing a lot of sleep.

Carrie cut back on the work she was doing for her own company and she assumed most of the daily financial duties for the Pomeroy Group. Then she and Bob began to look for a way to increase revenue. They did not have to wait long. The solution was right in their own back yard.

Less than two months after the Manulife deal closed, Bob and Carrie were in Hinton with Bob's sisters and their husbands. When they checked into the Holiday Inn, they were disappointed to find run-down rooms, dirty bathrooms and uncomfortable beds. They could not help but notice that, in spite of the conditions, the hotel was fully booked. Shockingly, the room rate was $40.00 a night more than at any of the Pomeroy hotels.

The next morning, they all discussed the difference in the accommodation.

The Pomeroy Group was now operating with 800 "doors" (rooms, in hotel vernacular). Bob's hotels were meticulously clean, the beds were top-of-the-line and each hotel offered a full breakfast to guests.

An increase of $40.00 per night at even the minimum operating level of 60% occupancy overall meant an immediate increase in income of almost twenty thousand dollars per day—more than a half million dollars per month—over $6 Million a year.

When they got back to the office, the hotel managers were advised that the room rates were being increased immediately.

In early 2006, less than a year after the Manulife deal closed, Kent Kirkpatrick called Carrie about the income statement he was reviewing. In his words: the "figures are scaring me."

In the original financial projections, the income from the nine hotel properties had been estimated at four million dollars for the full fiscal year. That estimated income was strong enough for Manulife to become an investment partner. According to Kent's statements, in the single month of March, the nine hotels had brought in two million dollars. Manulife was very happy with their new investment partner.

Both Bob and Ryan are clearly attuned to every nuance of negotiation and they had both impressed everyone they met with their business acumen.

Today, Tom calls Bob ". . . a strong example of a true entrepreneur. He welcomes hard work and he is a contagious optimist. He sees problems as challenges, not hurdles." He continued, "Knowing his background and his journey to success makes you respect him."

A person who gets one idea for a project, completes that and succeeds immediately is not really an entrepreneur; he is just a lucky guy with one good idea. An entrepreneur is a person who continues to have visions and then pursues each one of them. If he fails with one, he uses that failure to learn and then he tries again. He keeps doing what he knows or loves best and makes sure to avoid making the same mistakes.

Bob does exemplify the model of a true entrepreneur. When he wakes up, he tells himself that this is going to be a good day. Like a true entrepreneur, he knows that when he has a setback, he can recover. Just fifty percent of success is based on tangible properties. The other fifty percent is based on the entrepreneur's mind and Bob's mind is set on "Go" each and every morning.

Twenty-Nine

"It is work, work that one delights in, that is the surest guarantor of happiness. But even here it is work that has to be earned by labor in one's earlier years. A man should labor so hard in youth that everything he does subsequently is easy by comparison."
—ASHLEY MONTAGU, "THE AMERICAN WAY OF LIFE' PUTNAM 1967

Bob has never fit the mold of an executive and he, perhaps unknowingly, has run his business and his life according to J. Paul Getty's premise that "no one can possibly achieve any real or lasting success, or get rich, by being a conformist."

Being a non-conformist in daily life can lead to a person becoming known as a free spirit; in business, being a non-conformist can lead to great successes. In today's politically correct world, being a non-conformist in employee relations can lead to trouble.

In the former office in the Focus building, one female employee was very well endowed. According to several staff members, while the girl professed shyness, she continued to dress provocatively. Bob is always very gregarious and friendly around the office and occasionally he couldn't help but notice her physical attributes with a smile. One day, when her outfit was very tight and revealing, he couldn't help but say "Uh, your shirt is very nice today."

Carrie usually tolerated Bob's jokes but on this particular day, she reached the end of her patience with him.

The situation was already sensitive as it was a long weekend and some of the employees had been asked to come in and help move files to the new office. When Bob's remark seemed to embarrass the girl, Carrie snapped at him with, "Stop it, Bob. She's a virgin." Although Carrie's words were intended to advise Bob of the girl's innocence, they were said loudly and abruptly. They were also said in front of coworkers and were taken as an insult. Embarrassed, the young woman resigned and then reported the incident to the Labor Relations Board.

A few days later, Susie and Raphael were in Bob's office when he got a call from the government agency. When the labor rep asked Bob if the company had a sexual harassment policy in place, Bob didn't have a clue what he was talking about. He indicated to Susie and Raphael that he was lost. The concept of having strict guidelines and policies for employees had never been necessary before. Bob's company had grown faster than he had anticipated and the growth brought him into a whole new world of administration. Needless to say, the new and improved Pomeroy Group soon developed a sexual harassment policy and put it in place in all the hotels, restaurants and job sites as well as the corporate office.

Carrie continued to fume over the complaint to the Labor Relations Board. She felt that the former employee had been fully aware of how she was dressing, had been less than cooperative at work at the best of times and she had taken Carrie's words completely out of context. It is unknown if Carrie ever did sign the policy statement, but the Labor Relations Board did not pursue any action and the matter was dropped.

By this time, it was 2005 and the company was still moving forward.

Bob and Carrie, along with Cam Christianson, wanted to buy four Boston Pizza franchises: one for each of St. Paul, Wainwright, High Level and Fort Nelson.

The Boston Pizza franchise manager did not feel comfortable about selling franchises as far north as High Level so he turned the initial application down for that location. Bob would not accept that decision and he pursued the matter further up the administrative chain.

Fortunately, one of the original founders of Boston Pizza used to drive trucks north of Fort St. John and he knew the potential of the area. He interceded and told his manager to approve the contract. Bob and Cam got all four franchises they wanted.

Based on Cam's projections, Carrie had found enough investors to form a group to build the four restaurants.

Cam chose St. Paul and High Level as the first two locations and he built them as quickly as possible. Unfortunately, once they were completed, the costs were over budget by more than one million dollars. When Carrie got the records for the projects, she saw that not only was the funding going to be short for the proposed four properties, but neither Bob nor Cam had turned over payment for their equity.

Carrie was not happy and neither were any of the other investors. The investment group split into two factions. Cam took the St. Paul restaurant and the rights for Wainwright; Bob and Carrie with their investors took the High Level restaurant and the rights for Fort Nelson. In other words, each investment group retained one operating restaurant and one pending franchise.

In High Level, Bob's group of investors was doing well with the Boston Pizza they had built near the Super 8.

In Fort Nelson, Bob looked for another investor and found one in Doug Andrews. Doug owned the IGA in Fort Nelson and was an astute businessperson. He knew the food trade and he knew the people in the area. Not only did he become an investor, he also assumed the role of managing partner. The Fort Nelson location of Boston Pizza was built relatively quickly. It is still owned by Bob, Carrie, Doug and a few others.

Soon Bob started looking at expanding to High Prairie.

The perfect spot for a hotel was owned by the Peavine Metis Settlement.

Although the Peavine Group was already associated with the Pomeroy Group through the Ramada partnership for Clairmont, they were not prepared to sell Bob all the land they owned along the highway in High Prairie. They were even hesitant to sell the ten prime acres that the Pomeroy Group wanted to develop.

Fred Cunningham sat on the Peavine council at that time and he clearly recalls the arguments that ensued before a deal could be reached. The Metis, like many aboriginal groups in Canada, had learned to be extremely cautious with any deals involving their land holdings. The land was all that the Metis actually owned so they were even more suspicious of any overtures. Unlike Indian reserves, the Metis settlements were given only the land and the usage rights to one foot below the land. While the Indian reserves owned all the mineral and oil rights under their land, the Metis could just live and farm on theirs.

Their income is produced by leasing properties to oil companies and granting access across their land.

Any other income for the settlements has to be carefully negotiated to protect the future generations.

When the Pomeroy Group first submitted their offer to purchase land for a hotel, the offer was rejected. The members of the Peavine council were not about to give away their only asset.

Then Bob stepped in personally.

He sat down with all the Council members and told them about his childhood, his struggle to make a living, and his sense of purpose for the future of his children. He told them that he was not there to argue or to make demands; that, if they spoke together as equals, surely they could work out an agreement that would be good for both sides of the table. Fred was convinced of Bob's integrity and soon the other members came around.

Eventually a deal was struck.

The Pomeroy Group and the Peavine council would share ownership of the ten acres of land; the Pomeroy Group paying their ownership portion to the Metis Settlement in cash.

The Peavine Group would then invest with the Pomeroy Group for the hotel: the Peavine Metis Settlement becoming 66% owners and the Pomeroy Group retaining 34% ownership plus being contracted for all the management.

The open, down-to-earth style of negotiations sat well with the Peavine Group and they have stayed partners with Pomeroy. Less than three years later, the Peavine Metis became major investors in the new Best Western in Dawson Creek.

Bob's easygoing nature has made him a friend of many of the Peavine members, especially the Cunningham family. Fred became the coach of the Peavine Men's Fastball Team in 2005 and the Pomeroy Group was the team sponsor. When the team captured the Canadian National Men's Fastball Championship that year, the players were proudly sporting the Pomeroy name on their jerseys. More recently, at a dinner at Bob and Carrie's one evening, when Fred's daughter mentioned her dream of some day owning her own horse, she was told to "come out to the barn tomorrow." When the whole family took a tour of the new stables the next morning, there was a surprise waiting. Bob's Arabian, "Zhivago" had a new owner: the beautiful grey horse that Bob had bought for $35,000 just a year earlier now belonged to Angel Marlo Cunningham.

Bob's generosity was a factor in the gift, to be certain, but giving away the horse was also an example of his immediate "quick fixes."

Zhivago is a beautiful stallion but he simply did not live up to Bob's high expectations for the breeding program. Based on veterinarian and maintenance expenses, the horse became an expensive pet instead of a valuable asset. Bob decided that a generous gift was a good solution.

Bob has always had a knee-jerk reaction to problems and sometimes he barks orders before assessing the larger situation.

Case in point: In the fall of 2005, Susie had worked into the night in Grande Prairie one week to correct some bugs in the system for a restaurant. Then, before six AM the next day, she drove to Fort St.John to attend to some IT problems at Egan's.

When Susie checked in to the Super 8, she found the place in turmoil. It had snowed a lot overnight and many of the housekeeping employees had not turned up for their shift. All the rooms were booked and the manager was pulling his hair out trying to keep on top of things. Susie threw her bag and computer in her room and pitched in to help with the room turnover chores. Mid-morning, Bob called her cell phone and started blustering loudly about problems at the restaurant back in Grande Prairie. Susie was knee-deep in cleaning supplies and she interrupted him to say, "You didn't need to call me about that. I fixed the problem last night."

Bob did not like her tone and responded with "I don't need some girl to talk to me like that. Get off your high horse!"

Susie was tired and more than a little fed up.

For a brief moment, she considered the "up side" of being fired and she yelled right back with,

"The equipment here is crashing, your hotel is a mess and your GIRL on her F***ING HIGH HORSE is in the middle of cleaning toilets right now so leave me alone!"

Then she hung up.

About an hour later, Susie received a second call, this time from Kevin Person of Cool Line Refrigeration. He sounded amused—and impressed. "Boy, you must have a lot of pull with Bob because right now I'm on his plane on the way to Fort St.John to fix some equipment for you."

Bob arrived the next day with ten investors. He did not say a word when he met Susie in the lobby; just gave her a hug and smiled sheepishly.

A storm blew in with a fury just after the plane landed and everyone was snowed in for three days. The snowfall may have been an act of karma.

Every room was booked at the Super 8, the restaurants were bursting at their seams and travelers were turned away at the desk. The Super 8 was always full, in fact. The investors could see clearly that Fort St.John needed another block of rooms.

These investors had all been shareholders of the Super 8. Through the Watershed/Manulife deal, they had all made sizeable profits when Bob bought their shares.

By reinvesting with Bob in a new hotel, they could save on capital gains taxes and, more than likely, make even more money down the road.

Bob got the go-ahead for the new Pomeroy Inn & Suites.

Thirty

> "We must overcome the notion that we must be regular . . . it robs you of the chance to be extraordinary and leads you to the mediocre."
>
> —UTA HAGEN, FAMOUS QUOTES

Allison Lloyd had been educated as a teacher and, before she became involved with Ryan and the Pomeroy family, she had fully expected to work in the school system. She knew that Ryan had given up his original dream of playing professional sports so she found it easier to reconsider her own career plans. Their relationship progressed from casual to serious to fully committed and finally they moved in to the house next door to Bob and Carrie.

Being with the family "twenty-four seven", Allison began to really appreciate the critical staff shortage in the office and the stress this was creating for everyone.

Ryan was putting in long hours and the young couple hardly had time for each other. Allison agreed to work over the summer in Accounts. That way, she would at least see Ryan at the office and she would also be helping with the labor situation.

The die was cast.

Although she was offered a job with the school board that fall, she was already feeling a loyalty to Bob and Ryan. Her temporary summer position became full time.

When the general manager of the new Holiday Inn quit unexpectedly, Bob asked Allison to take over. She told him that she did not feel qualified for the position and, more to the point, she did not really want the job. Bob begged her to help him.

When he promised to look for a replacement as soon as possible, she agreed, albeit begrudgingly, to be a temporary fill-in. She knew in her heart that she would have preferred to resume teaching but she had become a part of Bob's family and she made the decision to step up to the plate.

Allison went to the hotel with Bob to see just what the job entailed. They spent about an hour walking through the property and then he left. Allison stood alone at the front lobby—the new General Manager of the Grande Prairie Holiday Inn.

Her headaches had just begun. Not only had the manager left, the head housekeeper had left as well. The hotel was 95% booked and the banquet facilities were fully reserved. Allison felt herself becoming physically ill and she called Ryan.

They both dug in. Allison attacked the hotel management and Ryan took over the housekeeping detail. He drove over from the office with Andy Doucette, his Director of Sales and Marketing, and the two of them, still in their business suits, pulled dirty laundry from the chutes until they were neck high in linen. And they are both well over six feet tall!

The men did laundry until eleven the first night and Ryan continued as head of housekeeping for over a month, staying at the hotel from seven in the morning until almost midnight every day, keeping the same long hours as Allison.

Six months later, Allison was still at the same job and working grueling hours. At the Managers' Summit, June 2006, she broke down in tears, suffering from sheer exhaustion. Bob took note and finally started to search for her replacement. It took a few months but finally Bob told her that she was relieved of her position as General Manager of the Holiday Inn. Her joy and relief were short-lived. Bob was promoting her to Division Manager of Hotels for the company. The responsibility for one hotel had now multiplied to four.

In spite of the obscene hours and oppressive workload she handled that year, Allison does not regret a moment. She feels it gave her inner strength as well as enormous self-confidence.

At the same time, she would never, ever, want to repeat the experience.

Businesses in northern BC and Alberta could not survive if they operated strictly within the labor relations standards in large metropolitan areas. The extreme shortage of labor, especially in the service and hospitality areas, demands that employees work long hours under less-than-perfect conditions. (For many employees, this is an opportunity to make more money so no one makes waves!)

Management in these industries also has to be flexible and it is virtually unheard of for anyone to work nine-to-five or have just a five-day workweek. It is not unusual at all to find a restaurant or hotel executive waist-deep in laundry, garbage or dirty dishes.

When Julius finally arrived in Grande Prairie on December 6, it was a Friday night and he called Bob to tell him he was finally in Canada. He did not know if the position was still available after a four-month delay with immigration but, if it was, he was ready to start work whenever he was needed. Bob said, "Great. See you at 6:15 at Ricky's on Monday morning."

On Monday, Julius reported to the restaurant on time wearing an open-neck shirt. When Bob asked him where his tie was, he pulled one out of his pocket.

Bob was impressed that Julius had come prepared for whatever the dress code happened to be. Ryan arrived and, after a quick breakfast, the three men drove to the Holiday Inn to introduce Julius to Allison.

After a few quick introductions to the staff at Barcelona, Ryan and Bob left. Julius was puzzled and asked Allison when he would meet the restaurant manager to be "shown the ropes." Allison could not help but laugh when she said "Welcome to the family! Deb is the manager and she is away for the next two days. You're solely in charge." Then she returned to her duties in the hotel and Julius began doing whatever he thought was needed at the restaurant.

Two weeks later, Bob took the whole family to Hawaii for Christmas, including Allison. The day before leaving, he stopped by Barcelona to talk to Julius. Quite matter-of-factly, he told his new employee to "keep an eye on the hotel while we're all away." Bob knew fully well that Julius had no experience in hotels but he instinctively recognized a strong work ethic. He new he had the maturity and intelligence to be able to handle anything thrown his way.

Barcelona was part of the Holiday Inn property and the hotel's usual full-capacity status required one server to be dedicated solely to room service. One Saturday night the room service employee did not show up, so, after working all day as manager, Julius put himself at the station. He ran his legs off.

The calls were non-stop and he made forty-six deliveries. On one call, when his service was particularly fast and the order quite extensive, he was not tipped.

At that moment, he found a new appreciation for the person who usually did the job. Many times during the evening, he was ready to throw in the towel but he persevered. At one-thirty, he called it a day; tossed the $126 of tips he had earned into the staff tip jar and drove home. He finally crawled into bed at two and was up at six to get back to Barcelona to set up for the Sunday Brunch.

The restaurant had created quite a following for the weekly brunch experience. They served 250 to 350 people each and every Sunday and, due to the wild popularity, it took a lot of work. The staff shortages had continued so Julius found Allison to be a Godsend. She could usually be found in the hotel doing housekeeping on the weekends and she would drop her own work to help him set tables.

After the last brunch table was cleared away, Julius would head home for a power nap. He rarely got more than an hour because, by the five o'clock shift change, there was always at least one employee who failed to show up. Julius was quickly out the door to cover the shortfall until closing. There was no point in warning or disciplining employees for missing shifts because, if they were fired, they could find another job the next day.

Due to the ongoing critical labor shortage, staff loyalty was a rare commodity and managing any restaurant under these conditions is both stressful and exhausting.

It can also be character building for anyone who has chosen hospitality as a long-term career. As Julius puts it, "The spring of 2006 was the best four months I would never want to do again."

Bob has always joked around with staff members, especially those who have been with him for many years and who know him well. Over the years, he has become a conscientious CEO who not only adheres to the new rules of "political correctness" but who also ensures that all his staff adheres as well. If he makes a "faux pas", it is unintentional and he immediately moves to correct it.

In 2008, for example, he was mildly admonishing Ashar for expecting excessive work of a newer employee. He referred to the new man as "not being her slave'. Unfortunately, it was a poor choice of words as the employee was: a) a recent arrival from Africa and b) the former recipient of some actual prejudice.

The man walked out of the office and Bob was flummoxed. He knew he had been trying to protect the man from extra work and he truly did not know what he had said that was wrong.

When it was explained, he acted quickly. He got in his car, drove to the man's home and apologized sincerely. He was not trying to avoid a complaint. He was truly, deeply upset at himself for inadvertently hurting someone's feelings.

Some of Bob's employees have learned to use his political "incorrectness" to their own advantage. Case in point: Getting Bob's attention.

Susie needed some contracts signed immediately but Bob was in a meeting with financing consultants from Toronto and Vancouver. The clock was ticking and she had a deadline to fax the agreements. Each time she would quietly open the boardroom door and try to get his attention, he would wave her away. After more than an hour had passed along with five attempts to get his signature, she was at her wit's end. She knew the meeting was important but she also heard enough to know that it was not at a crucial point; Bob just wanted to keep talking to a captive audience.

Finally, she grabbed a bright neon post-it note, and wrote, "I need a signature NOW." She stuck the note on her snug trousers directly on of her pubic region and walked boldly into the room. Bob looked up angrily, blustered, "I said NOT NOW", and turned back to his visitors.

Susie stood her ground and firmly asked, "Want to take a closer look?" and pointed to the post-it.

Bob stopped talking, exasperated at her impudence and looked her straight in the eye. Then he followed her gaze downward to where she was pointing. After reading the post-it, he burst out laughing.

Bob asked the men to excuse him for two minutes. Susie handed him the documents, he signed them and returned them to her without another word.

Appropriate? No. Efficient? Yes.

He may appear to be rough around the edges but, at heart, Bob

Pomeroy is a caring, sensitive man who appreciates his employees. When he insists on doing things "his way", he will always stop to explain why. He believes in giving people a second chance, even when they truly do not seem to deserve one. He expects employees to work independently and he will back them up on decisions. He allows staff to question his orders and to speak their minds. He tries to treat people fairly and he offers them the opportunity to do better.

If Bob could be faulted, it could be his expectation that everyone is happy to work seven days a week like he does.

He does not understand that people who are in salaried positions, those who have no ownership or profit-sharing, need time with their families.

Although most employees (both past and present) would comment on the company's reluctance to give salary increases, there have been a few instances when Bob suddenly took positive action.

Julius got a phone call from Bob at eight one Sunday morning asking him to come and have coffee with him as soon as possible. It took Julius less than an hour to get to the office but, when he arrived, Bob had already started a meeting with Ryan. Bob asked Julius to wait "a bit."

Julius kept himself busy in his office until Ryan finally left. It was 11:45. Bob walked in, sat down and began to talk about life in general. After an hour of non-work-related conversation, he stood up to leave. As an almost after-thought, he announced, "Oh, by the way, I'm giving you a raise."

A few years ago, Susie convinced Bob to take her to Egan's Pub for a drink after work. Without his knowledge, the whole staff had gathered there to announce that Bob was chosen as the "Developer of the Year" for Grande Prairie and area.

Bob stood quietly amid the loud applause, genuinely embarrassed to be the centre of attention.

As far as he was concerned, the award meant that the entire group of employees was doing a great job.

Bob would rather have people poke fun at him than praise him and he has always been a fan of the practical joke even in the office.

As part of a community campaign a couple of years ago, a live auction was held at the Holiday Inn to raise additional funds for the chosen charity. The auctioneer was Kevin Albers, a personality from the local rock radio station, and he knew Bob well.

The bidding started at $100, then rose by hundred dollar increments. $200. $300. $400.

At that point, Bob raised his hand to bid.

Kevin stopped dramatically and stared at Bob.

"What the hell is that supposed to mean, Pomeroy? $ 450?"

The crowd erupted in laughter once they took a closer look at Bob's raised right hand. It was the hand with the half-missing finger. No one laughed harder than Bob.

The next year, when the Pomeroy Group sponsored a customer service conference in Grande Prairie, the guest speaker was Dr. Cledwin Lewis.

For the first half of his address, Dr. Lewis described questionable service practices in the hospitality industry. He continually used Bob's name as a bad example, totally ripping him apart at times.

Bob loved it! He laughs at anyone and everyone who takes potshots at him as long as it is funny—or based on some truth about his idiosyncrasies.

Take, for example, his dependency on his phone. Bob does not "do" email or computers.

Bob relies on a small pocket notebook, his meticulously handwritten reminders and his cell phone. It is rarely, if ever, turned off. Sometimes he has two going at the same time.

A few years ago, Bob received a letter from Telus telling him that, due to his high usage, they were giving him two new upgraded cell phones. He just had to drop by the closest Telus office and present the letter to receive his bonus gifts.

Bob and Raphael Bohlmann were going out to lunch that day, and Bob took him along to the Telus store enroute to the restaurant. When the young girl at the counter pulled Bob's file, she was amazed at his monthly cellular usage and she asked what kind of work he did.

Bob proudly told her, "Raphael here manages restaurants and I build hotels."

The young girl was not impressed.

She flatly responded with "Hmmph, looks like all you do is just talk on the phone."

Thirty-One

"Know that it's your decisions, not your existing conditions that determine your destiny"

—*TONY ROBBINS*, FAMOUS QUOTES

Once the ball started rolling, there was no slowing Bob down. Having more equity and cash meant that he could go ahead with almost anything he conceived.

In High Prairie, the Pomeroy Inn & Suites had opened but still needed a restaurant.

The members of the Peavine Settlement Council were uncertain about investing more money so Bob flew their representatives to Fort St. John to experience Egan's.

They loved the restaurant and they loved the food. Fortunately, both the dining room and the pub were busy during the visit so the Peavine group became majority partners in the new Egan's as well.

Meanwhile, Sid Tissington and Hank Scheunhage came up with the idea that Grimshaw was the "next big thing" and could support a new hotel on the highway.

Nestled between Peace River and Fairview, the little town boasts a large trading population from the farming community and it supports an active business community. With the mention of a possible nuclear plant for the near future, it seemed a good time to jump in with both feet. After meeting with Bob, they decided that they would build and operate a Pomeroy Inn & Suites franchise.

The Pomeroy Group made a relatively small investment in the project but the franchise agreement required that only Bob's sub-trades could be contracted. Red flags went up initially when work began without even a definite budget on the table. Further, the Pomeroy tradesmen were not hired. The end of the relationship occurred when a shell for a restaurant was built without Bob's knowledge or approval.

Before Bob and Carrie would commit to investing any more money in the property, they got Rick Vieira to go over the plans and come up with a more factual costing forecast. The variables were too high to ignore and too large to continue. It appeared that the project over-runs could end up being well over two and a half million dollars.

Sid kept reassuring Bob that he had investors coming on board but months passed and none appeared.

Finally, Hank's daughter was successful in getting a few investors to join the partnership. Bob and Hank bought Sid's shares and took over the property.

The Grimshaw Pomeroy Inn & Suites was completed in the same first class manner as the other Pomeroy hotels. Each room is comfortable and attractive. The amenities are generous and high quality. The pool and waterslide area is a popular spot for local kids and their birthday parties.

Breakfast is a hot, satisfying meal, not merely a cup of coffee and a doughnut. Like the other properties, guests can enjoy complimentary waffles, yogurt, muffins, bagels or wide choice of cereals.

A discerning traveler or honeymoon couple can choose to stay in the sumptuous African Room—a magnificent suite comprised of three large defined rooms complete with a lounge area, Jacuzzi-style tub, enormous four-poster bed and full kitchen.

(Although the hotel is thriving, at this writing, September 2009, there still is no restaurant operating in the large space alongside the foyer.)

Both Yadminder and Mohinder Minhas were friends and clients of Carrie's and they wanted her to convince Bob to invest in a hotel project with them. The Minhas brothers had made a conditional offer to buy the Northwest Inn in Slave Lake. They had the financial capability to buy the Inn but no hotel management experience. In a nutshell, they told Carrie that, if Bob did not become part of the project, they would not proceed with their offer.

Bob was in the midst of a few hefty deals of his own but he liked the Slave Lake location. He wanted to take a third of the deal but his cash flow was not accommodating enough at that moment. As well, because Manulife still owned 25% of the company, everything had to fit with their vision as well. When Bob hesitated, the Minhas brothers made him an offer that he could not turn down.

Yad and Mo would lend Bob and Manulife the one-third equity if the Pomeroy Group would become the managing partner. They only requested that interest be paid monthly on the principal. It was a deal.

The Pomeroy team went to Slave Lake, fired the former manager and changed the computer systems.

With better control over the operations, and great appreciation from the Minhas brothers, the company increased the revenues for the Northwest Inn by more than $200,000 in the first year.

The Northwest Inn was doing so well, in fact, that the company took a look at the Slave Lake Super 8. In spite of that hotel always being busy and showing excellent volume, the owner wanted to sell. Carrie did a cash flow analysis and budget and then called Manulife. The numbers fit the criteria that Manulife required for purchasing new properties so Bob made the offer.

(Less than two years later, the Slave Lake Super 8 was sold as part of the Holloway purchase package.)

Bob heard that the owner of the Garden Court Motel in Manning was retiring and wanted to sell. Manning was the next stop after Grimshaw so it made sense to take a good look at the financials. The Garden Court was a small business, operated by the owners and showed a solid, steady income. When the owner offered to carry the mortgage for a year, Bob made an offer. Originally thinking of expanding the property, Bob had Tom Vukota from Manulife fly up and appraise the situation. Tom liked what he saw and he gave permission to proceed. After doing some redecorating and repairs and adding a new IT system, the company raised the room rates. Then, seeing that the place was making a good return in its present size, the decision was made not to expand, but to continue operating the same number of rooms.

The Garden Court was not included in the Holloway purchase package as it was still too new to assess its potential value. It remains part of the Pomeroy portfolio.

In Clairmont, the truck stop and hotel were doing a brisk business but Bob felt that they still needed to add a truck wash.

The GP Truck Stop Partnership Limited, formerly the Ramada Group investors, (Bob, Lyman Brewster, the Peavine Settlement and a few others) started to raise money.

Bob planned to build the truck wash himself but changed his mind when a company from Edmonton guaranteed that they could build one for less. He gave them the contract but it was not long before he questioned his decision.

The builders' liens started arriving before Bob had even received the balance of the financing.

The truck wash was completed but it will never rank among Bob's favourite projects. In late 2009 the property was for sale.

Thirty-Two

"If you don't drive your business, you will be driven out of business."

—B.C.FORBES, FORBES APRIL 1974

The Holloway deal was not a fluke. Nor was it accomplished without a great deal of groundwork. And, of course, there was Bob's incredible sense of timing.

The Cendant (now Wyndham) Preferred Owners' Event in Atlanta, Georgia, was an important occasion for the Pomeroy Group. Not only was the company awarded for exceptional service but it also received some very interesting attention from other, larger hotel consortiums.

Marc Staniloff had also gone to the Georgia event and, between meetings, he and his partner Ian McAuley introduced Bob and Carrie to Glen Squires of the Holloway Group. The energetic, thriving company impressed Glen and he wasted no time in showing his intent. When Bob and Carrie returned to Grande Prairie, they carried a one page "Letter of Interest" from the Holloway Group. Two days later, Glen contacted them with a basic preliminary offer to purchase a group of properties for $213 Million.

After some negotiations, however, that offer did not close and Holloway ceased communication.

The seed of a huge transaction had been planted, though, and Bob, Carrie and Ryan gave a lot of consideration to selling a group of properties.

The cash generated would allow the company to continue development without the need for adding a large number of investors.

Months later, the company contacted the Temple Group in Winnipeg to invite a proposal. That company submitted a Letter of Interest but, before any progress was made, the Holloway Group realized that they had some competition for the properties. They came back to the table.

No doubt hearing through the hospitality pipeline that the Pomeroy Group had become a hot commodity, they quickly put together a solid offer.

As negotiations went on in Toronto, Bob had many heated discussions with the lawyers representing the Pomeroy Group. Bob still has about as little regard for the legal profession as he has for life insurance. He would prefer if he never had to speak to any lawyers. Often, Carrie would call the lawyers to give direction on behalf of Bob.

Frances Macklin, Pomeroy's key attorney during the negotiating, stated, "I think Bob came around to view the fact that I am a lawyer as a flaw in my character, but not a fatal flaw."

Her initial impression of Bob was that he was a "just get it done" kind of man with little patience for paperwork, details, formality and legal complexities—all of which he associates with lawyers. In his business dealings, Bob would prefer to rely on personal rather than legal documents.

Bob does not like anyone speaking for him, particularly lawyers and so, when Bob was present during negotiations, he would take the floor and not hesitate to override recommendations and advice from lawyers or any other members of his team.

Bob readily tells people that he only has "half of grade twelve" (his way of stating that he only completed grade six) but by no means does he consider himself uneducated. He is, in fact, justifiably proud of reaching such a level of success without formal education.

The legal team representing the Pomeroy Group held him in high esteem. As Frances says, "To underestimate Bob is a mistake. He is clearly a very smart man with an astute business sense. His timing for business deals is enviable."

During the negotiations, an old acquaintance made an appearance.

David N. Grieve, the same executive that had helped Bob put together the financing for the Nomad Inn deal in Fort McMurray many years prior, was still with Merrill Lynch and he became involved in the Holloway transaction as well.

The proposal was for the Holloway company to purchase 10 hotels and 2 restaurants for $215 Million, Pomeroy Hospitality Services to continue the management. (Within six months, Holloway would buy out the management contract and simply operate the properties under the franchise agreement.)

Not so surprising, in 2007, when the Holloway deal was announced in the newspapers, the gossips and naysayers in Grande Prairie went into high gear.

Within days, the rumor circulated like wildfire that Bob was going broke and forced to sell off his assets. Had any of the critics bothered to surf the internet or read national newspapers, they would have realized that the exact opposite was true.

Respected publications like the Financial Post were printing positive columns about the strength and foresight of the Pomeroy Group; companies like GE Capitol and Manulife Financial rated the Pomeroy Group as a preferred client.

They still do.

Bob Pomeroy, the chastised student who couldn't get past grade six in school had managed to build a company of such enormity that, when the Holloway sale was entered into the economic records of Canada, it was recognized as being the second largest hotel transaction in the country.

The deal, $ 215 Million in total, set a new Canadian record for the highest price paid "per door" for a limited services hotel purchase.

Thirty-Three

> "He wants to live on through something—and, in his case, his masterpiece is his son . . ."
> —ARTHUR MILLER, ON WILLY LOMAN, NY TIMES 9 MAY 1984

Charlie Grubisich said, "Every facility built by Bob Pomeroy is a monument to him and to his attention to detail."

Perhaps that is true but monuments are not legacies and, for Bob, his finest legacies are his children.

He may have been an absent father for much of their lives; he may have been a poor role model as a husband. The plain truth is that no one receives a manual on how to live, how to love or how to be a parent. Anyone who has been raised in a home without positive example must adapt his own rules. Some succeed, many fail.

In spite of childhood trauma and a lack of education, Bob made his way in the world. In spite of a failed marriage and numerous relationships, Bob taught his children responsibility and commitment. While most of the credit for child-rearing must go to Marj, it is an accepted truth that children look to their father for leadership. Bob must have done something right.

When Ryan was appointed as President of the Pomeroy Group of companies, there were more than a few people who raised an eyebrow.

To some, it may have seemed no more than blatant nepotism. This opinion couldn't be further from the truth.

Not only is Bob's faith in his son's capabilities remarkable but it is valid.

Ryan is well deserving of his father's trust and he has earned his position.

He spent as much time in the hotels and restaurants as he did at home and in sports while he was young—perhaps more. His conversations with his father, even before he reached his teen years, were conversations between two men about the business. Bob never talked down to any of his children and he never disregarded their comments or ideas. The maturity level of all of Bob and Marj's offspring was far beyond their years.

When Bob named Ryan as his successor and turned over the massive job of running the company in such a growth period, many people were watching to see how the new president would cope.

Some of the company's associates, those who have not known the family for more than a few years, were expecting to see him fall flat on his face.

According to many of the company's employees and associates, as well as all of Bob's friends, Carrie made her opposition clearly known and she remains very vocal in her resistance to his position and authority.

During the Manulife transaction and then the Holloway purchase, however, Ryan made his mark and established himself as the rightful president.

In Toronto, executives initially considered Ryan to be a very bright, very intuitive young businessman, with emphasis on the "young." Some wondered aloud if he was ready for so much stress and responsibility.

By the time the negotiations had concluded, the entire "Eastern faction" had been won over. It had become obvious throughout the months of discussions that Bob's decision was the right one and that he had taught his son well.

Ryan was willing to forego his personal interests for the sake of the family; he recognized his father's need for creating a family dynasty and he knew that he was the right person at the right time.

Bob is justifiably proud of all of his children. Tim excelled at whatever he did, whether it was working in the hotels or on a construction site.

Kim overcame serious injuries and personal tragedy to build a career in college sports and to raise a loving, stable family.

Connor has defied the medical odds pronounced at his birth. Not content to be a fragile invalid, he participated at soccer through elementary school, and, after high school, pursued various jobs until he, too, may be on the verge of joining the family business.

It was, however, Ryan who was destined to be the public "Pomeroy kid"; the man who would lead the company into the future.

His first project was to build the first Pomeroy Hotel from the ground up and he knew where it had to be—right back at the beginning in Fort St.John, BC.

While it is true that Uncle Ralph put the Pomeroy name on a hotel, it had been a hotel purchased from an original owner. The new Pomeroy Hotel would be one hundred percent original and it would be first class.

A few years earlier, a group of investors from Prince George stated their interest in building a gaming centre in Fort St. John. Under the Lotteries Administration rules, there can only be one gaming license in an area with the population of the city and area so the Prince George group could not proceed.

The gaming licence for Fort St. John was held by Glen Guise and he was using it to operate a successful bingo centre.

Glen owned a huge tract of land on the Alaska Highway—exactly where Ryan and Bob wanted to build the new hotel—and all parties agreed that it would be a perfect location for a huge commercial complex; one that could encompass a restaurant, a gaming centre and a first-class hotel.

Under the BOSA (Bingo Operational Service agreement), both the Municipality and the Lotteries commission must approve any and all aspects of a project and the partners before the license can be upgraded to a CGCOSA (Community Gaming Centre Service Agreement) so it was no simple feat to put any proposal together.

This was not just a case of finding financing, making an offer, buying some land and building a hotel. With the government involved on a grand scale, the old way ("Bob's Way") of doing things—start to build first and get approvals along the way) simply would not work.

First, of course, was to structure a deal with Guise that would make the land available to the Pomeroy Group and make turning over the gaming license profitable to Guise.

At this "conception" and early stages, Bob and Ryan worked as a team. Bob raised the initial investment capitol needed to move forward and the two of them met tirelessly with all the principals to get a deal structured.

Guise wanted one lump sum for the zoning, the land, his gaming (Bingo) license and what he perceived was the value of the business and income. His price for the land alone was $2.75 Million, or $400,000 per square acre. The total price for the package was almost triple.

It was a huge undertaking for Ryan's first project and the lessons learned from his father proved very valuable. It would not be a one-step deal.

The purchase would eventually be comprised of several stages beyond the initial cash purchase for the land and the gaming license.

Guise would become both a lender and an investor in the business component, being paid not only interest on the loan portion but also generous management fees for up to five years. The initial amount for the business would be slightly less than his asking price but the contract structured in a bonus schedule whereby, if the video terminals net higher returns than the provincial averages had netted in the past, the payments to Guise would end up being more than his original asking price for the business.

It was a win-win situation for both parties. If the video terminals didn't meet the goals, Guise would still receive the original price. If they exceeded, he would be well-rewarded for his patience in waiting five years for the remainder of the proceeds.

The hotel project was developed with the Pomeroy Group and a new investment partnership, with mortgaging through the Bank of Montreal. It was much more than just a hotel, however, and the impact to the skyline of Fort St.John became obvious when the structure began taking shape.

The lavish new "Chances Gaming Center" was the first area targeted for completion. It was designed as a well-appointed, modern entertainment destination featuring one hundred and fifty video gambling terminals, a Bingo room, a high-roller room and an attractive cocktail and show lounge complete with stage, sound system and giant screen. During the initial construction of the complex, Allison had been promoted to the position of Purchasing and Design Manager and her decorating touches became evident. The new "Chances" would have no similarities to any vision of a "northern Bingo hall" but would be better compared to an upscale Las Vegas resort.

While the hotel complex was being built in Fort St.John, plans were underway for a new Holiday Inn Express for Grande Prairie.

Bob had started the initial financing and planning but now that, too, was turned over to Ryan.

On April 30, 2007, Ryan added a seasoned Chief Financial Officer to the staff.

His management team now included the appropriate balance of education and industry experience to support his determination to succeed.

Carrie was no longer part of the administration but she stayed on board until the end of June, the conclusion of the Holloway deal. After that, there was a definitive separation. Carrie returned to focusing on her own accounting firm (Langstroth and Company) and spending more time in Scottsdale.

At the end of June 2007, Bob also stepped back from the daily management of the Pomeroy Group. He remained as CEO but for the next year transferred his focus and energies into building the equestrian centres in both Scottsdale and Grande Prairie.

The ball was now entirely in Ryan's court and he was up for the challenge. He assumed complete responsibility for coordinating trades, final design and openings of both the Pomeroy Hotel in Fort St.John and the Holiday Inn Express in Grande Prairie.

The Gaming Centre opened to wild popularity in September 2007.

In July 2008, Tony Roma's restaurant opened alongside the gaming centre and, in September of that same year, the company's first Pomeroy Hotel opened it doors to the public.

Fort St.John now could boast of having a choice of well-appointed meeting rooms, a comprehensive convention center, an elegant grand ballroom and some of the most deluxe, most unique hotel suites in the province.

One wall of the hotel lobby is reserved to honour the family—photos of Bob Pomeroy and Ralph Pomeroy hang side-by-side along with a photo of Ralph Pomeroy's original hotel.

The ballrooms are named for people whose memories are still alive and strong: The Ralph Pomeroy Grand Ballroom breaks down on the right into the Marie Pomeroy Room and the left, the Scotty Pomeroy Room. The secondary ballroom is the Tim Pomeroy Ballroom, which divides into the Sterling Pomeroy Room on the right and the Kenny Pomeroy Room on the left. Massive chandeliers enhance the architectural ceilings; the muted décor designed to compliment the color themes of any wedding reception or important event.

On opening day, when the ribbon was cut, speeches were made and the photographs were taken, Bob stood beside his twenty-nine year old son with justifiable pride.

The opening of the hotel coincided with the end of the first year's operations of the gaming centre—and the deadline for the first profits-sharing payment to Glen Guise. The provincial average for video terminals is $250 per terminal per day. That figure is split with the provincial government receiving 75% and the licensee receiving 25% out of which salaries and all other operating costs are paid.

If the machines simply met the provincial average for the full year, Guise would make more money than in the original asking price for that reporting year. If the machines hit "up to" $350, he would earn more; over $350 and the bonus would get extremely lucrative.

In the first month of opening, the terminals averaged $350.

The next ten and a half months, they averaged along the provincial numbers.

With just 5 days left to the year end reporting, there had been $13.5 Million in wagers at the gaming centre and the forecasted variance was less than $30,000, or .002%.

A teeny little difference of less than 51 cents per day per machine could mean the huge difference in the bonus the company would have to pay. It was too close to call and too much of a risk to take to simply take a "wait and see" stance.

The contract for paying the bonus had turned out to be slightly ambiguous. The terms stated that the year was deemed to be 365 days but there was no clarification about non-operational days such as Christmas or extra days with Leap Year. With five days to go and a lot of money on the line, as well as too many variables to consider, Ryan took things in hand and called Guise.

He asked initially if they could agree on the final day for the end of the first year. When the conversation got bogged down with month-to-month variables and possibilities, Ryan offered a second option. He suggested that he could buy insurance to cover any unusually high performance in the spirit of a good future relationship or Guise could just accept a flat, non-conditional payment.

They settled.

The Pomeroy Hotel and Gaming Centre complex had a total project cost of over $37 Million.

It was the largest single project in the company's history. The amount of cash equity raised ($15,050,000.) for a single project overshadowed all the Pomeroy projects up to that point. The transaction was the largest commercial real estate development in the history of the city.

The Chances Gaming Centre in Fort St. John is the largest in the province of B.C.

Marc Staniloff and his group of investors participated in this project just as they did for many past projects. The list of the other investors included the familiar names of others who have profited with Bob over the years: Ray Yenkana, Ernie Patterson, Brian Surerus and, of course, Kim.

For the grand opening of the hotel complex, the company launched its first Charity Golf Tournament and Poker Event. In the new president's style, the company did not award a car or other lavish gift to one person to mark the event. Instead, Chances Gaming Centre, the Pomeroy Hotel and Tony Roma's sponsored the weekend celebration event and, with the generosity of corporate partners, raised over twenty thousand dollars for the Hospital Foundation in the city. The commitment has been made for this to continue as an annual occasion to benefit the community.

The Holiday Inn Express opened in Grande Prairie soon after the hotel opened. It was a smaller project than the Fort St.John complex but, nonetheless, an important addition to the portfolio. The investors included some of the "regulars" as well, but a few new faces were attracted by the track record of the company and the profile of its new management.

In keeping with Bob and Ryan's demand for the very best of amenities, both of the new properties were fitted with top-of-the-line linens and bedding. Their supplier for over a decade for all of their properties remains as Eden Textiles of Edmonton. That company is very proud to manufacture the only bed in the world to be honoured with a Royal Warrant. (The new Palais Couberg in Vienna recently issued a press release stating that they had refitted with Eden's Kiwi Collection because it "embodies the extravagant luxury associated with world-class hotels.")

The association with Eden Textiles, according to Steve Rice, is based on mutual loyalty. Steve added that, "Bob understands loyalty; he knows it goes both ways. Bob's word is his bond and he's never let us down."

In addition to comfortable beds and luxurious linens, the Pomeroy hotels also provide spa quality toiletries to guests and, although some other hotel chains are cutting back on amenities, the Pomeroys continue to add to their services.

The Pomeroy Group is now recognized and acknowledged throughout North America.

The company's hotels are known as being at the top of their class, beacons of good service and quality accommodation.

The Pomeroy properties, under Bob's direction, have received accolades and awards nationally and internationally.

It would seem that history will repeat itself under Ryan's helm.

Thirty-Four

"The biggest human temptation is to settle for too little."
—THOMAS MERTON, FORBES, 4 AUG 1980

After all these years working with Bob, Rick Vieira should not ever be surprised by last-minute changes. He does keep hoping that eventually one project will get from A to Z without any bright ideas showing up at the last minute.

With the Pomeroy Inn and Suites in Dawson Creek, construction was moving along on schedule. The crew was already framing on the third floor when Bob decided the hotel should have another floor added. Everything had to stop. Having four floors created the necessity of a second elevator. The first elevator shaft was already completed with the in-ground pipes in place.

To add a second elevator meant abandoning the original pipes for the elevator piston and changing the specifications to allow the installation of two hole-less elevators. It also meant reframing a large portion of the three floors already done.

The framers went nuts, to put it mildly, and Rick wasn't feeling too happy either.

The elevator change was not the only obstacle to adding a fourth floor. The Dawson Creek property was being built close to the city airport and there was the wee problem of height restrictions to contend with. Rick had to apply for new building permits, wait for approvals from the airport authority, and all the while, surreptitiously continue with construction to keep on schedule.

To save time and money on construction, the company did the site work and built the foundations for the Pomeroy Inn and Suites in Dawson Creek at the same time they had been working on the Best Western. The property sat as a concrete pad for a full year.

The Manulife deal was completed after the Best Western had opened. The company had retired the large group of investors, restructured mortgages and was operating on cash flow alone. GE had provided the mortgage for the new Pomeroy Inn & Suites and, with revenues from the other hotel properties providing all the cash needed to complete, the project went very smoothly.

In Chetwynd, the same process was going on but with a different group of investors. Money was not a problem but there were loads of other headaches.

Six months before opening, the company was approached by a mill that was doing a shutdown. They guaranteed to book 100 rooms for a month but they needed a definite "hard date." They had to know that, when their crews arrived, they would have rooms.

Ryan gave them his word.

The economy in the area picked up even more and experienced tradesmen were scarce. When the original site supervisor moved on, the company had no choice but to turn over the position of contractor to the framing company. The completion date kept being pushed back. It was the peak of the "boom" and eight man crews became three-man crews augmented by local teenagers. Any time the fill-in contractor got an idea for moving things along, things actually took longer.

With the Chetwynd Pomeroy Inn and Suites being built at the same time as the Dawson Creek property, and the construction already having "issues", Rick could only hope that Bob was too busy to fiddle with both plans. Wrong.

The week after Bob had made changes to the Dawson Creek building, Rick stopped by Chetwynd to check on that project. He discovered the framers changing all the specifications on the second floor.

They were installing the exercise room there and refitting the main floor location as a party room. The first words out of Rick's mouth were, "What the hell?!" His second words were," You don't have to say a thing. Bob was here, wasn't he?"

With two months to go to the promised opening date, Ryan called the furniture supplier to confirm that their order was in production and that the delivery time would be met.

He hit another wall. The furniture company was also in a boom and they had not even started the order. With their factory running at maximum production and orders backing up daily, they had looked at the past history of orders and had assumed that the hotel would not open for several months. It was a logical judgement call but one that should have been confirmed by phone.

Sixty days to opening—the building was not ready and there was no furniture arriving.

Fortunately, the designer found a hotel furniture supplier in the U.S. that had available stock. The good news was the quality and price were comparable and the furniture would arrive on time.

The bad news was the shipping costs were exorbitant!

The furniture arrived just before opening. Usually, after all the furniture has arrived, a hotel needs a full week to ten days to prepare for guests; installing lamps, desks, beds; hanging drapes, making beds, stocking bathrooms. The staff at the Chetwynd property had three days.

Bob's sister, Judy Kramer, supervises all the final preparations and installations for openings of all the Pomeroy properties and she would best describe the opening in Chetwynd as chaotic.

There were no phones and no television sets in the rooms. There were no toilets in the rooms on the main floor. The crew from the mill had arrived and they were guaranteed beds to sleep on. Fortunately, the building inspector approved the building if the main floor rooms were closed off. They were, and the doors were opened.

With such a messy opening and such a lack of amenities for the guests in the initial weeks, the Chetwynd Pomeroy Inn & Suites was heavily criticized by the local businesses.

The negativity was turned around, however, and Ryan gives sole credit to the employees that work at the property. He never hesitates to comment on the calibre and enthusiasm of the Chetwynd staff, right from front desk to housekeeping and maintenance.

Even in the current slowdown in the hospitality industry, the Chetwynd Pomeroy Inn & Suites maintains the highest occupancy in the area. That is arguably due to the efforts of the "hometown" employees who seem to have made it their personal goal to make their hotel the best place to stay.

Prior to selling the large group of properties to Holloway, the Pomeroy Group was owned twenty-five percent by Manulife and seventy-five percent by the Pomeroy Group.

In late 2007, the company bought out the Manulife position and was now the "Grand Hospitality Limited Partnership", solely owned by Bob Pomeroy, his wife Carrie Langstroth, and Bob's three children, Ryan, Kim and Connor.

It was public knowledge that the company was set to grow again and they had the resources to do it.

Although Bob's usual mandate was for top-of-the-line accommodation, he varied from his norm and decided to build a budget Motel 6. The franchise owners of the large chain had flown to Grande Prairie on a look-see and somehow convinced Bob to try a new brand.

The cash was available so the company went ahead.

In 2008, the Motel 6 was built on the north end of Grande Prairie. Once again, the company saved financing costs by using the healthy cash flow from the other hotel properties.

Even though the bank financing had been approved well in advance, the company built the hotel with cash and delayed drawing on the mortgage until just before opening. The first draw was over $7,000,000 and that was immediately transferred from the Motel 6 mortgage proceeds back into the company to repay the cash used in building.

Building the Motel 6 did not mean that the company was moving away from first-class accommodation.

In Canada, in certain cases, a taxpayer may postpone or defer adding a capital gain to reported income.

When a person sells a business property, for example, taxes may be deferred if the profits are re-invested in a similar, replacement property within a reasonable period of time. "To defer reporting the capital gain or recapture of CCA, you must acquire and you, or a person related to you, must use the new property for the same or similar purpose as the one that you are replacing." (Sic)

In Slave Lake, the Pomeroy Group had been in partnership with the Minhas Group—Yadminder and Mohinder Minhas– in the Northwest

Inn. When that property was sold in the Holloway transaction, both partners did very well financially.

The Minhas brothers had logging and trucking interests and they always had difficulty finding accommodation for their employees in Valleyview. They had found a large piece of land directly on the main highway and decided that this was a perfect time to build a hotel. By re-investing their profits from the Slave Lake sale, they could defer their capital gains taxes and solve their accommodation problems at the same time. The Pomeroy Group could re-invest as well so it seemed like a wise decision to move forward.

Just after the site work commenced, a huge hole was discovered below ground. In the hole was an old corroded tank. Work was halted until environmental studies could be completed and the tank removed from the property. This added a large cost to the initial budget.

Then, as the building resumed, the economy began to wane.

All the contractor pricing and contracts had been done during the peak times so the expenses were higher than normal. No bank financing had been arranged as, optimistically, the company had gone ahead under the assumption that the work would be paid through cash flows in the same way the last two projects had been completed.

The economy worsened faster than anyone could have predicted and hotel revenues were drastically reduced. Any revenues for the company were now needed for operations and management. There was no extra for building new property.

Consideration was given to stopping the project but both Bob and Yad wanted to keep going. Consideration was given to removing one floor, reducing 107 rooms to 77 rooms. The plans were redrawn for the smaller hotel concept but, after the costs were reviewed, it did not seem to make a lot of difference.

By removing one floor, the entire project would save almost $1.2 million.

Bob and Yad did not think that was enough of a saving and, against the protests of Ryan and Mohinder, the plans were changed back to four floors.

The Pomeroy Group still had money and the decision was made to financially support the project to ensure a spring opening. The logging industry was suffering a lot more than the hospitality industry at the time so, when the other partners had delays with their cash inputs, the company kept paying the bills.

In spite of delays and extra expenses, the hotel opened in March 2009.

The Valleyview Pomeroy Inn & Suites was Allison's first total design project. Both Ryan and Bob were proud to complete the hotel as her showcase.

The spring and early summer of 2009 was a black hole for hotels and restaurants all over North America. Valleyview was no exception.

The service station in the adjacent lot was just in the beginning stages; the proposed restaurant next door came to an abrupt halt and business for the hotel was slower than hoped. In spite of the circumstances, both the Pomeroy Group and the Minhas partners felt they could manage to survive through the slowdown by subsidizing the project with more cash.

They had no way of knowing what would happen in the months ahead.

A major investment partner of the Pomeroy Group suddenly had his own business downturn and he was hit with major financial losses. When he could not meet his commitments, the company initially covered his portion of expenses. Soon it was obvious that the situation was far worse than expected and the backlash had a serious effect on many areas of the company's own operations.

The result was immediate. Ryan had to take steps to stop the haemorrhaging of money in Valleyview in order to protect the other properties. He went to have a face-to-face talk with Mohinder, a "state of the union" summit, so to speak.

This was coming at the worst time for everyone. Logging was in a deeper recession and the banks were turning down every proposal for borrowing. The Minhas brothers managed to turn over $300,000 but the monies owed to the contractors was double that amount.

There was still another $300,000 needed for those invoices and the Pomeroy Group wanted repayment of the extra cash they had contributed to the hotel.

Ryan stressed the fact that, if builders' liens shut down the property, it would be the 70% owners (the Minhas brothers) that would suffer the most.

In the midst of the stalemate between the partners, Mohinder Minhas went to India on a family matter, became grievously ill and died. Weeks passed before anyone wanted to bring up business problems to the family. Even with his brother alive and working with him, Yadminder had been putting in sixteen to eighteen hour days. This was a crushing blow to him. The family had to arrange not only a funeral but Mohinder's daughter was set to be married the week after her father's death.

The family decided to go ahead with the planned event.

Two weeks later, Yad travelled back to India with his late brother's ashes.

During this personal upheaval for the Minhas Group, their accountant phoned Ryan to say that, prior to going to India, Mohinder had expressed his desire for Yad to deal with the Valleyview concerns as soon as possible. It had been causing him stress and he did not like the tension it was bringing between their company and the Pomeroy Group.

When Yad returned from the second trip to India, he met with Bob and Ryan and told them that the Minhas Group wished to take over full ownership of the Valleyview property. They would keep the franchise intact, operate as a Pomeroy Inn & Suites and pay royalties on the revenues.

It was not the best deal for the company.

By accepting, the Pomeroy Group would take a 30% loss on their cash investment.

That was huge.

On one hand, it was not a great financial move and it did not make either Bob or Ryan happy.

On the other hand, by going ahead with it, they knew that their tradesmen and suppliers would be paid and the friendship between themselves and the Minhas family would be retained.

They did the deal.

Thirty-Five

> "They look upon retirement as something between euthanasia and castration"
> —LEON A.DANCO, PRESIDENT, CENTRE FOR FAMILY BUSINESS,
> NY TIMES JUNE 1986

The past few years have brought a lot of change to the Pomeroy Group. Bob's appointing Ryan as President of the company was the beginning of that change and certainly a clear sign of Bob's belief in his son.

Bob has always worked with an open door and any mistakes he has made have been there for all to see. In his studies at university, Ryan was learning business from lectures. Alongside his father, he was learning business from example. In both instances, he learned both what to do and what not to do.

Bob has always espoused the ethic of hard work and he has passed this strength to his children. He not only gave them an education, he gave them business experience and an appreciation for the value of manual labour. He also taught his children maturity and acceptance.

Even when they were very young, still in elementary school, he spoke to them as adults and trusted them to make good decisions.

Being raised in the "old school" tradition himself, it was just his sons that he took to work in the hotels; just his sons that he expected to assume the mantle of management when he stepped down. When his first born, Tim, was killed in a tragic accident, he focused his mentoring on Ryan—never thinking that Kim might become a partner in the business.

He was pleasantly surprised when she not only became an investor but also a manager in a couple of the hotels.

Just like so many other successful businessmen, Bob found it difficult to set aside family time while he was building his company. He rarely found time to take actual vacations with his all of his kids. The one trip he took to Hawaii with Ryan included Bob's friend and his children and even then, the kids were usually on their own. Ryan recalls one overnight camping trip when he was twelve and a very recent day "tubing" at the lake as an adult. He does not count hotel conventions as being a vacation because Bob was there to work and Ryan was along because it was "dad's turn" in the child-sharing schedule. Most of the weekends they shared were spent driving from one job site to another. In fact, Ryan remembers spending almost every minute of one entire weekend sitting in Bob Lewis's office while Bob and his attorney hammered out the Nomad deal.

Ironically, because of the times that Ryan spent at work with his dad, Ryan knows every detail and every job site of Bob's progression to success. By watching his father, he learned his skill for listening to people and analyzing situations. Moreover, he knows that, although the circumstances were not always the most fun for a young boy, Bob was always happy to have him by his side. He never once felt like he was a burden or imposition.

Bob was just marking time until "his boy" would be his partner.

After high school and university, Ryan was enjoying his professional career in volleyball. He was a recognized and accomplished player internationally and, arguably, he may have preferred to continue in the sport.

Ryan was also Bob Pomeroy's son.

He fully appreciated the fact that his education, travel, income and lifestyle were a direct result of Bob's hard work and he knew instinctively that, with his older brother gone, he had to show responsibility and work in the family business.

He was not coming in as a novice. From the age of five, Ryan had seen every aspect of the hospitality field. He had bussed tables, cleaned rooms, greeted guests, washed dishes, removed garbage and hustled on job sites.

By the time he was twelve he knew how much money could be saved by minimizing the construction schedule.

By the time he was fourteen he knew ways to maximize the profits. He was as convinced as his father was that excellent service, immaculate rooms and a full range of amenities would bring repeat business much more effectively than advertising.

Before he left for university he was already very well educated in the nuts and bolts of managing hotels and restaurants. When he returned, he began a two-year intensive internship in the grease and oil of the business, the financing and expansion process.

During the massive growth period, Bob and Carrie had been putting most of their energies to restructuring the ownership of all the companies. They traveled to hotel association conferences and financial meetings with brokers across Canada. One evening, as friends were sitting around a bonfire, the talk got around to the changes expected in the corporate profile.

Bob said he had an announcement to make. He began his announcement by saying that plans were underway for some corporate restructuring. Without further pause, Bob emotionally announced that his son Ryan was leaving his sports career and joining the company.

When Ryan returned to the fold, he worked alongside Bob, taking on added responsibilities and representing the company in more and more financial meetings. Ryan continued to take a larger role in running the company but another year passed without any formal announcement.

Eventually Ryan's new business cards appeared and his role in the corporate structure was in print for all to see.

Although Bob and Ryan are both committed to achievement, their approaches to goals differ.

Bob makes decisions based on instinct and experience.

Ryan follows more of the professional business model: structure, procedures, job descriptions, streamlining, reports, and budgets. He makes careful decisions based on the facts he has accumulated for the probable return on investment and economic predictions.

Bob eschews email and computers. Ryan uses technology wherever it produces productivity.

Bob is content with his cell phone and notebook and prefers to concentrate on northern Alberta and BC. Ryan's blackberry keeps him tuned to the world and he follows business trends on a global scale.

Ryan reads business journals, researches on the Internet and follows other corporations. His mind is like a sponge and he is constantly absorbing information. He built his own management team, adding experienced executives to assist him in taking the Pomeroy Group to the next level of development.

Father and son share a mutual appreciation and pride in each other's accomplishments. When Ryan was travelling the world playing professional volleyball, Bob was the textbook "proud papa" constantly updating his friends with each of Ryan's accolades. He would never hesitate to remind people that one day Ryan would be working with him back home, that he had been learning the business all through his life and that his education and travel experience would make him even a better partner.

On his part, Ryan watched his dad struggle through economic setbacks, risk every cent he had in his first developments, work with pride for another employer when his own businesses failed, and then seize the opportunity to rebuild. He saw his father work two or three, even four, jobs at one time to be able to support his children and to invest in new ventures.

It is one thing to turn over the reins of a company but it is another thing entirely to hand over corporate direction completely.

Bob built his company on personal style and Herculean effort and, while it seems that he has accepted the changes Ryan has made, he has not done so without some reluctance. He knows, however, that he has taught his son well and he does not hesitate to express his support for the new directions being taken.

Father and son grew up in different times, in different social and economic climates. Ryan had the advantage of a formal education and an introduction to an established corporate entity. Bob had to be more ruthless in his pursuit of business, surviving by his wits and making the most of anything he could grab.

Even their personal lives differ.

Bob has had great difficulty in maintaining permanent relationships; his physical needs usually been met without careful consideration; his happiness and contentment never fully realized. His chaotic childhood and puberty never included a parental guide for managing his emotional wellbeing. After his divorce from Marjorie, he has stumbled through his personal life, never being certain if his appeal to women was personally or financially motivated.

Ryan, on the other hand, was raised in a more stable home and had his father's example of what issues to avoid. While being, arguably, a "great catch" in every sense of the term, he gave much thought to his future and the life he wanted. Tall, handsome, educated and affluent, he was able to travel the world and meet an abundance of potential partners. He wisely looked to his home turf and found a woman who, not surprisingly, espouses all the virtues of his own mother.

Caring, intelligent, hardworking, generous and supportive, Allison was raised in a loving, stable family home in Prince George. Educated and secure in her own abilities, she initially rebuked Ryan's overtures and was always more interested in his character than his wallet. Working alongside him as he builds their future, she has become the perfect partner that Ryan could choose to share his life.

Although their wedding in October could have been the event of the year with no stops pulled, it was a beautiful, intimate ceremony with family and close friends. The girl who could have had anything she wanted as she became Mrs. Ryan Pomeroy ignored the lavish Vera Wang creations and sensibly selected a locally-purchased gown. No prima donna here. Her gown was a mere $500 and she "rocked it"!

Ryan has always been proud to be a Pomeroy but he acknowledges the existence of some less than flattering public perception of the company. He knows there have been some issues in the past and he is determined to build a strong, positive presence in the community. He has already begun to resolve any old grievances, whether they be valid or not, and he is working very hard to avoid any future negativity.

Bob turned the Presidency of the company to Ryan in the belief that his son was ready for the responsibility. He told everyone that he would step back and provide support and advice; that he was ready to concentrate on horses and semi-retirement.

That is what he "said" but he is finding it much easier to spend time in the office and to plunge into another project than it is to retire.

As Ernie Patterson says, "He may have turned the reins of the company over to Ryan for day to day management but as long as he has eyes in his head and as long as his sixth sense keeps kicking in, he will be coming up with more locations for hotels or services."

Bob is a workaholic and cannot relax. He micro-manages. He works. That is all he knows. He could never sit still by a pool in Scottsdale and wait for annual reports. He would always be wondering how the business was doing, what he could be doing. He absolutely trusts Ryan's judgement but that does not stop him from getting ideas and wanting to be involved.

If Bob does decide to step back eventually, he need not worry about how other companies feel about his son. Even with the economic slowdown in Canada, the Pomeroy Group is still considered a preferred client of Manulife and other investment leaders. An executive from Manulife in Toronto recently emphasized, "They continue to explore new opportunities with the (Pomeroy Group) and have complete confidence in the new management team."

Bob's pursuit of his dreams has made him an important factor in the economy of the entire Peace area. His wish to create a company that would provide a stable future for his children has been realized.

The legacy Bob was creating has become a reality not just for his family but for the city of Grande Prairie as well. His hotel rooms and hospitality services have been recognized nationally and have upped the game for others in the area. The Pomeroy Group, indisputably, is one of the area's biggest employers (second only to the municipality) and has helped shape the infrastructure of the community with added services and amenities.

Bob invested in Fort St. John when others pulled out and, today, the Pomeroy Hotel stands as a beacon to the future.

In Fort McMurray, he saw potential where others saw problems.

In Grande Prairie, he saw the opportunity for growth.

He is, according to Charlie Grubisich, "an entrepreneur extraordinaire."

No one really believes that Bob will ever slow down but if you ask him to outline exact plans for the next five or ten years for himself, he does not have a concrete response.

Bob does know what he wants for his children. He wants them to be near him and he wants his grandchildren to feel secure and loved.

His property on the outskirts of Grande Prairie is referred to as "Bob's Town" not just because it covers a lot of land but because it has been designed to reflect Bob's insistence that everyone he loves live within shouting distance.

Anchoring the property is a massive multi-million dollar equestrian centre. To call it a barn would be a gross understatement.

The rows and rows of horse stalls are marked with shiny black steel gates, each one embellished with brass trim. The floors are cushioned for health and comfort. Each horse has ample room to walk or lie down. It more resembles a "hotel for horses" as it is always kept in pristine condition. Bob planned the veterinarian area of the center to be world-class and available to other horse breeders in the community.

The training center is huge and a supply of panels on one side can transform half of the area into a dance floor or trade event. The commercial size kitchen is appointed well enough to satisfy the fussiest caterer or chef. Elegantly furnished offices just off the main entrance house the workplaces of the managers.

In the centre of this impressive structure is an entertainment room complete with fireplace, enormous bar and big screen television. Because of the privacy as well as the ambience, it has become a favourite place for many companies to hold their social events or corporate meetings.

On the hill above the equestrian centre is the start of Bob's new house. Designed for the life of a country gentleman, the home, when finished, will be a jewel on the landscape.

Along the main paved roadway, there are three other driveways, each leading to properties designated for Ryan, Connor and Kim, each one marked with a street sign indicating which Pomeroy will (hopefully, eventually) live there.

Kim and her husband Rod Gravengard have already built their home on "their street" and their three children delight in running down to see their newest foals or visit with Grandpa when he's around.

Just down the road, at the edge of the property, Grandma Marj and her husband Herb have settled into their own home—close enough for the grandchildren to smell cookies baking.

"Grandpa Bob" is digging a small lake on the property and he has already started acquiring miniature livestock for a petting zoo.

Any weekend could find a group of 4-H club members on a tour of the facilities or a few developmentally challenged teens visiting the horses and enjoying the fresh air.

When the Southam family began Spruce Meadows Equestrian Center south of Calgary many years ago, people predicted early failure. This was "cattle country" and the idea of pleasure horses being trained for competition seemed ridiculous.

Time proved the Southam family to be right and Spruce Meadows has brought hundreds of millions of dollars to the city of Calgary through media, hotels, tourism, breeding, services and advertising. Their facility hosts events that are televised world-wide.

Grande Prairie is proud to be the Home of the World Chuckwagon Champion, Kelly Sutherland. If the impact made on the city of Calgary through the efforts of the Southam family and their Spruce Meadows Equestrian Centre is any example of how the show horse world can drive the economy, then perhaps the city should keep a closer eye on the Pomeroy family.

The equestrian centre has not yet been open for a full year and already the Grande Prairie facility is known by Arabian breeders throughout the US and Canada.

When Bob's stallion, Major Jamaal, was named as the 2008 Canadian National champion, the horse had already been named as the 2006 US National Reserve Champion Jr. Stallion.

These awards put Pomeroy Arabians International on the map. Bob's newly completed equestrian centre on his property in Arizona equals the Grande Prairie site in scope and quality.

This is not a guy who loves horses and has a nice barn for them. This is a man who has a passion for the Arabian breed; a man who will exhaust his own funds to build something that the entire community can enjoy and proudly boast about as being "theirs."

In Grande Prairie, Bob has earned respect. His hard work and determination are finally being appreciated in this forward-thinking city.

The innovation and success of the Pomeroy Group, along with the national and international recognition of the calibre of the service the company provides, has brought financial attention and investment opportunities to the entire northern area. There is more on the drawing table.

When Bob Pomeroy told people that he would be a rich man one day, they laughed at him. Everyone in Fort St.John told him that he had big dreams for a stupid kid with no money.

It is a good thing that he didn't listen.

Thirty-Six

"You can read the life you've lived but you cannot change a word."
—LEONARD COHEN, CBC TELEVISION INTERVIEW, 2009

March 2009. I am flying to Grande Prairie to spend some time with Bob about the final draft of the book. My seat partner on the plane is having an animated conversation with another man and, when the woman across the aisle joins in, the three are speaking across me so it is impossible not to overhear.

It becomes obvious that they all know Bob and I mention the book. Immediately they show interest, start laughing and ask if I have included the story about the "moose head", that no book would be complete without it.

I thought I knew all the stories so I ask for more.

They all chime in with various parts of the story: that Bob had hidden cash away from creditors inside a moose head; that he had burned down his hotel but had saved the moose head and the cash; that when the firemen arrived, Bob was standing in front holding the moose head; that the hotel had burned to the ground.

I laugh and then pause before telling them that there never was any "moose head" it was, in fact, a buffalo mascot costume. The costume was used to promote a restaurant, not a hotel. The restaurant he managed had a large fire that was caused accidentally in the kitchen and the verdict of the courts substantiated that fact. I added that any insurance benefits would have gone to the bank, as Bob was just an employee at that time.

My fellow travelers seemed disappointed. They had been enjoying the gossip about Bob for so many years and now they had been told that he was not an outlaw after all. The colorful tale had been destroyed like a popped balloon.

Orson Welles said, "When you're down and out, something always turns up—usually it's the noses of former friends" and this would seem to be the case with Bob. The irony is that most of the rumors about Bob started when he had lost everything in Fort St. John.

Some of the idle gossip borders on the ridiculous.

In the early stages of writing this biography, a woman from Fort St.John was anxious to tell me "what she knew about Bob Pomeroy." When we met, she divulged, in hushed tones, the story of how Bob and his best friend got their stake in business. She said that it was public knowledge they had transported and sold drugs in Fort St.John in the early eighties, that both acquired enough cash to start legitimate companies and that both men were "druggies."

When asked how she knew this incriminating material, she said, "I heard it around the campground."

When asked how long she had known Bob, she admitted she had just met him casually at a reception a week earlier and, in fact, she had just recently arrived to the Fort St.John area.

Pursuing the source of this arguably libelous rumor became a comedic diversion. People who have known Bob since puberty burst out laughing at the very suggestion of him selling drugs.

Even a couple of men who dislike Bob shook their heads and ended my enquiry with ". . . but that drug rumor is just nuts."

Bob is not only vehemently against street drugs, he does not even smoke.

I have completed well over one hundred interviews in the past two years, trying to unravel the twists and turns of Bob's life, to separate the truths from the lies, to discover what makes him tick, to find out what makes him happy and who he really is.

I have omitted some very personal things that people shared with me—not to protect Bob but to save others from embarrassment.

People have told me some things in confidence just so that I could better understand Bob and his strong bonds with his friends. I have honored these requests because, ultimately, they would not change the story.

When the hard work and risk-taking of a man results in his success, it is a foregone conclusion that some disgruntled non-achiever will invent a juicy bit of gossip. There are always enough ears around a beer table to listen to unfounded rumors, and enough small minds to spread the distorted facts as gospel truths.

One of Bob's former partners would not participate in the book. He said that Bob "has probably won you over with his charms." He felt that the book would be honey-coated and that there would be nothing told about Bob's poor choices or bad behavior.

He was wrong. Bob has not hidden a thing. If truth were to be told, he has bent over backwards to protect the privacy of other people, often at his own expense.

Bob was very candid because he feels that his life has always been an open book.

He has never claimed to be a saint and he knows he has been a sinner.

He confided about his personal history in the hope that his children would understand him and try to forgive past transgressions.

He provided details about his wheeling and dealing so that others could see just what he felt he had to do in order to succeed without money or connections.

Bob's biography would be incomplete without mentioning his relationships with women.

It is not a secret.

It is part of his personality, it is part of his past and it remains a part of his present.

Anyone who has known Bob for more than fifteen years also knows that, although he "loves them and leaves them"; he never cuts them off from his largesse. His door and his wallet have always been open.

He gave Marj a house when they parted and Bob would still move heaven and earth for her.

Although never married to Janice, Bob dissolved their relationship just as though they were a legally recognized couple. He put a generous down payment on her townhouse and provided child support when Connor lived with her. He continued to provide her with financial assistance well after he assumed full custody of their son.

Susan moved closer to Grande Prairie and continues to keep in touch with Bob. Although he unceremoniously dumped her to marry Carrie, and possibly because of that fact, he continued his financial generosity towards her over the years.

It would seem that, if a woman has shown love to Bob in the past, she has created an invisible bond with him for the future. If his insecurities made him susceptible to misplaced affection, then they also created a very soft heart.

Bob's attraction to the opposite sex could have been the inspiration for "Scent of a Woman" because he has never been able to resist women of any age, shape or color. This is probably Bob's worst kept secret and his friends delight in reminding him about his weakness for the ladies.

He seems, however, to treat women with the four "L"s: look at them, lust after them, love them, and leave them.

A cynic might add a "P" to the list because he usually ends up "Paying for them."

A few years ago, Bob's good friend Dave Thompson, presented him with a personalized board game, his own version of Monopoly called "Pomeroyopoly."

The properties all referred to Bob's hotels, restaurants, homes and the game cards were, as with Monopoly, divided in two stacks; receiving payments or being charged high fees. One of the "make payment" cards bore the words, "Another divorce/breakup; pay for new mortgage insurance."

There is an old axiom that states, "Them's that can't do, teach."

That certainly fits here. Even though he has not been good at managing relationships of his own, Bob tries to counsel others on ways to avoid his mistakes.

Because her family felt torn apart when her parents divorced, Kim was very cautious when her first husband, Mike, proposed to her. They had a long engagement. She knew that her mother had missed out on university life and a career. Because Marj confessed to her daughter that she occasionally regretted becoming a wife and mother too early, Kim had valid reasons to wait and be certain.

Despite the failure of his own marriage, Bob still believed in the institution and he wanted Kim to be happy. When the engagement seemed to be lasting a long time, Bob finally asked her why she did not want to set a wedding date, why she was so reluctant to make a commitment.

Kim took the opportunity to tell her father what she had been thinking all those years. She looked at him and quietly responded, "I am only going to say this once, dad, because I love you but, really, you haven't exactly been a good role model."

Bob walked away and ignored Kim for a couple of days. The discussion was not mentioned for years.

Vern Boyd recalls a trip to Fort McMurray with Bob years ago. During their flight, they talked about business and how much a man had to sacrifice to build a successful company, how many risks had to be taken to achieve goals.

That was the first time that Bob had ever shown any indication to Vern that he realized the trade-offs he had made in pursuit of the almighty dollar.

When Vern told Bob that he and his wife were separating, Bob took his friend out for a quiet dinner. The evening was not about business.

Bob asked how things were going in Vern's life and then he advised him that, whatever he did, he had to be fair to his wife; that it was more important to keep her as a friend than to save a few dollars.

Bob turned over a Corona beer coaster, took out his pen and drew a vertical line down the middle. He wrote Vern's name on top of one side and his wife's name on the other and then told him emphatically "If you two get along, then do not go to a lawyer. Write down what you can manage with under your name and what she deserves under her name. Then get a mediator and write it up and sign it."

That dinner meeting was more than seven years ago and Vern still has the Corona coaster in his file cabinet. The couple did go to a mediator and their terms ended up being pretty much the same as the "coaster contract" that Bob had outlined. They remained friends just as Bob has remained on friendly terms with Marj.

Women—and his horses—have been Bob's biggest weaknesses and, as his attorney Bob Lewis said,

". . . both have proven to be very expensive."

Although much of Bob's colorful reputation involves his many liaisons, it is important to know what historian Robert Rupp said, regarding President Harding's legacy.

His words were, "It is time to stop counting his mistresses and start counting his accomplishments."

Bob's accomplishments are many.

Hotels, restaurants, buildings, horses, homes in two countries; children, grandchildren, friends—they are all fact. The good deeds he has done are fact. The positive effects his companies have on the economy are fact.

No amount of "charm" can discount any of those.

Men who approach business like a game understand the rules. They have the prize well in their sight. Those who play the game well always succeed and Bob plays the game well.

There are no grey areas. Once he gets an idea in his head, he has tunnel vision. No matter how much work is involved, or how many financial hoops he has to jump through, he will pursue his objective as a challenge. It may begin with the prospect of making money but ultimately, it is the pursuit.

When Bob starts a project, he always offers an investment opportunity to people he has worked with before or to people he knows well. He is always upfront with the risks and makes no bones about the fact that, if the project fails, you lose your money and he will not pay any losses from profits made on other projects.

At the same time, if Bob makes money, everyone makes money.

On May 24, 2009, Larry King was interviewed on CBC Television. He was discussing his autobiography and the reporter questioned Larry's openness and candor about his past.

Today a well-respected television personality, Larry wrote frankly about his eight marriages, drug and alcohol use, even an arrest for grand larceny.

He responded to the question with the same honesty.

"You can judge me, you can respect me, you can dislike me—but this is my life. It is real and nothing can change it. I realized early in life that I would rather be the boy who 'fesses up to breaking a window than the one who hides and gets found out later."

The truth is always the truth and it is far better to take a pro-active approach with any person that you hope to do business with now or in the future.

Bob has never declared bankruptcy. He has left some unpaid debts behind when his own business attempts failed but he has always paid back any personal loans. When investors lost money on projects, Bob lost money as well, usually even more than anyone else did.

If he failed, Bob kept trying. He never let one loss prevent him from continuing to play the game.

Economic swings have created temporary havoc but suppliers and tradesmen who began working for Bob and investing with Bob more than a decade ago still eagerly accept work from the Pomeroy Group.

Many of these contractors have become millionaires directly because of their association with Bob.

There is no deception with Bob. He is, like Larry King, the "boy who 'fesses up." He is very upfront with investors and tradesmen alike.

If he wants a company to participate in a project and he does not have the full financing in place, he discloses the facts directly. If the tradesmen or suppliers decide to take the contract, they will be paid. It may take time. It may take a long time. Nevertheless, Bob is true to his word. This is something that Eden Textiles and many others have learned over their long association with the Pomeroy Group.

He keeps his ear to the ground and he uses instincts to make decisions based on bits of valid information that other dismiss. He is always thinking; always open to new ideas and ventures.

His cousin Mike says, "The difference between Bob Pomeroy and others is that Bob will not only follow through with an idea, he will work twenty four hours a day to make sure it works.

If something starts to fail, he works to make it succeed. If a venture collapses, he does not stop. He starts over and works harder."

An experienced investor, at any level, knows that wins and losses are not only a part of the investment gamble; they are a reality at any level of business.

The reason people continue to invest is that they hope to make a larger profit than they would in conventional saving plans. When people invest with Bob, they are hoping to win big—to make substantially more money—and they usually do.

There are always shifts in the economy and Bob always survives them. He has taught his son well and Ryan will not accept failure any more than his father would.

If Bob's house burned to the ground, he would start to rebuild immediately. He would also start a company to get the wood and sell at enough profit to cover his own requirements.

Ryan would react in the same way but he may pause before starting work to ensure that the proper building permits were in place and the mortgage company had signed the financing documents.

They both see opportunity where others see catastrophe.

Bob will do anything and everything he can to protect the Pomeroy name. He keeps a small notebook in his pocket and he keeps a record of when people do him a favor or help him win a deal. He will search for a way to show his gratitude no matter how long it may take.

In the fall of 2007, Ray Yenkana stopped by Bob's office to discuss a new project. While he was there, Bob handed him a cheque and Ray questioned the reason for the money. Bob responded by saying that he had profited so well from the sale of the hotels, he wanted to pay Ray the commission on the Igloo deal.

It had been fifteen years since Ray had waived his commissions to help Bob get the project he wanted and Ray had long since considered himself repaid under their "free rooms" agreement. He refused the cheque but was touched by Bob's personal integrity and generosity.

Bob operates on the concept that debts and financial commitments are just incentives people need to work harder.

After he sold the group of hotels in 2007, at lunch with Willie Kempin, he joked, "Well, do you think a man can live on $100 Million?"

Willie gave his friend Bob a resigned half-smile and shrugged, "Bob, you've probably already made commitments to spend double that."

Willie offered his thoughts on a world without Bob.

"If anything ever happened to Bob, his entire family would suffer the most because he is their "go-to guy", their rock, their source of dependability and support. Other people would miss him as well. As for the financial and business community, he would be missed there too because, like him or not, Bob Pomeroy's life affects a lot of people."

It would not be fair to dismiss all the rumors about Bob without including one that is absolutely, undeniably true.

He is a terror behind the wheel. He drives fast, uses his cell phone continuously and even writes notes to himself as he barrels down the highway. In spite of Kim's accident, in spite of Tim's tragic end, in spite of his own many accidents, Bob has only two speeds—fast and stop.

On one particular occasion, Bob and Hank Scheunhage were returning from Chetwynd and Bob was doing his usual multi-tasking as he sped around the mountainous curves of the old highway.

Hank's uneasiness soon turned to abject terror and he finally shouted to Bob to stop the car immediately. When Bob questioned the urgency, Hank told him he was not going any further and preferred to get out and hitch a ride. Bob was shocked at first but then grinned in amusement. He told Hank to take over the driving so he could continue to take calls and get some work done.

Hank was not accustomed to the power of Bob's Mercedes and he went a few kilometers alternating between speeding and braking. Just as he mentioned to Bob that he was having a lot of trouble keeping the car under 150 kph, sure enough, the blue and red lights of a police cruiser flashed behind them.

When the officers approached, they suspected that alcohol might have been involved due to the erratic manner the car had been driven over the time they had been trying to follow. After speaking to Hank, they were satisfied about his explanation and did not demand a breathalyzer. They did, however, give him a $182 speeding ticket.

Bob Pomeroy is loud, gregarious, and imposing.

He is confident; he is strong-willed; he is focused.

He can be intimidating.

You either dislike him intensely or love him like a brother.

Bob is a skilled promoter who can make any dream sound realistic. He also works unceasingly to make the dream a reality.

Bob believes in the strength of the human spirit and the power of human will. He is a survivor. He faces life head on.

He wants to go through it first class and he will work his butt off to stay in first class.

Bob Pomeroy will not accept second best.

His life is testimony to the opportunities available to anyone with a dream, to the fact that a man can start with nothing and win everything.

When Bob gets a vision of the end goal, he pursues it relentlessly, always seeking innovative ways to accomplish a task and to maximize profits while maintaining quality.

When faced with a problem, or choice, he makes a decision and then sticks to it.

He believes firmly that no decision is the worst decision of all.

The schools in northern Alberta in the early 50's were ill-equipped to even attempt individualized education and so, as with many other children in similar circumstances, Bob floundered in the classroom and became a frustrated, angry young man. He left school at age 13 with just a grade six education—or, as Bob prefers to say, "Half of grade twelve."

The plain truth is that the education system failed, not Bob. He entered the workforce with a minimum ability to read and a maximum chip on his shoulder yet he has managed to create a fortune and a legacy for his children

There is no doubt that Bob has a strong work ethic.

He asks no one to do any more than he will do himself.

He also has a total understanding of business. Whatever industry he enters, he immediately "gets it." With a memory like an elephant, Bob can multi-task several multi-million dollar projects using just a pocket size notebook and his mind.

He also has an uncanny aptitude with figures.

Although he has little formal education he has been blessed with a brain that can calculate at warp speed and he is rarely, if ever, wrong.

All these attributes came in handy in 2006 when the company exploded.

That year the financial and business community across Canada discovered the Pomeroy Group.

The company was named in Profit Magazine's list of Canada's fastest growing companies.

In the Venture Fast 50, the Pomeroy Group was number nine on the list of company's with over $20 Million in annual revenue.

At the Wyndham Worldwide Hotel "Preferred Owners" function in Atlanta, the company was honored for "Top Quality and Overall Performance." (For both the U.S. and Canada!)

In late August of 2007, Bob and Carrie, Ryan and Allison, along with a group of family members and friends, took a cruise/land holiday to the Mediterranean areas of Dubrovnik and Venice. They had chartered two small yachts for the trip and Bob, as usual, was the ultimate generous host.

One early evening, anchored in a quiet bay, the group was enjoying a cocktail hour and talking about the beautiful scenery. Bob became very quiet and sipped his Johnny Walker Blue in deep thought. After a few minutes, he cleared his throat and, with deep emotion, said, "Who would ever think that a poor kid from Fort St. John would have all this!"

He was not bragging. He was not fishing for compliments.

Bob Pomeroy was simply making an observation; a statement to reflect the true appreciation he has for everything in his life, family and friends included.

Years ago, when travelers checked into a Hilton Hotel, beside the usual copy of the Gideon bible, there was a biography of the hotel chain's founder, Conrad Hilton. The intent of the biography was to give guests a sense of knowing that a real person was behind the room they slept in. It let them know just how hard a man had worked to ensure that they would have a good night's sleep.

This biography will, hopefully, accomplish the same goal.

It has been an interesting journey getting to know Bob.

His life has been a lesson in perseverance, in the strength of the human spirit.

His story is a clear example of the "circle of life."

In 2005, Bob Pomeroy bought property on Spring Creek Road—the large tract of land that has become the home of the impressive Pomeroy International Equestrian Centre and the future home of his children and their families.

The price? A cool $950,000.

Bob bought the land from Helen and Cliff Innes, the same couple that—over forty-six years ago—gave a skinny fourteen-year-old boy his first job guarding their sheep.

Acknowledgements

Very special thanks to Bob's family for opening your hearts and sharing your memories.

Thank you to everyone who took the time to remember anecdotes and events from the past sixty years and to share them with me during the writing of this biography. Your trust is much appreciated and your input very valued. Thank you to Harj Panesar for his professional photography and for helping restore and prepare old photographs for use. And thank you to family and friends who took the time to find the photographs and lend family albums.

Bob's life, and this book, were touched by: Kevin Albers, Ron & Gail Barker, Darlene Black, Don Blonke, Raphael Bohlmann, Vernon Boyd, Marjorie Brent, Debbie Brewster, Lyman Brewster, Grant Brooks, Les Collier, Helen Collier, Terry Collier, Fred Cunningham, Joseph Fodor, Steve Good, Susie Goodwin, Dona Gretzinger, Charlie Grubisich, Al Hunt, Bill Jenkins, Susan Jorgensen, Willie Kempin, Wayne Korol, Bob Lewis, Allison Pomeroy, Frances Maclin, George & Starr Martin, Janice McKinnon, Earl Millsap, Ashar Minhas, Yadminder Minhas, Ethel Mohr, Ernie Cathy Patterson, Viggo Pedersen, Kevin Person, Glen Pomeroy, Mike Pomeroy, Ross Pomeroy, Denis Rochette, Bob Rogers, Hank Scheunhage, Brian Surerus, Dave Thompson, Fred Tissington, Gerry Tucker, Darrell & Shelley Urban, Julius VanWyck, Rick Vieira, Tom Vukota, Dave Will, Tom Wright, Mike Yenkana, Ray Yenkana.

Also thank you to John Pomeroy, the main genealogical researcher and source in England for his cooperation and clarification regarding facts and records from the Pomeroy history.

Some contributors preferred to remain anonymous.

My life and career would be impossible without the love and support of my husband Serge and the encouragement of my son Bob. The memory of my son Michael keeps me strong.

I would be remiss if I didn't thank my wonderful Nelia and Jonally who keep our home comfortable and secure and our fragile daughter Stephanie safe and loved.

—Madeline

Disclaimer

Names of partners and investors in projects were researched through public records in corporate registry and/or land titles or by access to records provided by the Pomeroy Group. In the case where there were variations in spelling of names, the version most often found was used for this book.

The author actively endeavoured to contact everyone who has been mentioned in the book and chapters of the manuscript were available to anyone who responded and wished to edit their interests.

Some names have been changed in an attempt to minimize embarrassment to parties whose alleged actions may be portrayed in a less than flattering light. No malice was intended.

No situation or story was included based on just one person's observations or gossip; indeed, only if several people relayed similar information was an incident included in the telling of Bob's story. Each person interviewed signed a disclaimer releasing their statement for use in the book. If a story sounds familiar, it is coincidental and most likely that Bob or another person provided the same story. If any story was not used in the book, it may have been left out simply for editing reasons or duplication of information.

The author is not related to Bob Pomeroy or to anyone in the Pomeroy family. Any and all observations have been based on over two years of interviews and discussions.

SOME REFERENCE SOURCES USED IN THIS BIOGRAPHY ARE:

Northwest Business, December 2005

Alberta Venture, January 2007

Holloway Lodging Real Estate Investment Trust News Release, May 30, 2007

Holloway Lodging Real Estate Investment Trust News Release, January 2008

Canadian Lodging Outlook, November 2007

Canadian Press May 30, 2007

Various Canadian financial newspaper items from Google and Yahoo searches, verifiable public knowledge sources.

Contracts and documents from corporate files

LINKS

www.pomeroygroup.ca

www.pomeroyhotel.com

www.pomeroyarabians.com

www.writer44.com

MADELINE HOMBERT enjoys the dual residency of Surrey, British Columbia and Grande Prairie, Alberta. Married for over thirty-eight years to her husband Serge, she is the mother of Michael (deceased), Robert and Stephanie.

Madeline has dabbled in stage performance and standup comedy. Some say that she is a moderately good poker player. Her family would mention that she is a great cook.

Her cv. includes experience in banking, marketing, politics, film and television production, winemaking and travel but she has always been a writer.

Her credits include film, television, newspaper, magazine and advertising. Although she has previously had true-life experiences published as anthologies in book form, this is her first full length biography.

Two new books are currently in development.

www.writer44.com

BOB POMEROY steps onto the sprawling deck of his rural home. Just meters away, two dozen fine Arabian horses are contentedly munching sweet grass, the newest colts resting in the shade of the world-class barn. It could be a scene from "Dallas" but this is Grande Prairie, Alberta. And, unlike J.R. Ewing, Bob Pomeroy didn't inherit his fortune—he earned it.

This is the story of a real Canadian. It is the record of a man who would not let his dreams die. It is the account of a man who continues to prove that ambition, focus and an unrelenting drive to succeed can take an uneducated boy from the life of abuse & uncertainty to a position of wealth and respect.